ICEFALL

ICEFALL

ADVENTURES
at the WILD EDGES
of OUR DANGEROUS,
CHANGING PLANET

JOHN ALL *and*
JOHN BALZAR

PUBLICAFFAIRS
NEW YORK

PublicAffairs books are available at special discounts for bulk purchases in the U.S.
by corporations, institutions, and other organizations. For more information, please
contact the Special Markets Department at the Perseus Books Group, 2300 Chestnut
Street, Suite 200, Philadelphia, PA 19103, call (800) 810-4145, ext. 5000, or e-mail
special.markets@perseusbooks.com.

Book Design by Jack Lenzo

Library of Congress Cataloging-in-Publication Data
Names: All, John, author. | Balzar, John, author.
Title: Icefall : adventures at the wild edges of our dangerous, changing
planet / John All and John Balzar.
Description: First edition. | New York : PublicAffairs, 2017.
Identifiers: LCCN 2016029165| ISBN 9781610396936 (hardback) | ISBN
9781610396943 (ebook)
Subjects: LCSH: All, John. | Global environmental change. | Adventure and
adventurers—United States—Biography. | BISAC: BIOGRAPHY &
AUTOBIOGRAPHY
/ Adventurers & Explorers. | NATURE / Environmental Conservation &
Protection.
Classification: LCC GE149 .A45 2017 | DDC 915.496 [B]—dc23 LC record available
at https://lccn.loc.gov/2016029165

First Edition
10 9 8 7 6 5 4 3 2 1

FOR:

Meggo, the next chapter—10/15/16

Oakster, so that you will know me better

Mom and Dad, thank you for the strength and obduracy

Asman, I'll never forget

Balzar, the steady voice

Caroline, I followed your advice. . . .

And my climbing partners: Medler, Rech, Sloan, Nelson, Goldstein, Trainor, Laughton, Leftwich, Benningfield, Harris, and Holmes

Contents

PART I

ICEFALL

Chapter One

Alone on the Ice

On the morning of May 22, 2014, my plans were in tatters. For starters, I was supposed to be on the Everest massif, many days' travel east and south of Mount Himlung, where my tent was now staked on fresh snow at just over 6,000 meters (19,685 feet). But I had been driven off by a climbing disaster, at the time the worst in the history of Everest. So I'd journeyed to this peak instead, known to serious mountaineers but not many others. I should have been in the company of the skilled, highly energized team I'd brought to the Himalaya on an expedition to collect evidence of the causes of climate change. But after the Everest disaster, their morale had taken a beating, a team member had a worrisome health problem, and for the moment they were scattered elsewhere. I was alone.

Finally, it was seriously late in the South Asian climbing season. Each day brought the dreaded monsoon closer—imminent weather that would up the odds for trouble as it approached, then instantly end any hope at all of reaching a mountain summit. The prudent move would have been to retreat for the year. But too much had been invested in this expedition. Sacrifices had been made, big ones. And our work was important, more so all the time. I was not ready to give up.

And besides: I had a spring morning to bask in. I was four miles high in the glory of the Himalaya. A benign sun reflected brightly off the ice. No wind to speak of. The white-tipped fangs of mountainous Nepal soared into the thin sky for as far as I could see, which was hundreds of square miles. I was thinking of coffee.

I wriggled out of my sleeping bag. I pulled on my boots and stepped out of the tent onto the small, flattish snowfield that I had chosen for Camp 2. Cold, bone-dry Himalayan air scalded the lining of my lungs. I grabbed a plastic garbage bag. Mountains are one of the few places on Earth where you must gather fresh water like you're berry picking. I'd fill the bag with powdery snow, melt the contents pan by pan on the camp stove, and brew. It was a tedious process, but it meant that the coffee would be all the more wonderful. While I was at it, I figured I'd get a head start on the day's scientific work and collect the morning snow and ice samples for our study. These too would have to be melted, then filtered and carefully stored so that we could later analyze the accumulated dust and ash and other residue of human industriousness from far-distant cities, farms, and mines. Bit by bit, when analyzed in the laboratory, these samples help us decipher the exact consequences of industrialization on the world's highest elevations, where climate change is under way in dramatic and, regrettably, life-threatening fashion.

Because I wouldn't be venturing far from the tent, I dressed "minimalist"—with just wind pants, a T-shirt, a light jacket, and thin gloves—no hat, no parka, no headlamp, no satellite phone. Just a quick jaunt out and back. Fill the garbage bag. Light the stove. Then, here on the roof of the world, await that splendid first sip of hot coffee.

Being alone on a Himalayan peak was unwise, and venturing by oneself onto the compressed, fissured, and perpetually moving ice of a glacier was manifestly dangerous, stupid even. I teach mountain safety, and I cannot imagine how many times I'd emphasized that fundamental lesson. You had to be skilled, knowledgeable, confident, smart, *and* lucky. In a place like this, anything less could kill you. This campsite had been methodically scouted. It was plainly the most stable area around. And I'd turned the prayer wheels at monasteries down lower as I trekked from Kathmandu.

I stretched, limbered up, and gulped deep breaths to raise my oxygen level. I looked higher up the mountain, and for a moment my thoughts drifted to the climbing route that would await us in a couple of days, after the remnants of my team returned here to Camp 2 from lower elevations. Ice cliffs directly above me meant we would have to pass to one side or the other. I pondered the choices. To my left and not very far above, I saw a flat area of snowpack that would provide a different vantage on the upcoming route. Plus, it was a perfect spot to gather snow samples and fill up the garbage bag.

I set out in that direction. One step . . . another. Another. I was not counting.

I took one step too many.

Vertigo. Blackness. So fast. Impossibly fast. My footing vanished. My face smashed into jagged ice. I disappeared into the guts of the glacier. Sliding. Bouncing.

There's no accounting for the shape of a glacial crevasse. It could be a simple narrowing V that pinned you in place before you reached the bottom. Or it could be an irregular crack that descended for a thousand feet. Or a small crack might open into a giant cavern. Honestly— how would you know? Until you fell in.

Smash. Pain.

I plummeted, but not straightaway downward. I crashed into one uneven, abrasive side of the hard ice, and then bounced into the other side and careened back. Crunch. The parallel sides of ice widened instead of narrowing. And wherever the bottom might be, it was farther down still. Way down. Down and down and down more, into blue-blackness deep in the heart of this ancient ice.

Automatically, I stabbed out with my right arm to break the fall with my ice axe. The only thing that broke was my arm, and my shoulder. I felt the bones snap. I tumbled and bounced off the granite-hard ice, one side to the other. I could not stop.

I was being battered to lumpy meat. I was picking up speed. Faster, and hopelessly faster still. Ten, twenty, maybe thirty miles an hour, gravity pulled me down. Four stories. Five. More. How far to the bottom? No telling. Did it matter? I was dying.

My velocity might have been increasing, but the old cliché turned out to be true: time slowed. Or perhaps my senses grew keener. Whichever. How, I somehow had time to wonder, could I have been so damn foolish?

All these years. So many expeditions. Now to die ignominiously, never found, buried inside a mountain of ice, all because I wanted a morning coffee and was careless and ventured out alone.

My side smashed into ice. Whomp. The sound was thunderous, but there was no one else to hear it. Then I wasn't falling anymore. I wasn't moving at all. Not even breathing. Death. My last thought was to recognize the end. How fitting.

No, wait. I struggled to inflate my lungs and regain breath. In the sudden quiet, the first sound I heard was myself moaning, a weak groan.

I wasn't dead. I felt intense pain. Pain meant I was alive.

A strange calm came over me for just an instant. Hope. Then reality. I gasped for breath. Oh shit, it hurt. I fought against fogginess. I needed to assess my situation. Just how bad were things?

In a word: bad. It took me a moment to understand that I had not reached the bottom of the crevasse. Far from it. I'd fallen seven stories down, to a spot just before the crack grew cavernous, where a jagged ice shelf had miraculously formed. I had landed on it, which had caused me brutal pain but was actually a blessing. It saved me from plunging deeper—endlessly deeper. I'll never know how far.

Lying sprawled on this ice protrusion as hard as concrete, I fought to breathe again.

Suddenly, I realized my feet were dangling over the edge. Vast and dark down there where the silence seemed all but overwhelming. I was keenly aware that not all of me was functioning. But there was no question that all of me was in agony. My survival instinct overrode the pain, and soon I pushed my foggy thoughts aside. My legs and one functioning arm should allow me to slowly push myself back onto the safest reach of the shelf. I tried to drive my crampons into the flinty ice. Slipping off this perch into that abyss would end the discussion.

I found myself positioned on my crushed shoulder and my right arm. Their only function seemed to be to give off shocking bolts of pain. I could not move that side of my body, or even turn my head to look in that direction. That fact told me just how badly I was injured. I was spitting blood, another unfavorable sign. It spread and froze, dirtying the ice in front of my throbbing face.

Maybe I would die after all. It would just take longer.

I was panting like a sprinter. My dry gasping whistled in my ears. I would have guessed that I already used up my adrenaline reserves. But the gasps came faster when I realized I was not on a shelf after all, but on a block of loose ice that had fallen from above and wedged itself into the crevasse. Perhaps loosely wedged. Perhaps wedged only for the moment.

God, I wished I could take back that last step. Just that one. How different things would be. I'd be boiling water up there in the morning sun, and coffee would not be far off. I'd look across a snowfield and not even know of this hidden crevasse below.

Now I was destined to be entombed here in this glacier—to emerge frozen in the distant future for people to ponder: *What happened to this corpse in a green nylon jacket?*

I looked up. Way up. In the distance, a glimmering hole. Tiny. And another beside it. I could see a pinhole of sky. Life. Hope.

I listened. I was breathing now, but I didn't like what I heard. The gasps had become labored wheezes. Respiration was slowing.

That was the signal, the alarm. I heard it and I was not ready to quit. Not without a fight. I still had command over some parts of my body, didn't I? In between waves of nausea, I rocked a little, testing my weight against my injuries. The pain was as hot as a live wire. I kept rocking. One way and the other. Reaching out, pushing, pulling. Holding back whimpers and yelps. Grasping. Moving. Exploring what I could do.

I gave it everything. A lurch that took my breath, and I was sitting upright. At least I thought so. My head was spinning, so I was not completely sure. My breath once again came in ragged gasps. But I had proven one thing: I could move. It hurt like hell, but I was not paralyzed. I took a moment to look around and collect my thoughts.

An idea struck me. I should record the scene. It was what I did, the reason I was up here in the first place: good science. Collecting imagery had become second nature to me, the same as collecting samples and recording my location wherever I was. Imagery added dimension and perspective to the exchange of information, helping us understand our universe. Perhaps the imagery from down in this crevasse would survive somehow and students would learn from my terrible experience.

I was thinking, too, of my mom. I wanted her to understand what happened to me in the claustrophobic, cold space I occupied during these harsh hours. I didn't actually consider the details of how these images might survive and reach the surface for others to see if I could not make it myself. I was partly on autopilot, which was about all I had the strength for.

A jacket pocket held my camera, a Sony HX7—my favorite of seven I'd tested this trip. I reached for it with my good arm. There it was. To my surprise, my fingers on this one good hand still functioned. More surprising, so did the camera. I started with a couple of still photos, but they failed utterly to convey the situation.

I moved the dial to video, aimed the camera toward me selfie-style, pushed the shutter button and spoke. Blood and snot and snow were smeared across my face. But my mouth was another thing that worked.

"Well, I'm pretty well fucked," I said.

I talked my predicament over with myself. As I looked overhead, I saw that climbing straight up was impossible. The crevasse was too wide and too vertical, and I was not functioning at a skill level that would allow me to scale an overhanging seven-story wall of ice. My only option, also probably impossible, was to traverse to my right where the crevasse appeared to narrow, and where I might have a chance to "chimney" my way up, using my body to span the narrower distance, pushing myself upward off the two walls. From what I could see, I'd need to advance hundreds of feet in that direction for any chance at all of gaining the seventy vertical feet to the surface. It seemed hopeless. Such a difficult, risky ice climb would be demanding even if I were intact and at full strength.

So, what was the alternative? I tried to calculate how long it might take for rescue from above. My teammates would not be coming back up to Camp 2 until tomorrow afternoon at the earliest, possibly not till the day after. It was doubtful they could rescue me themselves, and probably—wisely—they wouldn't venture far searching for me. They might not even realize there was a problem until it got dark tomorrow night and I still hadn't come back.

I was shivering already. I wouldn't live through a single night down here when the sun went down and temperatures plunged.

My thoughts returned to the stark choice: Climb or die.

This fateful plunge into a crevasse, of course, didn't begin just a few minutes earlier, seven stories above me on the snowy surface of a Himlung glacier. It was a fifteen-year journey of adventure, of scientific quest, of loves gained and lost, of learning and teaching, of facing wild beasts and living wild days, of struggle, of delight, of venturing high in hopes of doing good. The route had led me to the top of Everest just four years earlier. And to the summits of great peaks in the South American Andes. I'd gone deep into a mysterious Central American rain forest, which scientists had not visited in decades. And to the savannahs of Africa. I'd rediscovered the lost glory of a people who used to live just across the Arizona border in Mexico but who paid an awful price for environmental change. My journeys led to creation of a new organization that mixed science and adventure in equal parts, building an understanding of climate changes in the fragile alpine reaches of the world's highest mountains.

Then one lousy, lonely step too far.

Risk, though, is unavoidable in this business. Yes, I could have managed the danger better. But not exempted myself from it. Mountains are perilous places. And there are no reliable shortcuts for science up here. To fully understand what is happening on a mountain, you have to scale it, touch it, measure it. A satellite can convey details of, say, the mountains of the Cordillera Blanca in Peru. But only a mountaineer can get up there and bring back tangible evidence of what is occurring—what particulates, for instance, are being deposited on glaciers to hasten melting? And where have they come from? That evidence needs to be collected again and again, year after year, to accurately calibrate the extent and pace of climate change.

But let's take a step back. Why study mountains in the first place?

You can roll the whole thing up into a single word: water.

Mountains are the world's water towers.

Air currents are thrust aloft as they travel over mountains. Naturally, the air grows cooler along the way. This releases moisture. That is because cold air can hold less water than an equal volume of warmer air. The result of this lifting and cooling and moisture release is called orographic precipitation. Generally speaking, the higher air has to travel to pass over a mountain range, the more precipitation is produced. Up in these lofty reaches, precipitation is stored in vast quantities in the form of glaciers, snow, and alpine lakes. These are the birthplaces of the rivers that provide the hydrologic lifeblood for a large portion of humanity. Wet or dry years for the 22 million people of coastal Southern California are not determined by how much rain falls on Los Angeles or San Diego, but by the depth of the snowpack in the Sierra Nevada mountain range to the north and east. In just the same way, a huge section of Asia depends on water originating in Himalayan glaciers and snowfields—up here on peaks like Himlung. In South America, the eastern slopes of the Andes in Peru serve as headwaters for the world's greatest river system, the Amazon.

In addition to being water catchments on which entire cultures and peoples depend, these mountains provide gradients of soils, temperatures, precipitation, and ecological conditions in very compact geography. Moving upward in elevation means that in a compact space, the same environmental changes occur as those that will happen during long-distance travel from the tropics toward one pole or the other. That makes them handy terrain for the study of climate change. Beyond that, there is ample empirical evidence that environmental transformation as a consequence of climatic change is greatest at higher latitudes and elevations—where life is most fragile.

In short, mountains are our crystal ball. Understand them, and you get a glimpse of the planet's future.

We now know there are grave issues at hand. Accelerating environmental disruption has been visible all around us for some time. And complex challenges and social adjustments await us if we are to successfully adapt. The information that mountains can provide is crucial to our survival as a species.

Of course, these mighty peaks are also life-and-death places. For a few of us, the skill required to explore them, the exotic and extreme danger of doing so, and the scientific reward make them impossible to resist.

For all those reasons, I have spent much of my adult life in quest of evidence from all over the world to help fill in some of the scientific blank spots. If we had started this in-depth process in the mountains even forty years ago, we would understand our planet far better than we do today, and we could begin to think more concretely about what those adaptations might look like. It frustrates and saddens me that we've instead embarked on a decades'-long debate about whether climate change is happening, even as the ice melts beneath our feet.

Still, we should take heart from the spreading signs of global awareness—the recognition of both the facts and the impending uncertainties of climate change. Yes, there has been plenty of backlash along the way, but forward-looking political leaders continue to push for mandated reductions in carbon emissions as a step to slow atmospheric warming. The time has come for our leaders to devote equal energy to devising large-scale strategies for adapting to environmental alterations caused by shifts in climate—the next frontier.

To my mind, if I might borrow a crude trope, science is the headlamp that will help us find our way forward.

For the moment, though, my pathfinding challenge was hardly so ambitious. I was alone in the Himalayas, four miles up and seven stories down. Broken. Stuck. And a long way from anything like a headlamp.

Chapter Two

Lhotse

J ust a few weeks earlier, I'd been far from Himlung, pumped full of starting-line adrenaline, looking out across one of the starkest, most exciting mountain locales on the planet. I had arrived in Nepal to lead a team of five Western climbers and ten Nepalis headed for the roof of the world to gather research data. Our destination was the Everest massif—a mountain mass with several distinct peaks, including Lhotse, Nuptse, and Changtse. Our target was Lhotse, the fourth-highest mountain on Earth and sister peak to Everest.

We gathered on April 9 and headed to acclimatize at Everest Base Camp on the south, or Nepal side, of the massif, not far below the Khumbu Icefall, an ugly passage on the glacier of the same name. For a short interval each spring, this landscape of ice and sharp rock becomes home to a bustling burg built out of nylon and aluminum: a tent city, erected by a community of adventurers and thrill seekers, paid guides and Sherpas. People from all over the world—my tribe, as it were—convene here, climbers bound for Everest as well as the other peaks of the massif and countless trekkers who have come to see the great towering mountain close up. Whether this is the trekker's ultimate goal or the mountaineer's starting point, people who pitch their tents here feel special. Because they are special. Base Camp is at 5,200 meters (17,060 feet)—nearly 25 percent higher than the tallest mountain summit in the continental United States. It requires resolve and conditioning, time and money, just to get here. When we arrived for this expedition, the air was dry and frigid and breezes carried unexpected smells of baked goods, the hissing noises of camp stoves, the babble of conversation, and the keyboard clicking of people posting to Facebook. *Look Mom, I'm here.*

From Base Camp, it is a vertical rise of nearly two miles to the summit of Lhotse, which stands just 332 meters (1,089 feet) lower than Everest. Our plan was to systematically sample the dust in high-altitude snow and ice as we climbed. This fine, grayish material provides the means to measure the environmental effects of distant human enterprises. Commonly called "black carbon," this soot is the particulate residue of fossil fuel air pollution, surface mining, agriculture, and wildfires. As this anthropogenic dust accumulates on snowfields and glaciers, they grow darker, and therefore more heat absorptive. That hastens melting and runoff of stored water. The results include greater flooding potential downstream or higher likelihood of crop-killing summer droughts. Behold: climate change.

Our team was traveling under the banner of the American Climber Science Program (ACSP), originally created under the auspices of the American Alpine Club. The Program is an assemblage of mountaineers who are also ecologists, physicists, atmospheric scientists, biologists, glaciologists, geologists, physicians, and toxicologists—men and women uniquely trained to climb high into the mountains and precisely measure what is happening. We believed that our range of scientific skills would allow for a holistic analysis of how people and ecosystems are coping, or might have to cope, as a consequence of climate change. Such a strategy was new, and I was filled with optimism for what we could accomplish by merging our talents.

Our team for the expedition: Ulyana Horodyskyj was a PhD student from the University of Colorado who had been living in Nepal for a year doing her dissertation research examining the lakes that form on the surface of glaciers and in the scree as glaciers melt. When I met her a year earlier during an expedition in Peru, we had talked about an expedition to Lhotse. From that seed, the idea blossomed into focus as an important scientific and personal objective, and I set out to make it reality. Jake St. Pierre was a police officer from New Hampshire, also a climber, and the owner of a gym. Because a Himalayan expedition required an extended time commitment, Jake had little choice but to turn in his badge and resign from the force if he wanted to join us. It was a life choice to leave a career behind. But he exuded enthusiasm about the adventure and had decided to trust his future to fate. Because of his great physical strength and desire to learn to cross into the fabled "death zone"—those few places on Earth that soar higher than the benchmark 8,000 meters (26,247 feet), where mountaineers know that the fatality rate is highest—he volunteered to be our mule, carrying heavy loads of scientific equipment up the mountain. David Byrne was an architect who lived in Seattle and taught mountain safety classes as a volunteer. He had joined the American Climber Science Program Expedition in Peru the year before as safety officer. He had considerable climbing experience and, like Jake, dreamed of piercing the "death zone." He, too, quit his job in order to join the expedition. His plans were to climb with us and then look for employment as an expedition safety officer in Antarctica and other exotic locales. Dave talked his good friend and longtime climbing partner, Chris Cosgriff, of Seattle, into taking early retirement from his job as an engineer at Lockheed and joining the expedition. We were thrilled to have two team members with such good general mountaineering knowledge and climbing experience. We were also lucky because of the commitment that the team showed in sacrificing jobs or starting new phases in their lives to answer the call of the high Himalaya.

We had selected Lhotse, rather than Everest itself, because of simple economics. Everest was only marginally taller, but because of its popularity and cachet, it cost up to five times more to attempt, per climber, counting fees and other expenses. In day-to-day terms, Everest costs one year's salary for a newly minted lawyer and was beyond the reach of ordinary wage earners. On this expedition, such a premium price tag was too much by far. Someday, and soon I hope, the American Climber Science Program will not be restrained by financial limitations. But this year, we had only a small amount of funding from the National Science Foundation. And we were fortunate to have a chance at such a mighty and famed peak as Lhotse—hardly a consolation prize. Climbers on both peaks followed the Everest route upward a good deal of the way, including the spectacular "Lhotse face" of the massif, before peeling off to the south. We would not lack for opportunities to collect important data samples and, at the same time, increase our team's mountaineering skills—both goals essential to building the ACSP. And I, for one, was quite happy to face a new and challenging summit in a familiar locale.

I had summited Everest itself once before, on the north, or Tibetan side, so I understood the many ordeals that awaited our team, and the other mountaineers gathering at Base Camp. Or at least I thought I did. But seeking to understand and measure climate change in these fragile and hostile environs also meant exposing ourselves directly to the dangerous consequences of climate change. Fatal consequences, as it turned out.

On April 18, at about 6:45 a.m., a colossal boom echoed through the Khumbu Glacier valley as a block of ice the size of an office building, a huge serac, broke away from the high shoulder of Everest and thundered into the already dangerous Khumbu Icefall just above us. The ground trembled and then shook as a tsunami of powder snow and ground-up chunks of ice scoured down the mountain. Twenty-five men, most of them native Sherpas, were immediately buried in tons of jagged ice and compacted snow. Sixteen of them died.

The tragedy settled over Base Camp like a thick snow. There were Western mountaineers mixed in on the route with the Sherpa climbers this morning, but only the Sherpas paid the ultimate price—a capricious outcome that left others of us not just shocked but wracked with guilt. These victims were men we shared the evening with in Base Camp mere hours before they disappeared. One of them, Asman Tamang, was my friend and a member of our team, newly married and the proud father of a nine-month-old girl. This was his first trip up Mount Everest. He had been shy and we had teased him to bring him out of his shell. At night, we stood together near the tents, staring up at the looming, moonlit bulk of the Everest massif. I laughed with him about us racing up and setting a new speed record through the perilous icefall. Asman was so very excited. By earning a spot with this team and climbing with us on Everest, he would gain the experience and stature necessary to continue guiding and working on the mountain. For native Nepalis, that was a path to relative economic security and social standing.

Now our planet was getting warmer and warmer. And the mountains were melting underfoot. And ice was tumbling down. Killer ice.

And now he was gone. I was sick—heartsick—knowing he was on the mountain for me, for us, for our science.

All of us on the mountain were sick. The dead had belonged to the brotherhood of the rope, my brotherhood. I understood, and had witnessed, the killing power of Everest before. But not on this scale. Sixteen men, gone just hours after we'd seen them hike away. Two film crews at Base Camp made sure that it was also one of the most publicized of mountaineering disasters. Footage of the avalanche spread worldwide.

For me and my Nepali friends, it was personal. That morning seven of our team were spread across the Khumbu Icefall along with others, slowly climbing toward Camp 1. Near the top of the rugged terrain, one of the fixed ladders across a crevasse had fallen and created a bottleneck as it was laboriously being put back in position. Asman was at the ladder. Dipen—who was nominally in charge and a man with whom I'd climbed before—was following a bit behind. He looked up and saw the overhanging ice and the congestion of climbers. He told everyone on our team to drop their loads and run downhill. All but Asman obeyed. Dipen's split-second decision saved six people.

Asman, though, had not been accounted for. We waited for hours, our dread growing. Then the terrible news that he was among the dead. My friend. His youth, his exuberance, his dreams of a life in the high mountains. Gone. Unbearable.

His tent-mate and the person nearest to him during the icefall had been Dawa Lama, the highest-ranking climbing Buddhist lama at Base Camp and a man who had already summited Everest four times. Tears streamed down his face as he pitched a new tent, unable to sleep more than one night in the shelter he had shared with Asman. After the tragedy, Dawa led the somber Puja, or ceremony of purification for the entire Everest Base Camp community. A holy man of much strength and respect, Dawa's presence on our team brought us even closer to other survivors.

Season after season, the dangers on Everest are increasing. Sherpas and guides had come to dread the overhanging "ice bulge" up on the mountain's west shoulder. Occasionally, pieces had broken away—portents of the tragedy that had just occurred. This threat compounded the perpetual danger of the icefall, in which the moving

Khumbu Glacier drops over a cliff and breaks apart into a shifting maze of ice blocks and crevasses. Mountaineers have a special dread of such circumstances and places. In that kind of situation, skill accounts for little; luck will decide your fate.

In recent decades, mountaineering and attendant tourism have grown to be significant components of the culture and the economy of Nepal, employing more than a half-million people and transforming the nation into a global lure for serious adventurers. Now the Everest season was abruptly called off. Climate change violently ended the year's climbing before it had really begun, here on this most important mountain of all. My God.

I'm not what anyone would call devout, but I am a Buddhist, and serious about it. Dawa and the other Nepalis and I meditated for many days after the accident as we contemplated our loss. In memory of Asman, inside my left bicep I have a tattoo of a bell and inside my right, a tattoo of a *dorje* or *vajra*—traditional instruments of Buddhist meditation. These inked representations facilitate my meditations at high altitudes, freeing me from having to carry the extra weight of religious articles, and they help me continue to honor Asman and other friends who have lost their lives in the mountains.

Buddhists can sometimes forget their humility and be tempted to think they are invincible. Then one day the mountain itself breaks away, and the life-and-death nature of the high Himalayas gets rammed home in the worst possible way. And nobody—nobody—feels anything like invincible anymore.

After the disaster, Everest's ice wasn't the only thing hanging over the heads of climbers and those who labor in the nation's mountaineering industry. Politics came into the picture. On the surface, everyone in the climbing fraternity seemed drawn together in mourning. If there was any hint of friction, it was said to be between rich Western clients and the Sherpas, whose death benefits amounted to just $400. But I had loyal friends in the Nepalese mountaineering community, and they told a different story as shadowy people visited the tents each night after the tragedy. Nepal's bare-knuckle Maoist politicians had seized upon the fatal tragedy as an opportunity to try to fan Sherpa discontent with the nation's ruling political parties.

A tragedy became the foundation of a call for protest. Then to drive home the point, a Maoist functionary summarily announced that the mountain would be closed for the season. That deprived Sherpas of their livelihood without their consent. They were pawns in a political game—Maoists versus the ruling government. Some fumed. All mourned.

Foreign climbers found themselves stuck in the middle of the dispute.

Anti-Maoist leaders of the central government refused to acknowledge any issue—and declared the mountain to be open. Climbers had paid the government tens of thousands of dollars for official permits to attempt the summits of the massif. Now the government said it had no reason to issue refunds. Go ahead and climb, they said. We won't stop you.

But the Maoists would. They had no jurisdiction, only a political cause. But it was a cause enforced by dark threats of violence. Nepalis in city clothes began to appear—strangers to the mountains. Enforcers. Mountaineers and Sherpas alike were forced to heed the Maoist mountain-is-closed edict under the threat of having their legs broken or being beaten to a pulp. After a few examples, and given the violent history of this political party, the menace was taken seriously. Everyone was losing big-time and few of Nepal's leaders, if any, were looking beyond petty advantage.

For me, the mess was a sad reminder of the state of things—even with the deadly impact of climate change staring them in the face and threatening significant upheaval and suffering, politicians failed to rise to the challenge. They hunkered down to pursue venal rivalries. What of the stored water and traditional weather patterns of these peaks—the very lifeblood for two *billion* or so people who live in the ancient watersheds that cascade out of the Himalaya? That of course is the question that the country's leaders should have been asking. But politics once again obscured the bigger picture.

After the Khumbu Icefall disaster and political scrum, our team finally had no choice except to join a legion of climbers retreating off Everest; we were one of the last to leave. More ice avalanches rumbled down behind us as the mountain continued to melt away. We were numb and despondent, all of us. Many of the stunned Everest mountaineers from other groups raced, literally, to get home.

But home wasn't an option for our team, yet. We were in the Himalayas for reasons beyond climbing—and the tragedy of the Khumbu Icefall only underscored the urgency of our research. Ours was not work that could be lightly deferred. Not now, not for the foreseeable future. Just the opposite. Lives depended on it.

Our team had to find a way to proceed. We needed to get onto a Himalayan mountain somewhere; the higher the altitude, the better for our research. Too many information gaps existed in the global map, and filling those gaps could help us better understand and explain climate change and human impacts on our environment. In many regards, we were still assembling baseline data of current conditions—at this point barely able to calculate trends or estimate the pace of environmental alternations. I was determined to do whatever I could, whatever was possible, whatever *might* be possible, to add to our knowledge. Climate change wouldn't be taking the season off. Neither could we.

So, we held onto that thought, a hope really, during the long, shuffling trek back to half-old, half-new, noisy, sprawling, romantic, and always colorful Kathmandu. Our mood, though, was anything but romantic or colorful.

The first leg of our retreat was especially gloomy. Those who died on the mountain had left the remainder of us feeling deadened. No other word for it. Few seemed to be able to snap out of it. Nearly constant precipitation during what normally is the dry season added to the funereal mood.

Our first goal was the village of Lukla—several days' trek down the mountain but with the closest airport to Everest. The scene en route resembled the chaotic, hell-bent movement of refugees in full flight. During a normal year, people slowly wander down off the mountain after attempting the summit, the successful in high spirits. This time, climbers all but stampeded to flee the mountains, leaving behind a trail of gear and expensive debris. I'm accustomed to climbing on a budget, scrimping and scrounging for the equipment necessary to reach high altitudes, so it took my breath away to see piles of costly climbing gear crammed into huge duffle bags and left strewn across teahouse courtyards and abandoned in bags along the trail, a graveyard of once-shiny packs and rope and gear, as if the inanimate aluminum and nylon might be cursed.

Some people became downright desperate to escape this place of death. They summoned helicopter airlifts—to hell with the price. And the price grew higher and higher as poor weather closed in. Small fixed-wing airplanes from Kathmandu, high-performance craft that serve the mountain regions, were having trouble maintaining a schedule in and out of Lukla's sodden, nail-biting, cliff-top airfield—which is, as Himalayan veterans know, the scariest in the world.

Money talks loudly in this community of Everest climbers and trekkers—with the wealthiest having enjoyed unbelievably posh accommodations on the approach to Everest's summit. At Base Camp, those with the deepest pockets paid to have couches and satellite-connected TVs brought up to pass the time during acclimatization. They gathered in comfortable communal tents to dine on their choice of steak or pizza every night. Now, these same well-to-do climbers maneuvered their privileged status to the front of the line for the precious flights out. There was nothing subtle about the pushy entitlements claimed by the self-important members of this group. They seemed oblivious to the resentments they engendered as they split the once-homogeneous tribe of high-altitude mountaineers, and even trekkers, into those who, if I may be excused for generalizing, earned their way here and those who merely bought it. For pilots and aviation companies, though, this avalanche tragedy was an economic windfall without precedent.

We waited our turn at the end of the line. Finally, we lucked into seats on what turned out to be the only flight out to Kathmandu for the next ten days. I felt lousy that others were left waiting. Their nightmares were no less vivid and disconcerting than ours.

As we lurched down the single runway at Tenzing-Hillary airport, with full-throttle propellers fighting for grip in the thin mountain air and mountain winds knocking the plane one way and then another, I reflected on the tenuous nature of the mountaineering culture here. This avalanche would reverberate in so many ways for the Nepalis. When that huge chunk of ice lost its grip on a warming mountain and caused death and panic among climbers, it undermined the economy of the many towns and villages. Tourism—predominately mountain-related—accounted for more than a half-million jobs in Nepal, and its economic importance had been expected to double in just the span of a year, according to a study prepared by the World Travel and Tourism

Council. Now, that development trajectory was in jeopardy. The year 2014 would go down as the first time that climate change closed Mount Everest. I looked out the window of this small, bouncing plane and wondered to myself if people down there have the chance, the foresight, the leadership, to adapt to the environmental alterations now happening to their beloved mountains. What I had seen of Nepal's politicians did not fill me with optimism. And what about the rest of us humans—since we all face some version of that impending question?

Would we rally, lock arms, and make ourselves both strong and formidable? When?

When we reached Kathmandu, we pretty much had to start over. The first step toward every summit begins with governmental red tape—the scramble to obtain climbing permits. In a normal year, this would be done far ahead of time. Now, I could hear the clock ticking. Each spring, the extreme winds at high altitudes ease for a week or two before the arrival of the monsoon storms. That interval of calm, for the fortunate people who time things just right, provides a brief window for mountaineers to attempt summits on the big peaks. Because of the time lost already, the window would be closing soon. The monsoon was about to blow in and extinguish our hopes for productive work this season. The rush was on.

Our team met to discuss options. We agreed to strike out for a different peak, one for which we could get a climbing permit without too much added delay. Everest was located to the east of Kathmandu. We set aim in the opposite direction—to the region near the famous Annapurna massif and a peak along the Nepal-Tibet border called Mount Himlung.

Himlung is a mile lower than Everest but has similar characteristics. It would serve our cause well enough. We could collect baseline data on how soot and other particles in the atmosphere affect the glaciers and snowfields in this border region between the two countries. Plus, we would still have a chance to stand atop a worthy Himalayan giant.

In addition to the paperwork, we needed to re-provision and arrange the complex, and ticklish, logistics to reach our remote target.

Now my friendship with Nepali climbers who understood and believed in our mission really paid off. One after another, they penetrated the bureaucracy and kept us moving forward. Finally, on May 8, I went to my Nepali graduate student's traditional wedding in the morning and we headed toward our new climb just after lunch. As my student's honeymoon, he and his new wife would join us on the trail, doing interviews for his thesis research. The first section of our route would follow the path toward the Annapurna range. At one time, this was the most storied trek in the world. But progress replaced the charming trail with a barren, soulless dirt road. Off we went, on foot, back into the great Himalaya range, our spirits much sapped but not so our hopes.

Because this was the tail end of the season, we traveled a lonely route. And the Everest disaster left us with only a minimalist support team—a sirdar who also served as our cook, plus two other helpers. I couldn't ask more of my Sherpa friends to accompany us, not after the pain they had suffered. Yaks carried our gear slowly up the mountain paths. Typically, we traveled faster than the pack animals, which meant we had to carry heavy loads to assure our self-sufficiency— gear for a sudden snowstorm, water and food for a day, and so forth.

We walked. Days spent alone with our thoughts from the past few weeks. Then at a junction, we veered off the standard Annapurna route and entered a vast, mostly empty valley that was seldom seen by foreign visitors. In Nepal, there are two types of valleys—those that end in mountain passes that easily cross the border into Tibet, and those that don't. Generally foreign trekkers are forbidden to travel into the valleys that lead to mountain passes because of potential border incidents with China. But this route served as our approach to Himlung, which stood right up against the border. As a consequence, we had to carry a special permit, which we had obtained in Kathmandu, thanks to the amazing work of our expedition's Nepali expediter and my friend, Sujan Bhattarai. He had processed the extra paperwork and submitted the additional fees to get us moving in near record time. To tell the truth, I had been concerned that we would be denied permission on such short notice because the valley's border pass was unusually low and fraught with dangerous history. In the autumn of 1950, it was the primary escape route for Tibetans fleeing the Chinese invasion of their nation. Along with countless thousands of civilians, the largest part of the Tibetan army had fled through this pass—a historic occurrence that remained fresh in cross-border relations. In addition, we would be traveling along to what had been a major Himalayan trade route, another red flag for Nepalese officialdom. As we walked, we saw disquieting evidence of this not-so-distant past—a festival site, hundreds of tent platforms carved out of hill slopes, and, shimmering in the distance on a remote ridge, old and mostly abandoned Buddhist monasteries where merchants and travelers once prayed for safety on their journeys. It was a solemn, foreboding valley whose vibrant past was wrapped up in tragedy. If it held an omen for us, we were too distracted to pay heed to it.

Walking long distances gives the mind time to wander. It is one of the secret joys of Himalayan mountaineering. I've always loved the chance to feel my thoughts relax and expand with the landscape, even in one so laden with past miseries as this one. No matter how the route changed from rough to smooth, from steep to flat, my mind wandered easily, without the hurly-burly of cosmopolitan life. I contemplated the coming climb, the work we were doing, the life I had chosen, and the people I loved. On this occasion, though, my free-ranging thoughts kept returning to the tragedy of the Everest Icefall and what it might portend.

The weather continued to worry me, too. How much time did we really have before the deadly Asian monsoon? Was this a fool's journey?

We pressed ahead. I was not alone in battling gloominess. The struggle to scrape together the money and arrange the extended time off needed for this expedition had raised the stakes. We had planned and paid to tackle the most famous of massifs, Everest. And we had to admit it: science may not care which Himalayan mountain we studied, but the mountaineer in each of us did.

In high-altitude mountaineering, the "eight-thousander" is the standard by which elites measure themselves—8,000 meters above sea-level, where the "death zone" begins. Only fourteen summits on Earth reach so high into the sky, 26,247 feet or more. Lhotse was one. Himlung was not. Who could blame those among us who felt we were marching toward a consolation prize?

This wore on the team. Several of them had quit their jobs just for this. Their distress was plain to see. As I looked back on the Everest disaster, it was clear that I had been more deeply shaken by the deaths than the others, and the difference in our reactions had put us out of sync. And health was becoming a bigger issue, as often happens during long expeditions. Between the marginal food and the thin air, the long distances and the tension of a team under extended stress, no one felt well. Ulyana was exhausted after a year of working in Nepal and was battling a serious stomach illness.

Not that we lacked rewards en route to Himlung. This late in the season, we found ourselves the only foreign travelers for miles in any direction—traversing an otherworldly Himalayan landscape where snow caught the sunlight and glistened in the high reaches above bone-dry valleys. Where wind carried the sound of vast spaces. Where, during daylight, our small group could spread out along the path and rub shoulders with terrestrial infinity. At night, we gathered together to sleep in teahouses—small stone rooms rented for token sums.

Unfortunately, with the monsoon season approaching, many teahouses were closed. As we got closer to Himlung, I scooted out ahead of the others each day to search for lodging. If there was no handy teahouse, I knocked on village doors, appealing to the famed hospitality of the Nepalis to help us find shelter.

During our last day on the trail, we were pinned down by an early monsoon snowstorm in a village called Pho—which resembled nothing so much as a medieval stone fortress in the Transylvanian Alps. We were provided room to sleep in dusty storerooms crawling with bugs. My mood sank. And it didn't get any better as we waited out the storm for a second day, then a third, trying—not altogether successfully—to keep a grip on our patience.

While the storm raged, we learned that a village herder had died trying to get his animals to shelter. The people of Pho lapsed into mourning. Another menacing omen. Being the superstitious type, I pondered the worrisome signs that seemed to be stacking up around us. But, I reassured myself, something as important as our climate work simply had to be favored in the scheme of things, right?

When the weather cleared, we hurried toward Himlung. It was now clear that the cumulative stresses of this extended expedition had divided our group. David and Chris felt strong and decided to set out by themselves for a different peak. Ulyana was having a lot of problems and she and Jake stayed with me. When our trio reached the base of Himlung, we climbed quickly. Base Camp was established and we pushed onward to 6,000 meters (19,685 feet) to make Camp 2.

For all the hurry, the one thing we could not rush was acclimatization. The physiology was complicated but came down to this: the human body needs time to adjust metabolically to a reduced supply of oxygen, to thin air. That process cannot be hurried. Everything from breathing rates to the density of red blood cell production is significantly altered by the density of the surrounding air, or more importantly, to correspondingly lower oxygen levels. We planned to spend a week slowly climbing and acclimatizing, and to use the time to gather and process snow and ice samples for later analysis.

But again, troubles. Ulyana was not acclimatizing well, as she continued to suffer gastric distress. She was getting weaker with time, not stronger. Another unsettling portent. Jake volunteered to accompany her from Camp 2 back down to Base Camp, where she could rest before starting up again. Recovery occurred more reliably and more quickly at lower elevation.

With the monsoon and the end of the climbing season approaching, perhaps days away, I decided not to accompany them down. I would stay up here on Himlung by myself and arrange Camp 2 for strategic occupation. I was confident that I could collect the necessary scientific data and keep things moving while the other two descended for a time. That meant, of course, putting aside the normal, commonsense rule against splitting such a small group and leaving a team member alone at 20,000 feet. At the time, it seemed a reasonable move. We scouted our camp and ensured that I had a safe zone for work.

I wouldn't be honest if I didn't confess that I relished the prospect of some solitude. We had been crammed together for long, stressful intervals already —planning, arranging, eating, sleeping, and performing other bodily functions in close quarters. To me, low-pressure time with only the incomparable beauty of the mountain landscape to keep me company sounded wonderful.

That first morning alone, I found myself reflecting on the human dynamics of mountaineering. Stories get told of great achievements or great catastrophes. Excitement unfolds on a heroic scale in quest of summits, leading to the pure high notes of joy or the unfiltered anguish of despair. The tightly focused, life-and-death arc of the mountaineering narrative mostly separated climbers from ordinary mortals—or that's how climbers sometimes viewed it. But in truth, mountaineering was foremost a grind. The turmoil and illness in our team was no surprise. Seeking science at Earth's extremes extracted a toll on the best of people and on the closest of relationships. Too many long, taxing days. Too many frigid nights without sleep. Too many dangers, always too close at hand. Too much strain on the body and the mind. Sores and cuts and sunburns and frostbite were external signs of the struggle, but the unseen internal dings and dents were just as harsh. I knew from experience that it was impossible for a team leader to both survive and be reliably friendly, to be both safe and considerate, in the high mountains. The team could hug when we'd been to the summit and back. But until then, focus. Your life and mine depended on it.

What was it about danger, anyway? My thoughts turned in that direction as I set out alone to gather snow for coffee. As I took those first steps, little did I know just how close I was to real danger, to the glacier's icy jaws. Then I learned.

I'm gonna live till I die.

Isn't that how the song goes?

PART II

CLIMBER SCIENCE

Chapter Three

Adaptation

A decade ago, I was two years into a PhD program in renewable natural resources at the University of Arizona in Tucson. A fundamental realization hit me over the head like a cast-iron skillet: I didn't know enough. I didn't know enough to know what I needed to know. I had been learning so many facts and theories, but I didn't really understand the world—the big-picture world. When you've come to that understanding about such a yawning gap in your educational strategy, it's pretty hard to contemplate just carrying on as before.

Caroline came to the rescue. She was a vibrant young woman from Germany and we had been dating. When her visa expired, she headed home. Sadly, I took her to the airport. She flew out of my life. But she left me a gift by way of advice—a simple gift that changed my life forever. She told me to travel. To take the measure of the world close up. She promised it would open my eyes.

I would give it a try. I would venture beyond my native land. I would see what there was to see. I bought a one-way ticket to Mexico City. That summer, I had worked seventy-hour weeks in the cotton fields of Georgia to save up money. But instead of using the money for school, I would seek a different kind of education. My funds would allow me to travel for around a year, I hoped, and so off I went.

How many thousands of young people had gone before me, finding themselves giddy at their first exposure to strange geography, unfamiliar language, exotic perspectives, exciting cultures, fresh landscapes? How many of them discovered the lessons that eluded them in college? A life of purpose means life as a quest.

I arrived in Mexico City at midnight with a four-word Spanish vocabulary, an English-Spanish dictionary, no itinerary, and no place to stay. I took a deep breath, passed through customs and into my future.

After spending the night in a dingy hotel, I awoke and ventured into the historical center of the city. One of my first stops was the imposing *modernismo*-style palace housing the Museo Nacional de Arte. An 1880s painting caught my attention. A powerful and evocative landscape in the style of the age, it conveyed in looming detail the mountains surrounding the site of what was now this huge city. A visitor, though, could have been forgiven for mistaking the canvas as a work of fantasy. These same mountains had vanished behind a choking fog of pollution. Even the tops of tall buildings disappeared into the eye-stinging brown haze.

Adaptation hadn't become a crusade for me yet, but the idea was ripening. Mexico brought home the notion that people could shape their relationship with their environment or the environment would sure as hell shape them, and not necessarily for the better.

My journey south was about to change my life in another important way. Until Mexico, I had been content with—unquestioning about—a life divided into two distinct pieces.

There was the cerebral half, the indoor half. The classroom and library half. I had participated in academic competitions, for example, in Math Team, Academic Bowl, and Science Bowl. I won many awards—such as at the National Academic Decathlon in Los Angeles.

The other half of my existence was the physical, the outdoors piece—athletics from volleyball to rugby, along with plenty of hiking, canoeing, and eventually, climbing. I took monthlong camping trips with my father from our home in Georgia, venturing to Canada and the West. As I grew into my teens, I grew. I grew to six foot five inches during my freshman year of high school. And not just big, I was tough. I headed out for solo backpacking trips beginning close by and then farther off, to places like the Upper Peninsula of Michigan. Naturally enough, I developed an appetite for wild places. Then more than an appetite, a passion. The wilder the better.

Before long, mountains took hold of my heart. I started looking up high; aiming up high. Indeed, mountains were the chief lure of

Mexico and the reason I traveled here for my first exploration of the larger world. The country was famous for its towering volcanoes. I wasn't the first to fall under their spell. So after a week in the capital city, summits beckoned. I wanted to see, and climb, these great peaks hidden behind the smog.

After reading accounts of past expeditions, I chose Popocatepetl, which rises to 5,426 meters (17,802 feet) just forty-three miles from Mexico City. Then I discovered to my chagrin that climbers were forbidden on its slopes at that time. The volcano was belching toxic gases, and scientists expressed fears of an inevitable eruption. Ultimately, scientists were proven correct. In 2000, Popo erupted and forced the evacuation of tens of thousands of nearby residents.

So I chose instead to climb an adjacent and less active volcanic peak, Iztaccihuatl. A Mexican fable held that Iztaccihuatl was a princess and Popo a warrior, and the gods made the two lovers into mountains so they could spend eternity together.

I was learning that in almost every way possible, whether real drama or simple folklore, the peoples of mountain regions lived their geography and built their narratives out of the terrain around them.

Iztaccihuatl was my first 5,000-meter peak—rising to 5,230 meters (17,158 feet). It was a long, physical slog to reach such a lofty summit, but I had no real technical difficulties. Next, I traveled to Mexico's highest mountain, the majestic volcano Pico de Orizaba, elevation 5,610 meters (18,491 feet)—an intimidating climb by almost any measure. Two mountaineering teams were already at the base camp hut when I arrived, but conditions were unfavorable to move up. Two days earlier, a team had taken a bad fall. One climber was killed, the other injured. It seemed that the glacier, which marked the common route to the summit, lacked the usual cover of snow. It was said that snowfall was light this year and what did fall melted quickly, leaving bullet-hard ice. As a consequence, the difficulty of the climb rose dramatically. My time on California's Mount Shasta had prepared me for tough ice, and I was becoming better acclimatized to thinner air. Once again I reached the summit. Three and a half miles closer to the stars.

I was growing confident in my abilities. My strength at altitude pleased me. And it was at this interval that I came to the life-changing understanding that avocation and vocation need not be separate parts of my life. This was a big step forward in self-awareness. Not so long ago, when I moved to Arizona to finish my graduate studies, I had been a bifurcated man—half academic and half athletic. Half indoors and half out. Half work, half play. It seemed the natural way of things. I pursued both with mounting enthusiasm, but always separately.

By the time I arrived in Arizona, my interest in team sports had receded in favor of encounters with nature. I relished moving across new types of topography. My wilderness skills and confidence expanded accordingly. Looking back, I guess it was inevitable that I'd come into contact with rock. And rock climbing.

Hands grasping rough surfaces. Stretching, toeing for footholds. Shifting weight—first here, then there. The ballet of climber. Vertical vistas. Risk. Exhilaration. Reach. Toe. Some passions come and go. This one stayed.

Swept up with youthful invincibility, I journeyed across the desert, over the Sierra to Yosemite National Park. I would climb El Capitan, "The Captain," the 900-meter (3,000-foot) sheer-granite monolith that stands as the preeminent rock climb in the world. This was the proving ground of legends—climbers such as Warren Harding, Royal Robbins, Jim Birdwell.

I made the summit. But just barely. If things had gone wrong on that rock face, if I had been alone, I could have died—a battle with mortality that added shape and substance, and perhaps sober motive, to the man I was becoming. What happened was absurdly simple: my longtime climbing partner and friend, Eric Sloan, and I ran out of food and water after five days on the face. Eric was experienced and had set our water rations, but the weather had turned blisteringly hot on us. We had two more days to the top—days without water in 100°F temperatures. I suffered heatstroke and dehydration. But, through it, I learned about willpower—and what can be done if you have confidence in yourself, and if you refuse to succumb. I had always thought only heroic figures took on life with a knife clenched in their teeth. El Cap showed that ordinary me could do the same. It was a lesson I shared again and again with my students. Desire scratches out the "im" from "impossible."

I was hooked. There was much to learn, much to experience in the mountains. In my youth, my father had taken me to lonely Wheeler Peak in Nevada's Great Basin National Park for my first mountain climb. The power of that 3,982-meter (13,065-foot) desert peak moved me. I had read extensively about mountaineering—the collected canon among the most inspiring in all adventure writing. As John Muir put it: "Thousands of tired, nerve-shaken, over-civilized people are beginning to find out that going to the mountains is going home." There were big footsteps to follow up there. My focus grew sharper still on vertical landscapes.

From Yosemite, I took aim at far northern California and the volcano cone that rose almost two miles from the floor of the Central Valley, Mount Shasta. Here, I could take on something entirely new. Ice climbing. I had never worn crampons. If I was going to think of myself as a budding mountaineer, that just wouldn't do. There was a reason I was born with the demanding name All.

I chose the north side of the mountain, which was the most difficult, but safer—the ridge route was frequently soloed, according to the other climbers I had queried. I spent a fitful night before climbing. I was alone this time, and solo ascents do not allow for so much as a single error.

The route turned out to be hard and steep ice. Later, I was to learn that two people had fallen and died mere days ahead of me on this route. They slipped and couldn't self-arrest. For me, though, any danger of falling was overshadowed by the chop-bite feel of the axe into ice, the stab of toe points on one crampon and then the other, the rhythm of step-pull-step, the alive feeling of breathing, eyes up, the lure of the summit.

I discovered there was no sensation—really, none at all—to match the soaring of spirit when I reached the top after a hard climb. Why climb? To get to the top. I felt strong, increasingly capable, eager for more.

Rather suddenly, in Mexico, the two halves of me came together into a unified whole—and out of that, a single ambition. What brought me to this view was the sharp contrast between Mexico's searing lowland heat and the brisk chill and ice of the alpine reaches, and all the variety in between. What a perfect, compact laboratory—a layer cake of environments for the environmental scientist. Provided the scientist had the uncommon skills to climb up, over, and around these mountains, science and adventure could be pursued as one. What an exhilarating realization.

But also, at the moment, an exhausting one. I was bone tired. Gravity and lack of oxygen had taken their toll on my body after summiting two of Mexico's tall volcanic peaks in just a week. I wanted to rest and contemplate my emerging revelation. I retreated to the coastal Yucatán Peninsula and the island of Cozumel to look at our environment from still another elevation: below sea level. I earned my certification first as an open-water and then as an advanced scuba diver—and before too long I would earn rescue diver certification, too.

Coastal peoples, like mountain dwellers, often live day to day, very close to their geography. And like the alpine mountains, coastal oceans could be very fragile places, canaries in the climate-change coal mine, if you will. Favorable topography attracts people, but the confined space of an island environment means rapid resource deple-tion. The bounty of the sea can overcome this limitation—but not for-ever. I soon witnessed that the interplay of pollution and poor fishing practices, along with damage from occasional hurricanes, was chang-ing local ocean dynamics off the coast of Cozumel. And overfishing was startlingly apparent to divers. In another life, I might have become an oceanographer. The vast panoramic views of nature, the concentra-tion and skill required to explore them—it all appealed to me. But at heart I was still an apprentice to an idea that was becoming clearer all the time: Challenging vertical terrain would provide this budding climate scientist both personal and professional opportunities in over-flowing abundance. Not many people could venture to our planet's terrestrial extremes. I believed I could. And that's just what I would do. Of everything I had undertaken, of all I'd seen and dreamed of, the high, cold mountains beckoned strongest. And by chance, I turned out to be a better climber than I might have foreseen. So I resolved: I would plant the flag of geoscience as high as I could. Eventually atop the world—the summit of Everest itself. The oceans would remain a pastime, a retreat sometimes, but not a devotion.

C limate change confronts humanity with three fundamental tests. The first is to understand—to understand the dynamics of what is occurring in our atmosphere and its effects on the environment. That means figuring out both what can be divined and, importantly, what cannot, at least not without advances in science. This willing-ness to acknowledge unknowns is fraught with peril, of course. If we're not absolutely sure, then why rush to act? The answer is simple, even if the actions are not: because delay could very well be the end of us. Somewhere countless generations ago, our progenitors came to understand that certain foods would kill them—for example, colorful mushrooms or dead meat rotting in the sun. So they eliminated these items from their diet, not waiting for science to catch up and figure out the mechanisms of food poisoning. To continue the analogy, educated people today, all these countless generations later, understand that toxins exist in our environment but few of us actually understand how they work on the body to make us sick or kill us. Dear Mr. Congress-person: This tuna sandwich has been sitting in the sun for a week in the backseat of your car. Do you believe it has changed from healthy to unhealthy? Could you explain the biochemistry of what happened and why? Or are you willing to accept the word of science on it? If not, well, bon appétit.

The second challenge we face is to mitigate those factors that contribute to climate change. Environmental instability is not a winning formula for our sprawling and intricately industrialized social systems. Over the long haul, our planet's climate has not been static; we know that for certain. But does that mean we can be blasé about the changes under way? Does it matter if bananas come from Guatemala or Colorado?

Well, over the course of, say, 100,000 human generations, slow geographic migrations of agro-ecological zones might not matter all that much. But compressed into relative eyeblinks of geologic time, mere decades, such shifts will almost certainly destabilize our world. Put the other way, can anyone really envision an easy transition if we put matters off until the very end?

So why not do what we can? Why not agree that we should start now? US Army general Omar Bradley, World War II's greatest American field commander, was farsighted in warning that industrial advancement alone did not win the future. "If we continue to develop our technology without wisdom or prudence," he said, "our servant may prove to be our executioner."

The third test posed by climate change has received the least focused attention in our national conversations, and for understandable reasons. But it is no less crucial: human adaptation. Many smart people worry that opening the discussion of how we're going to cope with climate change means jumping too far ahead. They fear that it would amount to surrendering without trying to mitigate the impact that human industriousness has on our environment. I understand. And sympathize. But I also believe that if we're going to grow bananas in Colorado, then the people of the Rocky Mountains better start preparing.

Adaptation. A word with urgent possibilities. A do-or-die word. Adaptation is the challenge awaiting us, and it wouldn't be rushing things to raise the matter. Not now and not for the foreseeable future. Arguments by the flat-earthers only prove the magnitude of the task for our political systems, our social systems, our economic systems, our wisdom, and our courage. The National Oceanic and Atmospheric Administration (NOAA) issued a report projecting that by 2050 a majority of US coastal areas will be threatened by thirty days of flooding each year on account of rising oceans. One month out of every year. A "majority" of the US coast, the most densely populated part of the country. Spread the problem across the globe and the annual cost "not to adapt" to such sea level increases would annually exceed $1 trillion in flood damage by 2050, according to the World Bank.

Alaska, not normally a progressive pathfinder, already took steps to move the native village of Newtok to higher ground as part of a federal program to counter the effects of climate change, a process that did not unfold easily but which may become more commonplace. Of course, there was also the contrasting approach taken by unimaginative politicians and developers in North Carolina. There, state lawmakers earned the ridicule of scientists as well as comedy-show hosts for trying to beat climate change by voting it away. A state-sponsored scientific study concluded that North Carolina's lovely coastal barrier islands would be all but inundated by rising sea level by the end of the century—wiping out billions of dollars in property and the related tourist economy. Rather than begin to face this future, the legislature yielded to frantic real estate and business lobbyists, who were supported by climate-change deniers. Lawmakers voted to recommission the study, reducing its scope to only thirty years and not allowing scientists to project the effects of global warming on sea levels. To make the point clearer, the state prohibited policy decisions based on the first study—meaning that development could continue on its merry way, unimpeded by science, common sense, or even the destruction of recent storm events.

To my way of thinking, the only flaw in the original study was that it would have been more effective a few decades earlier, ahead of many billions of dollars in real estate investment. As it was, though, the whole crazy episode got reasonable people thinking about the need to hurry action along, not the opposite. Adaptation will not get easier or cheaper by putting it off.

For that reason, and because of the powerful human instinct for self-preservation, I try and lean to the optimistic side of things. We can learn a lot about the possibilities of adaptation just by poking around with eyes open. That has been my approach to environmental change ever since I interrupted my graduate studies to venture south of the border and see what I could see. One thing I saw pretty clearly was the resourcefulness that people, past and present, have exhibited in coping with their environments. My head spun when I wandered around the Yucatán Peninsula, which had been home to one of the great civilizations of the human epoch, the Mayans. From a contemporary environmental standpoint, this peninsula should be closer to uninhabitable than prime terrain for a storied civilization.

The peninsula is what geoscientists call a karst landscape, one composed of soluble rock. The easiest way to think of karst is the word *cave*—caves are common in karst and not many other types of geologies. Karst is generally limestone rock that weathers chemically instead of physically. This means that instead of surface rocks eroding into smaller and smaller pieces to be carried off by rivers, limestone melts away under the surface from the carbonic acids that naturally occur in organic soils and that are flushed deep by rainwater. The result can be seen in caves, sinkholes, cenotes, and other curious geologic phenomena. As a consequence, this terrain supports few streams and rivers. Its soils are thin and easily eroded. In many cases, fresh water is only available from that which floats atop seawater in sinkholes. Not hospitable terrain on which to farm or build. Yet the Mayans adapted to this landscape and thrived for centuries, building one of the most important civilizations in human history.

Of course, they had centuries. We might not.

During my year of traveling, I found that my interests were focused on the Andes and surrounding landscapes. The region fit

me both personally and scientifically. And why not? It was splendor-
ous and intriguing geography, and it was brimming with challenges.
It was vertical, and more. I developed a pattern where I would climb
a mountain, descend, spend a few days at the beach, maybe go scuba
diving, and return to the mountains. I was learning. About mountains. About joy. About balance in life.

Adventurous young people are free to tell their parents that I recommend some version of the same for them, the bolder the better.
Grabbing and hanging onto the tail of wanderlust can be a vital step in
a well-rounded education. Not only did I have glorious fun, which is
part of youth—and not a small part, either—my ambitions for myself
intensified and grew more focused.

In Equatorial Peru, the Andes were quite wet and jungles grew
high up the flanks of the mountains. As I moved south, away from the
equator, the climate grew drier. This shift was especially pronounced
along the narrow lowlands between the Andes and the Pacific. This
terrain is unique in all the world. It offered ecological gradients both
vertically, according to altitude, and horizontally, according to latitude. Really nowhere else could you be on an alpine ice field headed
to the top of a 6,000-meter (19,685-foot) mountain, less than one hundred miles from a warm beach. I kept both my parka and swimsuit
close by wherever I went.

Not only did the environment present great diversity, so did
the dozens of variously identifiable peoples of this region. Small native populations spoke their own tongues and practiced resource-
management strategies thousands of years old. The Atacama Desert
plateau of western Chile is one of the driest, and most environmentally stable, landscapes in the world. It is said that rain had not fallen
for four hundred years in some places. The small populations of humans who live here had many generations to adapt to what should not
be survivable. Not far away were fully modern peoples, the residents
of such cities as Lima and Valparaiso. The contrasts in the region
beckoned. I vowed I would return as soon as I could to this wondrous
natural laboratory that was richly diverse in both culture and environment. Now, however, it was time to return to finish my graduate studies. My year of travels had broadened my understanding of the world,
and my compass heading as a geoscientist was pretty much set. I was
ready to get to work.

Chapter Four

Paradise Lost

B ack in 1994, before I began my PhD studies, I had earned a law degree at the University of Georgia, with an emphasis on international and environmental law. In my mind, law was the pathway into the places where things got done—government and commerce. As the calendar clicked over into the twenty-first century, it was time to add to my resume a PhD in geography—specifically, the study of global climate change. Science is the pathway to discover what needed to be done and I intended to be as well credentialed and knowledgeable as possible to confront contemporary environmental challenges.

Professor Tom McGuire, an applied anthropologist at the University of Arizona, helped identify geography close to home that would be ideal for my PhD study of environmental disruption.

McGuire was an expert on community development strategies, and he showed me that some of the things I found compelling about human adaptation in the Andes could be informed—and contrasted—with the experiences of peoples of northern Mexico along the US border, where rapid change had upended the social and environmental status quo with alarming consequences. So I set my sights on the Colorado River Delta and the Sea of Cortez, just east of San Diego between Baja California and mainland Mexico. The high mountains would have to wait.

For now, this border region would prove an upbraiding lesson for anyone who was inclined to make light of rapid environmental change. Prior to the twentieth century, this delta was one of the premier desert wetlands on Earth. Here, the free-flowing Colorado River braided out into a vast estuarial system at the top of the Sea of Cortez.

Journals of early travelers described a teeming gallery of forests with huge flocks of birds and rare animals—all nourished by the river's surge of spring runoff from the distant Rocky Mountains. The Cocopah Indian Tribe flourished in this paradise. When Spanish explorers in the late 1500s encountered the tribe, they could count a population of nearly 25,000. At the dawn of the twenty-first century, the water had all but disappeared and so had the glory of the surroundings and all but a few of the Cocopah people themselves.

What happened to the water was a familiar story. As development swept the western United States, dam builders put their shoulders to the grindstone. By the beginning of the twentieth century, the Colorado River was the most engineered and contained major waterway on Earth. Dams held back irrigation and drinking water, creating recreational lakes and producing hydropower. What a wonderful human achievement! Except for the people, animals, and environment of the Delta. The Cocopah were driven from their homes and the lives they knew and migrated toward cities in Mexico, Arizona, and California. In short order, geologically speaking, the land became too barren to support all but a few holdouts, who struggled to scrape out a living. The rich estuary was reduced to a massive salt flat—baking in the sun until an occasional and unpredictable flood, like the one that came as a result of 1983's large-scale El Niño. Then, life-giving water momentarily washed over the land again and you could almost imagine the lush vitality of the past.

Treaties and water allocation compacts accompanied all this dam building and the related diversion strategies, of course. But the people who drafted and signed these agreements had not accounted for drought, for climate change, for El Niño–style floods. Perhaps they believed that doing so would be too politically messy. More likely, they were making decisions in the scientific dark, not accounting for increasing climatic variability. In the absence of knowledge, they answered to a simple maxim: water that found its way to the Sea of Cortez was as good as wasted.

My research was founded on a belief that wiser public policies, such as building resilience into human communities, required comprehensive environmental understanding. The Colorado River Delta was not just an example of arrogant power politics on the Mexican border; it was striking evidence of what happens to a landscape and its people when water distribution patterns are disrupted and residents do not have generations to adapt. What the dams and upstream urban development and agricultural irrigation did to this place in years past, climate change was sure to accomplish, in various forms, elsewhere in our future.

I believed the case would have to be as unassailable as contemporary science could make it—meaning it should be based on painstaking fieldwork, not just glib overview. This was not necessarily "Eureka!" science. I wouldn't be looking for answers in a laboratory with bubbling concoctions in test tubes and growths spreading across petri dishes. No, I was headed in the direction of shoe-leather science, the science of data collection, measurement, comparison, analysis, and from that, hopefully, insight. Success rested on two things: first, my wisdom as a scientist to determine what information would be of most value, and second, my ability to reach the places where those data could be collected. And, of course, to return safely.

So I packed my old Honda Prelude with notebooks, a GPS laser rangefinder, topo maps, a camera, and a good deal of youthful optimism. I knew enough now to get started. I drove south.

At its most rewarding, PhD research leads the student straight into the unexpected. That proved particularly true in this instance when it came to personal matters. Oh yes, I logged the geographical characteristics of this remote, often desolate landscape mile by careful mile. But the surprises came from a different direction. One day while conducting field studies on a cracked-earth Mexican salt flat that was once part of the Colorado River Delta, I found myself saying "yes" to a proposal of marriage. And the earth moved. Only it wasn't like you might think. And then, too, there was a half ton of cocaine piled up in the desert.

On this particular sojourn to the Delta, I was traveling with Sara Dalton, wonderful Sara, who was a fellow student and very much my romantic interest. We planned a quick trip—eight hours of precision survey work on one of the Delta's dry lake beds to prepare an accurate topographical profile for my dissertation research.

Only later did I come to realize that I was establishing a pattern. As much as I was drawn to fieldwork in remote and inhospitable places, I found it could be achingly lonely and dangerous during solo pursuits. My solution was to share the work, and the companionship, with like-minded scientific colleagues—friends and, sometimes, my loves. Over time, my belief in collective science broadened. The complexities of climate research demanded teams of researchers from many disciplines. And the places where I was destined to go were not those that could be reached and studied by one person alone.

That was ahead of me. For now, I drove the little car onto a vast salt flat known as Laguna Salada—once a vibrant marshland, rich in saltgrass and cultivated maize. Now the desiccated sand was packed as hard as concrete. After hours of driving, we were working near a thicket of tamarisk, and damp, salty mud had bubbled up just beneath a crust of sand. The car broke through and sank to its axles. Next thing, I remembered: Damn, I forgot the shovel. Oh well, at least I had two jacks in the trunk.

But one turned up missing. The other had no jack handle. This was not a proud moment for a guy with a supposed knack for logistics and a woman to impress.

I did not think of giving up, though. With the car bottomed out in brine in a far-off roadless area, with the tires spinning futilely, while my jack and jack handle and shovel were who the hell knows where, I took a breath and did what any soon-to-be-PhD would do. I dug with my hands. I used the jack with a wrench to turn it. I pushed. And swore, and pushed and dug and pushed harder. After a few hours of toil, or what seemed like a few hours, the car had not budged an inch. By then, it was late afternoon and our hike out was long.

Sara and I packed up the most valuable of our belongings because when you leave a car unattended in this part of Mexico, there are decent odds that it will be gone or gutted or even burned when you return. We saw several such carcasses during our time in the Laguna. We had passed army vehicles earlier in the day; maybe we could retreat and find soldiers willing to lend a hand. I took a GPS bearing so we could find our way back.

Sara had something else on her mind, though. She dropped down on one knee in the sand and unsnapped a ring from the gold chain around her neck.

"You will make me the happiest woman on earth if you will marry me."

Every man should have this experience once in life: his ego salvaged by a lovely woman's good heart and quick thinking. Love to the rescue. And who said scientists were coldly rational?

The ring was intentionally inexpensive, a "travel" wedding ring that would not tempt a potential thief in the world's poorest places, where we would of course journey in our future lives of scientific and romantic bliss. It had come to her to propose at this most unexpected of moments and give me the ring for a practical reason. She said we could now barter her gold chain necklace holding the ring in order to get help with the car if needed.

That was the kind of adaptive thinking I admired. A partner with forbearance, a great smile, and uncommon good sense.

What could I do except say, "Yes, of course"?

We retreated back to the road. The three miles took over an hour across the blistered earth. It was difficult to imagine that early in the twentieth century, this was a lush wetlands encompassing nearly 2 million acres. You'll understand if I give myself a bye for my next lapse. I reached for the GPS to take a second reading to help us find our way back to the car. My pocket was empty—I'd left it behind.

Kissing a dirty-faced girl who had just proposed had made me all giddy stupid. We traipsed back to the car.

Now, we were running short of time until nightfall, so we tried once again to move the car. We dug until it looked like an archeological site. We threw down a tarp and scraps of carpet from the trunk. With Sara at the wheel, I pushed. And darned if suddenly she didn't drive right out of there onto hard sand, with me chasing on foot.

So with that, the newly betrothed rode merrily off to safety, while visions of topographical maps danced in their heads.

Well, not exactly.

Our self-rescue left me feeling confident, and I am dogged in pursuit of a goal. With what was left of the day, we returned to our task, driving down the flank of the lake to make some more survey measurements of

the salt flat with the handheld laser rangefinder. Why not make use of
the time?

At one point, we stopped and got out to scout the route ahead. We
returned, and suddenly, the car was rocking and shuddering like
some phantom monster was trapped inside the hood. I looked at Sara.
She looked at me. We felt it.

"Earthquake!" she shrieked.

Great, I said, I always wanted to feel a big earthquake. I grabbed
the car and held on. Sara said I was grinning ear to ear.

We continued driving toward the mountains on the far side of the
Laguna. On this hard surface I could drive fast, and so we sped across
the salt. Again we took readings every half mile. After a bit over two
miles, I suddenly felt the wheels spin for a second. And then again.
And then we were slowing down with the wheels spinning. I tried to
downshift to control the spin but had no luck. We were stuck again!

What? It was smooth and rock hard. We got out and I saw a dis-
heartening sight. Below the salt crust was wet dark clay. The salt crust
had gradually thinned the farther we drove toward the low point of
the Laguna, now only half a mile away. Finally, we'd broken through.
We looked back and could see the clay begin to appear about one hundred yards behind the car. I wanted to cry in frustration.

Sara was very calm. She had the rare and valuable ability to remain serene at the important times (and panic over nothing). She
suggested we try pushing. No way that would work, I thought. But
I got in front and heaved. And the car began moving backward. All
right, I thought as I pushed and jogged along. But after just ten yards
our progress ceased. Damn. Sara had followed our tracks rather than
steering for new, unbroken crust. And the car dug itself into a rut.
Oh, well. At least we knew it would move if we worked at it. So with
an hour of sunlight remaining, we again jacked up the car and filled
in underneath the tires. Once more I pushed the car backward. We
moved about three feet before we stopped. Oh, no. We tried going forward but couldn't move an inch. The more we tried, the deeper in we
dug ourselves. Finally, all the way to the axle. Later Sara confessed

that she had the emergency brake engaged, ruining any chance of getting us moving. She was crushed.

Physically and emotionally spent, I began pulling out our sleeping bags while there was still a tiny bit of daylight. Sara futilely tried to jack up the front of the car in the darkness, refusing to accept that we would have to sleep here. We hadn't eaten since breakfast and all we could salvage from the car was a PowerBar, two apples, and a few crackers. We talked and looked at the stars. For the moment, fieldwork science didn't seem quite so romantic. I felt sad because I had led Sara into such trouble and was worried about tomorrow. The entire night passed in a light doze, as I dreamed of jacking up the car and digging in the mud.

When the sun finally began to peek over the mountains, I hopped up, ready to work. But I found that it was freezing cold, and stripping down to dirty work clothes and digging in mud wasn't very appealing. Sara had no intention of getting out of her bag in the chill morning air. She told me to walk over to the mountains and back. Perfect, I could look at the low point of the Laguna. I walked east, where dark, damp ground marked the middle of the Laguna. From there, it was only half a mile to vegetation on the far side. There, I saw clearly that the plants marked a high-tide flood line. Plants a few feet lower had been killed. The total elevation drop from the high-tide plants to the bottom of the entire Laguna Salada was fifteen feet. At least I had gotten some useful data even during this melancholy point in the trip.

I continued toward the mountains, looking for firm pieces of wood or stones that might give us traction to move the car. I walked for about twenty minutes and then saw a mound and something that looked like a stove. I walked over and the "stove" was a signaling device. And the mound was a 3 x 3 x 6-foot-high pile of plastic bags filled with a white powder and lightly covered with dirt. I tasted it and found that I was standing next to what I figured to be about 1,000 pounds of cocaine. It looked like it had been there for quite a while, but I decided it was time to leave.

I had encountered the drug trade during field research on this dangerous border region the year before and wanted no part of it now.

Back then, I was good friends with a fire ecologist named Mark Kaib. He was tough as nails and had fought fires and led fire crews for years before coming to Arizona to work on a PhD. For his research, he was fascinated by the relationship between the Apache Indians and fire in the desert Southwest. On the East Coast, Native Americans had employed fire to clear undergrowth and keep forest habitat prime for deer and other game. The Apache had used it for war. But in the 1880s when settlers and cattle had come into what was then US territory and the Apache had been driven out, fires disappeared. Some Apaches fled south of the border into Mexico. They took up residence deep in the Sierra Madre mountains and frequently raided the lowlands. Mostly, they kept the cattle out of the mountains and fires continued to burn in historic patterns until the 1930s or later.

So by comparing history as told in tree rings between the Arizona and nearby Mexican mountain forests, Mark hoped to form a record of differences in fire regimes and chart changes brought on by ranching and settlement. Everyone has seen tree rings and knows how they record a year's growth. For many trees, a good year is a fatter ring whereas a lean year is a thinner ring. By comparing thick and thin rings, dendrochronologists can create records of past climates. Trees also scar when they are burned by fires. The scars cut into the rings and then, if the tree survives, the rings heal around the wound slowly and grow over the fire scar. So if you are very lucky and find trees that burn without dying, you can use the rings to figure out the year of the fire. For his graduate research, Mark had sampled mountains across southern Arizona and now he wanted to sample the rugged and relatively unknown northern Sierra Madre. He needed help both to collect the data and to ensure his safety by not traveling alone. So he asked me and a former Special Forces officer turned conservation director named Roger Conjulio to accompany him. Roger was now in his fifties and worked in the pueblos of the lowland Sierras on forest conservation and had always wanted to visit the last strongholds of the Apache.

The trip was grand, and we spent several weeks collecting tree-ring data in the most remote part of the mountains. We found cliff dwellings and ruins throughout the area—if they were in the United States and were more easily accessible, they would have qualified as a national park. We saw the spoor of dozens of animals that are rare or completely gone from American forests. Finally, we prepared to head down the mountains toward some well-deserved hot food and showers.

On the last day, Roger and I decided to walk the last fifteen miles to the nearest pueblo. We wanted to follow a wild and uninhabited river gorge down to the lowlands, leaving Mark alone to drive fifty miles of winding donkey trails to reach the same place. The river was beautiful, and I have never seen another undisturbed waterway like this in the desert Southwest.

But it was not entirely undisturbed. After several hours we were startled to come across a thin black pipe, the kind that someone might use for drip irrigation in a garden. It ran down the bank along the river and puzzled us for several minutes.

We kept walking and suddenly Roger said, "Oh, shit."

The pipe ran to an isolated clearing that was filled with marijuana. Close up, the plants gleamed in the sunlight, and then blended into the canopy of the surrounding forest. It was too late in the day to retreat, so we decided to pass through as cautiously and as fast as we could. We saw no sign of habitation. I took a few pictures and we moved on quickly. Then we came upon another cultivated clearing. Then another. Each was quite small, presumably difficult to identify from the air by anti-drug agents. We didn't encounter anyone, so I kept taking pictures. Another clearing. A backpack sprayer next to a pile of drying plants. Roger said that in Mexico there were fewer regulations and that they used DDT and other toxic chemicals to keep the plants clean of insects. I thought it was sadly ironic that Americans smoking the weed were exposing themselves to dangerous pesticides.

We kept moving downstream, hoping the plantation would end. But it continued, plot after plot, now with piles of drying plants. It was an industrial-scale operation.

Suddenly Roger muttered, "Oh, shit" again, and then barked out a greeting, "*Hola!*"

I had been dreading this; meeting someone. I turned and saw a gun barrel pointing at us. It was a World War II–vintage carbine, and the man holding it stepped from behind a tree and knelt on one knee, keeping his aim on us. Nine times I have had guns pointed at me with deadly intent—and many of them have been in situations like this one—when you pursue science and exploration to the ends of the earth, you sometimes run into people who strongly object to your presence.

The man was very darkly tanned, with a long beard, scraggly hair, and a wild look in his eyes. He seemed to have only a few teeth in his snarling mouth. He had the expression of a man who hadn't seen another human in a while and was probably more scared than we were—two large blond men appearing out of the forest. Who were we? Federales? CIA? Drug Enforcement Administration? Or just idiots?

Thankfully Roger took command, shining at this moment. His Spanish was much better than mine, and he began explaining how we were just tourists out hiking and we had gotten lost. He acted like there was nothing wrong and asked where the trail was from here. The fellow looked utterly befuddled but pointed up a side trail and said to follow the creek. He could have said the moon was made of cheese for all I cared. All I wanted was to move on. Roger asked for detailed instructions, which seemed pretty insane to me. I slowly backed up, and repeatedly said, "*Gracias.*" I told Roger it was time to leave. We slowly walked away and kept looking back to make sure the rifleman didn't object.

For what seemed like an eternity, I couldn't shake that tense feeling of knowing a ghostly bullet was pointed at the center of my back. Then, we slipped out of sight and could begin to "*move with alacrity*" as I described it in my journal. But running was closer to the truth. Even as we fled, though, I found myself reflecting on the way the growers had integrated small-plot agriculture with the river and thick forest to protect and nourish the marijuana plants. I guess I've been interested in ingenious adaptation since the very beginning of my career in the field.

Now, once again, that bygone experience flashed in my mind and my heart pounded as I realized that here in the Colorado Delta salt flat known as Laguna Salada, I'd once again stumbled into the lair of the ruthless narco trade. I looked around, satisfied myself that no one was visible, and strode back toward Sara. Along the way I picked up a handful of good wood pieces to put under the car.

When I got back to the car in the warming sun, I said nothing about the cocaine to Sara. No point in both of us being on edge. But I worked as hard and as fast as I could when we began our ritual of jacking and digging and filling. We got the body of the car off the ground and filled in under the tires with the sticks and packed salt. After a couple of hours, we were pretty confident. Sara started the engine. I heaved. The car moved. About five feet. Then lost traction again.

We tried again. After a couple of hours, the car had moved only about another two feet. It was noon. If we wanted to strike out on foot for help, we couldn't dally longer. We took everything of value we could carry and plenty of water. We might not make it back, or the car might not be here when we did. We had about a six-mile walk to our dirt track and about fifteen miles more to the paved road. I was already cramping in my legs from kneeling and jacking for so long, but we had to go.

The walk was not too bad. We talked about fairy tales from our youth (Sara had grown up in Switzerland and had learned an entirely different set of stories than what we learn in America) and tried to make the monotonous time move forward. After a couple of hours, we reached the track. I craved shade and there was none. My legs were cramping badly from no food or salt and my empty stomach didn't want water. After a brief respite, we headed north toward the paved road. There were some bushes a few miles ahead where we could rest and find shelter from the sun.

The shade was wonderful. We rested for half an hour, I drank as much as I could and ate some crackers, and my legs began to feel better. We saw an army jeep pass several miles to the west, but the soldiers ignored us as we waved and jumped. Sara was determined to keep walking. And off we marched into the afternoon heat. We needed to make it *somewhere* before it was dark.

Several hours later, we saw another jeep again passing to our west. Bad luck it wasn't aiming our way. Again we futilely waved and jumped, and then kept walking. Sara and I had divided our lookout duties. I scanned the horizon in front of us, and she kept an eye to our rear.

"Dust," she yelped. Yes, there was dust rising behind us. But it was unclear who was making it and where they were headed. We kept walking. We were too tired and discouraged to get our hopes up. Sara kept glancing backward.

Five minutes later we could see them clearly: a black pickup truck advancing our way, filled with men in the back, staring at us coldly. We waved. I was very happy to recognize them as soldiers, not drug runners. But they didn't look pleased to see us. I explained our situation. A look of pain crossed the face of the man leading the group. They had a night on leave and were heading into town in clean uniforms to whoop it up. So instead of asking them to drive us all the way back and help pull the car out of the mud, I asked for a ride into the town of Mexicali.

That wouldn't end our troubles, but for the moment we savored the chance to ride instead of walk. Once we reached the paved road, the leader of the group got out and told us that they were going into town but would be returning to their base the next morning and would help us with the car then. Unexpected good luck. I asked him to drop us at a cheap motel.

Dinner, our first real food in nearly two days, was heaven. Beef and tortillas and beans. Wonderful. Sara kept her gold necklace, and I kept the engagement ring. Plus, we'd pocketed the science I needed. And I'd learned a thing or two about the unexpected challenges that arise during fieldwork in difficult places—a lesson that would eventually follow me around the world, for better and for worse.

The next day, the seven soldiers and I easily pushed out the car and they followed us back to the dirt track. Sara drove and I rode in the truck to reduce the car's weight and the chances of breaking through the fragile crust again. Before long the car began smoking. I could see consternation on the faces of the soldiers, who plainly wanted no further headaches from us. But it was a temporary problem. Sara had not released the emergency brake. Again. Once it was off, so were we, back to the land of plenty.

If you believed in omens, I was destined for exciting times ahead.

Interlude

Bugged

The tiny mosquito illustrates the pervasively high stakes involved with climate change.

In 1900, the leading cause of death in the desert city of Tucson, Arizona, had nothing to do with Wyatt Earp or wars between Apaches and settlers. The major killer was malaria, spread by females of the *Anopheles* mosquito.

Fortunately for the people there, Tucson was located on the extreme northern edge of the *Anopheles* range. That made it feasible to push the mosquito back, using techniques acceptable at the time, such as spraying DDT inside homes. The disease was declared eliminated across the United States in 1951, after three years in which no endemic cases of the disease were reported.

Now, however, warming temperatures and changing patterns of precipitation portend more favorable conditions for territorial resettlement of *Anopheles* mosquitos and a disease that each day kills 1,300 children around the world, according to the United Nations. Each day! A total of 500,000 human deaths, adults as well as children, each year worldwide. More than 100 million infections. And now a threat spreading into the United States.

The implications, as always when we speak of changing climate, are both local and global.

I learned this early in my career as a geoscientist. I helped develop a UN program on human health and climate change with Andrew Gotheko of Kenya, among others. He was chronicling the rate at which malaria was moving up in elevation across Africa as temperatures warmed and climate conditions became more welcoming for *Anopheles* mosquitoes.

This trend of rising temperatures has become a time bomb for millions of people. That is because the cooler highlands of the tropics have been islands of refuge from malaria for hundreds of years, leading to the growth of great and now potentially vulnerable cities such as Nairobi and Mexico City.

And as already mentioned, altitude correlates with latitude in matters of climate and environmental conditions. So as the deadly mosquito spreads higher and higher, it also is prone to reach farther into once low-risk, higher-latitude areas, like our own Sunbelt. The US Centers for Disease Control and Prevention (CDC) has warned of the possible reemergence of malaria outbreaks in southern states across the United States.

From this point of view, millions of Americans are finding themselves vulnerable to the life-or-death consequences of climate change.

And, as millions of people are learning, malaria is not the only disease threat. I worked with Duane Gubler of the Centers for Disease Control and learned of his concern about several emerging tropical diseases—a concern shared by scientists in other agencies, including the World Health Organization and the World Meteorological Organization. They worried that other mosquito-borne tropical diseases such as dengue fever and chikungunya fever were on the move into new terrain on account of warming climates. Likely areas for these homesteading diseases include the southwestern United States, Hawaii, the Gulf Coast, and the Mediterranean countries of Europe.

Seemingly out of nowhere, the eerie mosquito-borne Zika virus popped up on public health radar screens early in 2015, when the Pan American Health Organization issued the first Western Hemisphere alert about an outbreak in Brazil. Within just nine months, fear of the disease and potential birth defects in unborn children of infected mothers captured headlines throughout the hemisphere. The World Health Organization declared a global health emergency for only the third time in its history. In the United States, scientists identified the types of mosquitoes that could transmit the virus in the Caribbean, the Gulf Coast, and the Eastern seaboard as far north as Washington, DC. Unknown numbers of people altered travel plans as a consequence. The Centers for Disease Control warned, rather vaguely, "Zika virus will continue to spread and it will be difficult to determine how the virus will spread over time."

Once such diseases get a toehold, increasingly favorable conditions for mosquito hosts foreshadow growing public-health crises, that is clear enough. For instance, West Nile virus has become well established in the United States. Reports now say it will be a risk earlier in the year and remain later as a result of more inviting temperatures for insects.

In many places, such as the desert Southwest, the standard advice to protect oneself against mosquitoes becomes problematic. Heavy, long-sleeved shirts, long pants, and socks make for miserable summers in Tucson, Las Vegas, or Miami.

As might be expected, the trouble doesn't stop with mosquitoes. Ticks are expanding their ranges and consequently spreading Lyme disease and Rocky Mountain spotted fever to more of the nation. And, again, tick seasons appear to be starting earlier and lasting longer—although year-to-year variations may not be showing straight-line increases.

Then there's Chagas disease. Spread by the bite of the penny-sized *Triatoma* bug, Chagas disease was once confined to Latin America but is now described by the CDC as one of America's "neglected parasitic infections." *Triatoma* bugs, sometimes called "kissing bugs" for their habit of biting near the mouths of sleeping victims, have been found in the lower half of the United States from California to Pennsylvania—and scientists believe they are spreading north. The Chagas infection is difficult to diagnose, mimicking symptoms of lesser ailments and then lapsing into remission, sometimes for years, only to resurface with life-threatening consequences.

The fungal disease Valley Fever from Arizona might be intensifying and even spreading on account of changes in rainfall patterns and rising temperatures. This disease is endemic to certain soils and is spread in dust—particularly dust storms.

For those with a truly morbid streak, the CDC confirms that it is investigating potential links between climate change and the spread of the free-swimming freshwater "brain eating" amoeba associated with *Naegleriasis fowleri* disease.

Even seemingly unrelated maladies such as kidney stones are expected to increase. That's because rises in ambient temperatures are associated with corresponding incidents of reduced human hydration (that is, we don't drink enough when it is hot), which results in greater mineral concentrations in urine and, ouch, more kidney stones.

The World Health Organization is among many credible organizations and growing legions of scientists, physicians, and public-health workers who have recognized that changing and intensifying "infectious disease transmission patterns are a likely major consequence of climate change."

PART III

FIELDWORK

Chapter Five

Up and Up

I t took some years of tromping here and there across the world, perfecting my skills in both geospatial research and climbing, while also trying to inspire young people as a new professor, but at last, good fortune caught up with both my scientific credentials and my enthusiasm for mountaineering. I landed an invitation to join an expedition to my beloved Andes under the auspices of the American Alpine Club. My heart beat like mad. Founded in 1902, the club has become the nation's foremost voice on behalf of climbing. I had undertaken research in other places, but this expedition, scheduled for the summer of 2011, would be a homecoming to the mountains that had so inspired me—nature's perfect laboratory. Beyond that, the Cordillera Blanca Environmental Expedition was composed of climbers and scientists who shared my belief in the force-multiplier approach to environmental research, basically, the conviction that such research requires cooperative, multidisciplinary teamwork.

In short, this expedition was going to be something special. I just knew. I actually trembled with excitement. In the weeks before our departure, I prepared by flying north and climbing Alaska's Denali, the highest peak in North America at 6,190 meters (20,310 feet). I was feeling strong and well acclimatized for mountain altitudes. And I'd have the unusual opportunity as a scientist to carefully compare the ice and snow conditions that I'd measured on a high-latitude mountain with what we would find on the tropical summits of Peru. The Cordillera Blanca is the world's highest tropical mountain range, and

I might add that I found it breathtakingly beautiful—for me, beyond words. I had dreamed of climbing there. Now I would.

The expedition included seventeen volunteer climbers and climber-scientists, organized into various teams to explore and study the valleys and mountains of Huascarán National Park in the central Andes. Each team would climb and collect data for a series of scientific studies. At the project's conclusion, we expected to have assembled an effective characterization of the major environmental parameters of this park, which doubles as a World Heritage site. The work would be a cooperative undertaking of the American Alpine Club in conjunction with Peruvian government agencies. At lower elevations in the many approach valleys of the park, our scientific teams would record data on plants, land use, soil erosion, and meteorological variables. As we climbed higher, we would focus on snow and ice deposits to inventory and analyze atmospheric contaminants. We would allot three weeks to the expedition, a generous amount of time to allow us to cover plenty of terrain and perfect our collaborative research techniques without being slammed by tight deadlines. Our climbers planned to attempt the summits of twelve different peaks in the Cordillera. Yes, it was going to be the trip of a lifetime.

In June, still sunburned from my climbing in Alaska, I left my brother's welcoming house in Atlanta and boarded a flight for Lima. I was groggy when I landed. The hour was late at night, and I had to scramble to find a taxi outside the nearly deserted airport. I checked into a hotel and enjoyed myself with my longtime climbing partner, Bill Trainor, for a few days of wandering through colonial Lima. He came down for a short vacation prior to the expedition—a relaxed interval that allowed me to reset my mental gyroscopes for the excitement ahead. Then it was off to the city of Huaraz, 250 miles north and 3,000 meters (10,000 feet) high, the base of operations for travelers in the Cordillera Blanca. Our team gathered at the Café Andino—a coffeehouse, library, game room, and all-around comforting oasis run by American ex-pat and java-bean connoisseur Chris Benway. From the balcony, the view of the surrounding Andes is dizzying. It was pretty dizzying inside, too, at least for a fellow with my background and interests. When our expedition members finished introductions, we sat down with maps and notebooks for the utterly delightful task of fleshing out our plans for carrying science to the highest reaches of the hemisphere. The energy was so high you could almost hear it crackle. Before long, the logic of our single expedition began to expand. Why just an expedition? Why not an organization and many expeditions? The seed was planted.

"Frank" was our trip director. At least he started with that responsibility. Frank was an easy, welcoming person who helped pull us together and arranged necessary resources. A passionate advocate for bringing the power of science to bear for the good of the Peruvian people, he let dreams of climbing high peaks dance in his head. Unfortunately, he was neither a scientist nor a climber up to the challenge of these great mountains. Looking back, I might have guessed that Frank would lead us into problems. I just didn't know how big they might be.

The co-leader of the expedition was Ellen Lapham from the American Alpine Club. She was an organizational fireball whose reputation in mountaineering and conservation had us all looking up to her, even though she stood but five feet two. In the early 1980s, before Everest had become crowded with people who paid guides to get them up the mountain regardless of their climbing skills, Ellen had been on two teams that attempted to carry hang gliders to the very highest point on Earth. In her day job she was a businesswoman, and she undertook mountaineering with the kind of businesslike professional zeal and attention to the mission that few could match. Her nonstop smile and can-do gusto inspired us every day—leadership drawn from a deep well.

She wasn't the only star among us. Rebecca Cole was a restoration ecologist at the Institute of Arctic and Alpine Research at the University of Colorado, and her spouse, Carl Schmitt, was a physicist at the National Center for Atmospheric Research. This pair of world-class Nordic skiers became my enduring, foxhole-type friends before it was over. Our expedition roster included other scientists with commanding credentials, as well as people chosen primarily for their climbing skills; our wilderness-medicine focused doctor, Alex Stella; and Clinton Lewis, a friend and the professional photographer for WKU, who talked his bosses into allowing him to document our expedition.

Combined, this was the strongest and most notable group ever assembled to take science to mountaintops, at least in my experience. They were committed not just to themselves but to the larger cause of making a difference in the world. I had found my people, my tribe. I had traveled many years to reach this coffeehouse in the Andes.

It was my good fortune to pair up with Dave Truncillito from Albuquerque as a climbing partner for the expedition. Dave was a mechanical engineer with a special interest in climbing gear and a dream of making it his vocation. He was also, and I was seasoned enough to judge with confidence, a really great climber with deep inner strength. In preparing for the trip, we met beforehand in Washington state to get to know each other. We had planned to venture into the Cascades for some fairly easy "sport climbing." Both of us were aware that serious alpine climbing was more about endurance and hanging onto calm in the face of challenge and danger than scampering up overly protected rock pitches.

One serious sport climber watched us and then remarked to Dave, "How can you climb with this guy?" He nodded in my direction and added, "He isn't a very good sport climber."

Dave, bless him, gave the fellow the stink eye and replied, "Because we aren't going sport climbing."

I also found myself working on the climb with Kevin Grove, a math and physics instructor from Bend, Oregon. Kevin seemed to have figured out what really mattered in life. In that familiar debate over work-life balance, he chose to make the career rat race secondary so he could live in a beautiful place where he could ski and climb in his backyard. I confess, his example strongly influenced me.

Our first days around Huaraz were spent getting to know each other and acclimatizing to the 10,000-foot altitude. We visited the park office to meet Superintendent Marco Arenas Aspilcueta and his staff. They understood the concept of our work and the potential value of learning more about the park environment they managed. And they were happy to receive our gifts of computers and environmental monitoring instruments. We also visited the local university in Huaraz to conduct workshops, making friends and collaborators in the process. We prepared to set up a new weather station and begin air-quality sampling. All the while, we found our eyes looking out, and up. To the snow, ice, and rock of the not-so-distant peaks. Our excitement grew.

I didn't know our expedition director very well, or even much about him. But Frank presented the group with an ambitious climbing schedule, promising that we could accomplish a lot in a short time. He's the director, so he must know what he's doing, right? I would soon learn the error of that assumption. For the moment, though, I joined the others in making final preparations for climbing challenging peaks in an alpine wonderland of the tropics. The mountains of the Cordillera Blanca were among the most aesthetically pleasing in all the world. Peaks such as Artesonraju—the instantly recognized and breathtakingly beautiful 6,025-meter (19,767-foot) peak depicted in Paramount Pictures' logo. Artesonraju was also a famous climb in its own right, even though a long-standing route up the Southeast Face had been obliterated by a thunderous icefall in 2009. Nearly half of the entire mountain pyramid calved off in that colossal demonstration of high-altitude erosion driven by climate change. That left a real question: Was it possible to climb the peak at all anymore? Dave and I were given the plum assignment of finding out. We would have to search for a route up.

But first, another magnificent peak rose as our initial target—the knife-edge, 6,036-meter (19,816-foot) summit of Quitaraju. Dave and I would assist Frank's team there, and then head south on our own to Artesonraju.

Once again I unpacked everything and spread out my gear to give it a final going over. Fiddling mostly, to tell the truth. Mountaineering requires lots of stuff. Heavy-duty stuff. The kind of stuff your life depends on. I sometimes daydream of just once flying somewhere without three 49.9-pound duffle bags and two 49.9-pound carryon bags weighing me down. Hours spent at baggage claim and customs have left me with an abiding empathy for teachers trying to keep track of grade-schoolers on field trips. But without all this gleaming, alloyed, brightly colored stuff, I would be a mere tourist. So I went through it piece by piece. Glancing out the window, the upthrusting Andes were convincing reminders of how essential each item was.

Balmy weather at this altitude in the tropics added a layer of complexity to our packing. It might sound nice, but it can be debilitating for the unprepared. So I brought a special set of clothes for the treks through valleys to Base Camp—shorts, T-shirts, lightweight socks. Plus plenty of water bottles. Then, for Base Camp we needed to prepare for wild swings in transitional weather—anything from wind-whipped snow at night to sizzling sun during calm afternoons. Higher up, progressively harsher, colder conditions awaited us—with –20°F temperatures and winds over sixty miles per hour near summits.

In the end, my gear inventory included a midweight base-camp tent as well as a technical mountaineering shelter for high elevations, a featherweight sleeping bag and a massive –40°F giant worthy of Everest, three pairs of boots—from leather trekking boots to space-suit monsters made of foam and plastic. I couldn't do without three cameras—one for taking personal pictures, a GoPro for video, and a data camera to record the vegetation and landscape at each data-point stop. The load grew heavier with the addition of such everyday things as gloves, hats, socks, goggles, and so forth, along with a dizzying volume of hardware such as carabiners, a harness, a lightweight ice ax for easy peaks, and a pair of wicked-looking technical "ice tools" for the unknown dangers on steep, frozen mountain faces. My iPhone and earphones would serve as both journal and entertainment center, with music and a selection of recorded books. Portable solar panels would keep the electronics charged.

I packed up once again. Everything on which my survival would depend was stowed where I could get to it quickly. I was ready.

One of mountaineering's intractable rules: Don't count on things, even simple things, to happen according to plan. So it happened that Frank, our trip director, enlisted a local guide to plan and lead the ascent of Quitaraju—which looked something like a spectacular, icy scallop shell standing on end and reaching nearly four miles into the sky. The friendly guide, whom we knew only as Quique, presented himself as if he knew his way around this part of the Cordillera. Yet some of us, the most experienced climbers in our expedition, felt uneasy as he began to spell out the plan. For one thing, Quique did not seem to be allotting enough time for high-altitude acclimatization. As a result, his summit plan called for people to move up more rapidly than some of us instinctively felt prudent. For another, his apportioning of rations seemed skimpy. Still, over the years many of us had learned to respect local people and their knowledge. That tradition held sway this time, and those of us who had doubts kept them private.

Finally, we were ready. We loaded the gear and boarded a bus for the three-hour ride to the Santa Cruz Valley, which would lead us into the Andes. The Andes! Pushing off at the start of an expedition is one of the most exhilarating moments of the mountaineer's life. You don't just leave behind a town, or a room in a coffeehouse; you exit most of the known world and nearly everyone in it. Climb high enough, and your old life vanishes below.

In addition to the guide Quique, our subteam of six expedition members employed three rugged, mountain-savvy porters to help with the gear carry and camp chores for the two-day trek to 4,500 meters (14,764 feet) and Base Camp and then to Quitaraju. Here the real feeling of mountaineering took hold, as we craned our necks at the soaring spectacle before us. We acclimatized for a day in Base Camp. In hindsight, that was a major error. Most of the team was not ready for an all-out battle with the thin oxygen at higher elevation after such a pitifully short time.

Quique said we should make the long climb from Base Camp to a ridgeline saddle, or col, at 5,500 meters (18,044 feet) in a single long day. That would mean traveling very heavy all the way, ascending steep, crevassed, and technical terrain with just a few days' acclimatization. Not only would this add physiological stress to the technical demands of mountaineering, but it would surely test our mental stamina. We would be skipping past an intermediate camp at 5,000 meters (16,404 feet) and then pushing upward into technical ice. I wasn't alone in being troubled. There did not seem a good reason for the rush, and there were excellent reasons to go at a more controlled pace. But again: Who were we to challenge our expert guide, Quique, who surely knew what he was asking of us? To do so would cast a pall over our relationship for sure. We proceeded.

Coming from Denali, I was acclimatized and ready to go. Dave, too, was in shape for high altitudes by virtue of climbs undertaken in the weeks leading up to this. So we agreed to lead out ahead and fix ropes for Quique and the rest of the team. We ascended quickly and confidently through the crevasses and up the ice, fixing ropes as we went. It was a marvelous climb and we were eager. In places, the hard, clear ice draped down dramatically in the shape of frozen waterfalls. We reached a point just below the col after a final few hours of concentrated labor. That was around 2:00 p.m., and we relaxed in the blazing sun and waited for the others. In particular, we were anxious to see Kevin Grove, who was carrying the last of the ropes. Once he reached us, we could move ahead and fix the remainder of the route to camp. We could then start setting up a stove to melt snow for water and flatten out pads for tents.

Things seemed to be going well. Our rest and wait was a real luxury. We had made ourselves good and secure at this way stop with two ice screws lodged in the solid ice of a crevasse wall as anchors. Our perch at the mouth of this crevasse provided a stunning panorama. Why climb? Because there's no sight anywhere on Earth to match the vista of alpine mountaintops.

But then the sun moved behind the neighboring peaks. In the rose-colored shadows it grew chilly. Then cold. And colder. The difference in temperatures between sun and shadow in thin mountain air is always shocking. We dug into our packs for down jackets. This helped, but soon I could feel the cold penetrating into the core of my body. We had no room to move around and warm up. We began to fret. Where were the others? Finally, hours later, Raúl Gavilán caught up with us, pulling himself up the rope and kicking footholds with his crampons. Raúl was a Mexican government scientist studying air quality, and he did not seem to be doing well—although he was ahead of the others. Bad sign. He stumbled the last few feet onto our perch. We helped anchor him into place. While he struggled to recover, we continued to wait and worry about the others. Our concern was growing as the shadows darkened.

Kevin arrived as it was getting toward evening. He was climbing well but he had a splitting headache, a sure sign of altitude difficulties. The rapid ascent to this elevation had taken a toll. All of our team knew you simply could not rush the body's adjustment to reduced oxygen. Yet here we were. Kevin rested while Dave and I, finally, resumed climbing, using the rope he had brought up.

The route was almost vertical now. Over hard ice. This was the most difficult section of the climb so far. But I was grateful, because I warmed myself from the effort. I led, with Dave anchoring. The solid ice gave me good purchase to fix the rope. I reached the col, then Kevin came up, followed by Dave, then the local porters. Matters were becoming grave for the remainder of the team below as the light began to fade. I rigged up a solid anchor and began helping the next climbers up, rather than have them slowly hoist themselves up the fixed line. Dave, Kevin, and the porters worked to erect tents and set up camp. Our teammates below us were beginning to get hypothermic, the condition brought on when a person is unable to hold off the cold and the core body temperature drops. Even modest hypothermia increases the odds of someone making a mistake, because confusion, fatigue, and failing coordination are early symptoms. We all knew that frostbite would not be far behind. So the rush was on. We needed to get them up and into tents to warm them as quickly as possible. We labored at this until finally only Frank remained below, along with his rope partner, Brett Overcash, another member of the American Alpine Club.

It was now very dark and bitterly cold. Climbing one at a time might have been fatally slow for these stragglers. I yelled down for them to come up together. I would belay them on twin ropes. I rigged it so I could help haul them up the mountain as they also climbed. They needed every bit of lift I could give them. Brett was a big, strong man—but those muscles needed acclimatizing to this elevation of 5,500 meters (18,044 feet). At this point he was tired and suffering. Frank was worse—and now only semi-coherent. As he climbed, he knocked the headlamp off his own head, and it tumbled hundreds of feet before disappearing into a crevasse, an eerie reminder of the danger of a misstep. Brett traversed closer over to him so he could provide light for both of them. He encouraged Frank to keep moving.

Time seemed to slow for the three of us linked together on the ice. Each movement upward was all but impossible, and at the same time survival itself was in the balance. My arms screamed from effort. I could only imagine the agony of the two down below as peril engulfed them. Up and up. But barely. After what seemed an interminable struggle, I could reach and lock hands with one and then the other, and they staggered up onto the col to the camp. Frank was shivering uncontrollably. He said he couldn't feel his hands, so I gave him my heavy and pre-warmed gloves and sent the two of them scuttling into their tent. Thankfully, then Dave appeared to help me straighten the mess of the anchors and ropes before my bare hands froze. I was the last one to crawl into a tent and burrow into a heavy sleeping bag. We were cold and exhausted, but alive.

We had been way overextended, and that was inexcusable for such a strong team just starting out. It was a disastrous start to the expedition.

I had no way of knowing, of course, but these events on Quitaraju would become life changing for me. At the moment, my feelings merely toggled between blunt anger and total relief. Oh yes, and a little awe left over for this magnificent campsite. Under other circumstances, I might wonder if a living person could get any closer to heaven.

You could describe what happened next as a battlefield commission. I had taken charge of the climb in a pinch, and I wound up in charge thereafter—a consensus choice to assume leadership. The near disaster so early in the expedition had cast immediate doubt on the entire enterprise, and my teammates expressed faith that I could get things back on track. Gulp.

I agreed to try. I had led expeditions before with smaller groups and with lesser stakes. I was confident in my mountaineering skills. I also understood, as well as anyone, that our shared goal of bringing science into the high mountains was in jeopardy. If we couldn't pull together at this moment, our dreams would probably flicker out. Maybe for a long time to come. It was a big burden to contemplate.

Still, part of me felt about as awkward as a kid trying on a dorky set of new school clothes. Others regarded me as the "pro" on this expedition. On the inside, I was still in the business of learning, not yet an "expert." It was a lot of responsibility to shoulder, but I could see that I was the logical choice among our troupe. I had more high-altitude mountaineering and general climbing experience than anyone on the expedition other than Ellen, and she was working with me all the way. I was in the front ranks of mountaineering scientists. Others were looking my way. I guessed it was time to take myself more seriously. I hadn't planned this, but I'd wound up acting like a leader, so I needed to start thinking like one.

We awoke slowly on the col high camp, crawling out of our tents but still wrapped in gloom. My first task as leader was to get us packed and moving—downhill. We aborted our attempt of Quitaraju and retreated quietly down the fixed ropes to Base Camp, a solemn group. Later, we learned that our guide, Quique, was, in fact, a trekking specialist whom Frank liked but who was not qualified to plan and lead difficult summit climbs. We had trusted in Frank's judgment and Quique's claims about the mountain, and we had suppressed our doubts. Never again, I vowed, would I be so acquiescent when I knew better, or should have.

Most of the group, including Frank and Quique, headed back to Huaraz, carrying snow samples that we had collected. We had accomplished at least some scientific work. These samples, identified precisely by location, would be used to measure tiny particles of black carbon, heavy metals, and other pollutants. Analysis of those results would help government officials in Lima learn more about air-quality trends in a city ringed by open-pit copper mines. Snow is a giant dust collector, and we were using it to tell us about the particulates carried by breezes in this heavily mined country. We also had some preliminary meteorological data, but it wasn't enough—after all, we'd pulled up nearly 500 meters (1,640 feet) below the summit. Elsewhere in the park, other teams from our larger expedition were measuring levels of the primary greenhouse gas, CO_2, at different altitudes—a stratification study that was taking advantage of the steep mountain geography. When the air was still, we would find levels of CO_2 three times above normal along glaciers. This was the result of strong sunlight reflecting off ice, jump-starting the breakdown of human-caused, or anthropogenic, smog pollutants into CO_2.

Dave, Kevin, and I had also collected data on varieties, health, and densities of vegetation during the trek up the valley to Base Camp. Normally, this kind of information provides a starting point by which to chart subsequent changes over long intervals. But this time, our records proved quickly valuable: the next year a massive glacier flood would sweep through the valley and wash away virtually all plants and soil, right down to bedrock. By chance, we now had a detailed record of what had been lost.

While others of our group trekked back to town for showers and fresh food, Dave and I set out on foot, aiming south with a single porter. We weren't quite through climbing.

Walking. Or trekking, if you prefer. Whichever word, the process was good for me. The forward motion of feet crunching down on raw earth soothed the disquiet of the failure we had just endured. We walked, purposefully but in open country, aware of our own breathing, senses relaxed but not dulled, thoughts unmoored and allowed to wander according to their own compass.

My thoughts turned to a fuzzy memory: I am young and in my seat in the theater and the lights dim. The screen flickers, voices boom. It could have been a war movie or a comedy or a superhero film, I have no way of being sure. What has stayed in my head, a memory as vivid as a tattoo, is the profile of that great pyramid peak, the sun low in the sky, snow gleaming on the left flank of the mountain and shadows on the right. Paramount Pictures, the paramount mount towering high, ringed by stars.

When we crossed the Santa Cruz Valley, there on the other side, live and in color, was the mountain itself. Artesonraju. "Arteson," as we lazily titled it.

No ring of stars. Not really so much higher than the other peaks around. But nature's unmistakable and perfect pyramid.

Walking, I was reminded, can take you to the most wonderful places.

We passed through a marshy valley, stopping frequently to note our position and record environmental data. Because science slowed our progress, we acclimatized just a little more all the time, growing just a little stronger in the process—but remember, we reassured ourselves, "just a little" sometimes made the difference when the margins were small. Moving up, we walked into a massive geological scar from when glacial lakes burst through their dams and flooded the valley below, carrying away mind-boggling volumes of sediment that had been collecting over countless decades. The threat of such huge, even catastrophic, outburst floods grows each year in the world's high mountains as glaciers recede and their meltwater builds up behind natural dams, which are chronically prone to failure. Many people downstream are unaware and unprepared for this increasing danger resulting from climate change. As had happened in the past, this very place would be scoured by such a catastrophic flood the following year.

After an hour or so of steady trekking up the base of the mountain, we climbed out of the one-time lakebed and onto the lateral moraine—a buildup of dirt and rock left behind when the once-active glacier moved down the valley. Higher up, onetime feeder glaciers had created eerie hanging valleys above us. Here and there, we came upon sweet little remnant lakes from glacier melt higher up the mountain. The scale of the valley was enormous, the power of the now-gone glacier almost unfathomable, the 360° view overwhelming.

Of course, down-to-earth matters required our attention, too. From my journal during one stop:

> Dave is helping our porter fix his radio earpiece so that he can listen to the Peru-Chile soccer game on the radio. I will be surprised if he can get reception this deep in the mountains, but we shall see.

We enlisted the porter not to climb with us but to get us in position. Then he would take our big tent, main cookstove, and sleeping gear back to town. We would have to pare things down to travel up and over the fragile, snow-blown summit and down the other side, collecting what we guessed would be ten gallons of snow samples during the climb. Given the weight of wet snow, these samples didn't give us leeway for extraneous things up high. Not much room at all.

Finding a route up the mountain worried us. In recent years, unstable climate and weather conditions in the Cordillera Blanca had disrupted climbing. Entire mountain faces of snow and ice had peeled off, leaving broken rock behind. Frequently, heavy snowstorms had swept in from the Amazon during what historically were completely cloud-free months. Many classic routes had simply vanished. Unless they had up-to-date firsthand information from the current season, or even the current month, climbing guidebooks were increasingly unreliable sources. The irony was not lost on us. Climate change posed a rising challenge for those of us who wanted to study climate change.

Ever since the Southeast Face of Artesonraju cleaved off in that unimaginable avalanche of 2009, climbers had made attempts from the North Ridge, which required a longer and more difficult approach. Initially we planned to follow their lead, taking our samples on the side of the mountain facing the Santa Cruz Valley. On arrival in Huaraz, though, we were told there was fresh snow on the regrowing Southeast Face, which looked into the adjacent Paron Valley. That meant it might be possible to climb from the north, cross over the mountain summit, and descend on the southern side—a traverse that might be the first on the mountain. Of course this was still all speculation. Nobody knew for sure what awaited us. Snow and ice conditions were dynamic all through the Cordillera. If we were fortunate, a solid layer of snow and ice would make the steep face passable, whereas bare rock would require too much gear and too much time in frigid conditions. With all the melting occurring in this part of the Andes, though, who was to say whether a route was climbable without giving it a try? That's exactly what we intended to do.

We decided we would attempt the North Ridge. If it was climbable, we would top the mountain and inspect the Southeast Face for our descent. Risky? Sure. But exhilarating, too. On most great mountains in the world, every route and camp had already been plotted out, often years ago. To come upon a peak as celebrated as Artesonraju with the challenge of linking old routes and finding new ones through gaps would put us in the company of mountaineering pioneers.

And, as it happened, there was a strong scientific rationale for our planned traverse as well. By sampling two sides of the mountain in the same climb, we could collect data to compare airflow through and over the Andes from the Amazon Basin to the Pacific Ocean, as well as the reverse, and measure corresponding air-quality differences. The patterns were known to be complex—different on the Amazon side than the Pacific face. We hoped to start quantifying these differences.

At our camp before our porter returned home and we began our ascent, I made this entry in my climbing journal:

> Dave fixed the earpiece! And so our porter is very, very happily listening to the game. It is super warm inside the tent with the three of us—but the porter's sleeping bag has clearly never been washed and the smell is making Dave and me feel ill. I think we need a bit more air or it will get worse as each of us smell to some extent; but at least with our alarm set for midnight, we won't have to suffer long. We just heard a huge avalanche to the left of our route. Sort of scary . . . but the views we have had of the route itself look solid, so I think we will be fine. Mountains have always been unstable, but in recent years climate and weather changes have made climbing seem even more like roulette at times.

We snoozed an extra half-hour after the alarm sounded. And that was the last lazy moment for a while. Ahead, we faced an endurance marathon. At 12:30 a.m., in the beam of headlamps, we wrestled into our climbing gear. At 1:00 a.m., we started up. Our porter stayed behind with his malodorous sleeping bag and would strike the tent and carry it back on his own timetable. It would be hours before we'd even begin to see daylight, but this was going to be a very long climb. We got moving upslope early, light and fast in good weather.

Dave carried a featherweight sleeping bag and an extra layer of warm clothes. I was prepared to carry the snow samples, which left space for only an ultralight Megamid sleeping shelter and a jacket. If something went wrong up high and we were forced to bivouac on the ice, it was going to be a miserable or even deadly night.

Our plan was to reach the summit and descend on the other side of the mountain without stopping to camp. Many stories were told of climbers who perished for lack of a good sleeping bag and warm clothes. At a minimum, we knew we would have to get off the high reaches of the mountain, one side or the other, or we'd risk freezing and frostbite. Our margin of safety was truly unknown. Maybe small. Maybe impossibly small.

Dave took the lead, threading a path through and over seemingly endless crevasses. I provided a moving anchor. At six foot five and 240 pounds, I had it easy. Dave was only 130 pounds—not counting gear, of course. With every pitch of rope, the zigzag route grew steeper. We had been able to scout this section from our camp below in last night's twilight, and thus we dodged most of the large, problem crevasses. We could sense, but not yet see, the much larger spectacle of Artesonraju's mighty face looming above us. I was thinking about how tiny we were, making our way up, when we reached a portion of the mountain where prolonged action of sun and wind had created micro-penitents, or ice statues that rose up to several feet tall ahead of us. These became our friends, providing great footholds. Accordingly, we moved faster still.

Two hours into the climb, we reached the first cliff-band of steep ice, where climbing would become technical. Except we couldn't get there. A crevasse, twenty feet wide and hundreds of feet deep, opened up in front of the cliff, blocking our path like a moat protecting a castle. We could see no way around. The only possibility was a slender snow bridge across the chasm, maybe six feet thick, off to our left. We had no choice but to try. I set an anchor and Dave eased across. I followed. The bridge held. I wouldn't want to wait for the sun to come up and try again when the snow was warmer.

We expected to find a straightforward ice cliff above. It was not. What looked like a solid glaze of ice clinging to the mountain on the 75° slope turned out to be a frozen, honeycombed matrix. Bars of ice the size of baseball bats were latticed around openings that went deep into the ice sheet—as deep as my headlamp could penetrate. I had never seen anything like it. If this bizarre ice formation couldn't hold our weight, the climb might fail. We tested it. It seemed stronger than it appeared. We put weight on it, and it held. Up we went, two boys climbing a playground jungle gym of ice. Once again, I mused that we had climbed an obstacle that I would not want to try again when it was warmed by the sun.

At the top of the honeycomb, another formidable crevasse blocked our progress. It did not seem to have a bottom. Someday, the entire ice cliff below would peel away from the mountain at this juncture. But this was no time to wonder when. We scanned carefully with our headlamps and found, to our left, that a chunk of fallen ice had wedged into the crevasse only about ten feet down from the lip. We climbed down and balanced our way across the abyss. Ahead, the opposing wall of the crevasse was eerily overhung. Dave gracefully led us out. And neither of us dared look into the chasm directly below. The mountain was throwing us challenges one after another, but we had not been defeated. Of course, we were still a long way from the summit.

Above, a steep but smooth snowfield was easy enough to climb. We pushed upward as dawn broke, a faint glow blooming into a gentle blue penumbra, then suddenly hitting us with the force of a fireball. Every 500 meters (1,640 feet) up, we took samples of snow, filling both vials and one-gallon bags. We dug to get samples at different depths. We rested on a snow bench below a formidable array of glimmering blue ice cliffs. Being in a dramatic mood, we named them "The Cliffs of Insanity."

Now I led the way, moving around an intricate crevasse system by going far right, then far left, and then diagonally upward toward what we thought was a climbable opening in overhanging ice cliffbands. I soloed upward into the ice of the lower band and found myself blocked. Indeed, it appeared there was no possible way to get around or through the overhanging ice. I worried whether we'd have to turn back before reaching a summit—a second consecutive failure for the expedition. Then Dave caught up. I put him on belay and, fine climber that he is, he threaded to the left and then traversed over to a snow chute, or couloir, where we could resume climbing. I followed, once again grateful for such a partner.

We had been climbing hard for almost six hours, and the sun was warming the face of Artesonraju. People often ask me, How do I feel when climbing? I suppose I feel like a foundry worker pouring molten steel, or a navy pilot approaching the heaving deck of a carrier—much too absorbed with my dangerous task to indulge in feelings. Each foothold, each swing of the ice tool, each kick of crampons, each decision en route must be successful. Feelings are what you have later, down in the valley. If you're not so tired that you just fall into a dead sleep.

I led directly up the steepening snow and ice toward the North Ridge. This was supposed to be the "classic" part of the climb: a long, steep, beautiful couloir sixty feet wide and at least ten rope pitches long. Hey diddle-diddle, straight up the middle. The classic reputation referred not just to the topography but to the perfect conditions of firm snow, a veritable racetrack for climbing. Unfortunately, we did not encounter classic conditions. The snow was wet, warm, and sloppy. Footing gave way beneath us. We might as well have been stair-stepping in place. Our ice tools pulled away as if we were swinging at sand dunes. Progress went from slow to slower, and all we could do was try to swim uphill and hope that the whole damn mess didn't peel off the side of the mountain. Rather than have a standard lead climber and anchor, we simul-climbed together to speed up progress, keeping one anchor in place between us at all times, but both moving. At the top, Dave swung into the lead—up and then around a house-size snow mushroom to the "summit" ridge. We sensed we were closing in on the prize.

Except it was a false summit ridge. We had a long way still to go. Stopping en route for snow samples was slowing us down, and now we looked up the barrel of another long snow couloir. Conditions here were even worse. There were too many air pockets in this snow pack, unmistakable evidence of heavy melting. I doubted whether it would last much longer. Once again, climate change was playing hell with our research into climate change. It was like trying to climb in soup. No picket or anchor would hold in this slop. We simply couldn't climb together the way we had up the last couloir. Then I saw a tiny, isolated patch where the snow had melted away to reveal blue—the blue of solid ice. I struggled for it. Finally, I was able to set two good ice screws and belay Dave as he led up the last bit of the couloir to the true summit ridge.

Artesonraju was not through with us, however. Ahead was another large snow mushroom. Rounding that, we discovered that the entire snow and ice ridge had avalanched off, leaving only a dip of bare rock and a snow bridge that appeared weak with loose sloppy snow. After that, if we could overcome these obstacles, the final route up to the top awaited us. I set out, moving as fast as I could. We had been climbing for nearly eleven hours. Noon was approaching. We were behind schedule, by a lot. At this pace, we'd be caught in darkness, and darkness meant deep, painful cold. Cold that could kill us if we didn't keep moving.

I belayed Dave up behind me. He took the lead and cruised along, making the route look almost easy up the remainder of the summit ridge, past potentially fragile cornices. The summit was in sight—just three hundred feet ahead, then one hundred, then fifty, then thirty . . . and then, another deep crevasse blocked our way.

I could almost throw Dave across the chasm. I wondered whether those who had "summited" Artesonraju from the North Ridge in recent years had come this close and called it a finish? It would be a time-consuming struggle to cross this last obstacle, if that was even possible, just to cover the final thirty feet to the summit and then cross back over it again in order to descend.

As for us, we had no choice. To accomplish our traverse and reach the Southeast Face in hopes of finding a route down, we had to get across the crevasse. We searched for any possible path. The mountain resisted. Finally, I lowered Dave down onto the dangerously exposed, and unclimbable, East Face of the mountain for nearly the entire two-hundred-foot rope length. He located a tenuous snow bridge, crossed the crevasse, and then fought his way back up the other side in chest-deep powder snow to where he could anchor me.

We dropped our packs on the summit. We had climbed Artesonraju using a variation on the North Ridge route, with chunks of the high ridge gone. It was one of the best climbs of my life, and maybe I should cut the qualifier. This was mountaineering at its finest. We took photos, and an extensive set of snow samples. We ate PB&Js while Sublime serenaded us from the tiny speaker on the iPhone—"Summertime and the livin's easy . . . " We packed and contemplated the drop-away descent down the Southeast Face.

A week later, we met a group of climbers who had been in the Paron Valley below. They had been scouting for a route up the Southeast Face when suddenly we had appeared on the summit. They jumped and yelled in delight, recognizing that we were making a traverse. They watched during much of our descent. They told us they were inspired to push themselves.

Just below us, the face of the mountain was corrugated with runnels, or veins of ice. Farther down it broadened into a wide, nearly vertical slope—the face was still accumulating snow and was far steeper than it would be in a year or two. To be on the safe side, we supplemented our anchors with ice screw backups for rappelling. I went first. If the primary anchor held my weight, Dave would be plenty safe and we could remove the ice screws. They held fine and we bounded down. The rhythm of coming off a summit this way became hypnotic. Rope after rope. We moved through a few shorter pitches of steep ice and then undertook a series of twelve, two-hundred-foot rappels. We were, of course, coming down much faster than we went up, but still the day dragged. We interrupted progress to maintain our 500-meter (1,640-foot) sampling stops, and my load was growing heavier by the hour. This was the price I paid for being the biggest member of the team—I got to carry the samples! And snow was heavy—as anyone who has shovelled a driveway knows.

Afternoon shadows grew longer as we reached the bottom of the face. We moved onto downhill terrain that was not nearly as steep. We had been climbing for fourteen hours, but we were still quite a bit too high on the mountain. Stopping here would put us at risk from the cold. Ahead of us was the jumbled wreckage of the mountain face that had peeled away in 2009. These fused remnants of avalanche debris were a mix of rock, ice, and compacted snow heaped atop a glacier below—an odd, otherworldly surface on which to walk. There was no clear route, of course, so we zigged and zagged and looped and wound through the mess for hours. Finally, as daylight faded, we passed through the last of the debris field and reached a small cluster of tents set high on the glacier below. We had finished the last of our water long ago, so we were grateful to accept tea from a German team camped there.

Unfortunately, we were still too high to weather the night with our skimpy gear, so we pressed ahead. We finally reached the edge of this receding glacier at about 4,900 meters (16,076 feet). We gathered the final snow and ice samples of this climb, then resumed our journey down under the feeble, wandering beams of headlamps. We wanted to get below 4,100 meters (13,451 feet) to make our bivouac bearable. So we plunged ahead, and my sixty-five-pound pack seemed three times as heavy. We traveled over the loose glacial scree in inky darkness, asking ourselves if it would ever end. We were unfamiliar with this terrain—and it was plain now that we should have scouted this side of the climb beforehand. We had no choice except to blunder in a downhill direction, clambering over steep valley walls, all but stumbling, grabbing tufts of grasses to keep on our feet. We pressed ahead because each step downward meant warmer conditions. Thanks to exertion, we were not bothered by the cold at this point. But when we stopped moving, we knew it would hit us hard.

Finally, at the limit of our endurance, we reached the main Paron creek bed, which we followed to Lake Paron itself, the largest body of water in the Cordillera. After twenty hours of climbing, we dropped our packs on the beach. The nighttime temperature was around 20°F here, but it seemed almost balmy compared to where we'd been. We pitched the tiny sleeping shelter. Dave got into his bag and kindly gave me his jacket. Ropes served for pillows. I fell into the deep slumber of the exhausted, battling bad dreams about cold.

Stiff and chilled, we rose slowly in the morning. We burned up the remaining gas for our one-burner cookstove, melting the snow and ice samples, processing them through a quartz filter with a syringe to trap particulate matter. These tiny particles we kept for later analysis, the melted snow we discarded. During the tedious process, we tried to ignore the hunger that consumed us. Finally, we shouldered our much lighter packs, strode around the lake, and aimed for civilization. We traveled as quickly as we could. I wanted a plate of food so big that it would take two waiters just to bring it to me. I wanted a Coke. I wanted to be warm.

We arrived in Huaraz. What a great couple of rest days! I could remember little in my life to match them, or even come close. When we finally walked into Café Andino, our expedition colleagues greeted us as heroes. Dave went through the details of our climb. We listened to their stories of teams attempting four other mountains in the Cordillera. Sometimes everyone seemed to be talking at once. Out came filet mignon steaks that weighed almost a pound apiece for Dave and me, with a side order of a large pizza. And Cokes. The rest of the day passed in a blur of feasting and laughing and jabbering. How did I feel now? No one asked, but I felt like a man enjoying life to the hilt, among my own kind of people—purposeful, sunburned people with chapped lips and calloused hands and razor-sharp minds. I gulped down the Cokes. And I made a mental note to myself: This was one of life's perfect intervals. Standing atop a mountain of my dreams and then gathering here with new friends to celebrate.

Ellen took charge to meet the leadership crisis that had put the Cordillera Blanca Environmental Expedition in jeopardy. Solid and businesslike, she pulled me aside with the husband-wife team of Rebecca Cole and Carl Schmitt. Together we reformulated the objectives of this expedition to make it safer, and to build on what we had already learned to make our data more valuable. By now, we all knew that this would not be a onetime event. There in Huaraz, Peru, this gathering sponsored by the American Alpine Club would endure and morph into the club's scientific affiliate, the American Climber Science Program. The Program would send scientists back to these mountains year after year. I would become its first executive director.

But that was still down the road. For today, we had more mountains to climb in this inaugural year. All too quickly, our relaxing came to an end and we returned to business. Soon, I was leading a team up Huascarán Sur, the highest peak in Peru, at 6,768 meters (22,205 feet). Others fanned out to attempt five other peaks.

Never had so much environmental data been collected so high in such a short interval. One could only wish that early climbers had done more of the same during their explorations. We would have a far better understanding of changes in these mountains over the long haul. Old-timers here tell of countless routes that no longer exist on one peak after another. Contemporary guides describe each year as a chance for climbers to make first ascents on account of the loss of glaciers, of ice, of snowfields, and of huge rockfalls on mountains themselves. Relentlessly, conditions in the Cordillera Blanca and Andes generally are becoming drier and warmer. Occasional years of heavy snow interrupt the pattern, but the trend is clear.

However, we could not count on anecdotal, hand-me-down stories from the mountains to prod nations of the world into action against the status-quo inertia of today. If I believed otherwise, I wouldn't feel the need to climb and to lug full packs of snow samples down mountains.

And so we ventured up to Camp 2 at 6,000 meters (20,013 feet) on Huascarán, Dave and I and Carolyn Stwertka, a graduate meteorology student from Salt Lake City, Utah. We ate well that night and I enjoyed the sunset. It was bitterly cold and began to snow. Then harder. From my journal:

> [I]t got worse and worse. So we all three snuggled (boy, girl, boy) as tight as we could. It is such a nice warm comforting feeling to be with such good friends in a tent during a storm.

We struggled up to the summit, brought back samples from the highest point in the country for study, and met up with colleagues once again in Huaraz before heading home. It was not the end, but a wonderful beginning.

Luck, happenstance, karma—call it what you will: the tide of events during this expedition provided what may turn out to be one of the most important organizational engagements of my career— creation of the American Climber Science Program. Others had shared the idea that climate science, even the specialized realm of climate science at high altitudes, was too much for any one scientist or any single branch of science. The urgent search for understanding called for a swarm approach. Strength in numbers. Creativity born from the breadth of ideas. Camaraderie with a cause. In the army, this kind of assemblage was called a "force multiplier"—a team made stronger by the skilled aggregation of its individual parts.

That idea blossomed into reality in 2011 on the Cordillera Blanca Environmental Expedition.

Chapter Six

Here, There, and Beyond

I n my years of bio-geo-scientific fieldwork, I have collected, just guessing, maybe 10,000 separate samples and measurements of the environment parameters for given places across the Earth, each recorded by time and precise location by longitude and latitude and altitude. Add up all the data collected by all the scientists on all the expeditions I've been on, and you could expand that number fiftyfold or more. Small numbers in the world of Big Data, yes—but information obtained only by the difficult, often dangerous, effort of exploring extreme locations. Information impossible to duplicate.

This work and the research of the American Climber Science Program has added incrementally to the vast repository of millions of planetary measurements taken by satellites and space probes, in addition to more than a century's worth of increasingly detailed weather information; geological, hydrologic, and anthropological research spanning the globe; and the painstaking fieldwork of data collection and analysis by scientists elsewhere. Roll all of it up using the science of "geospatial analysis" with its principal tool, GIS, or geographic information systems, and one can begin to fathom the dynamic map of what is happening climatically and environmentally, over time, on our only planet.

These travels into the blank spaces on the map of climate change have taken me up, down, across, here, there, and beyond on our worldly planet. My companion all along has been adventure. But a curious thing about adventure. You'd almost think it doesn't mix with the other parts of living, like . . . well, you know, like love. Oil to the vinegar of ordinary life. Well, yes, Indiana Jones and Marion Ravenwood may have teamed up on the big screen to spice up their daredevil days. But most stories I've come across in the genre of adventure tended to skip over things like romance. As a scientist, I can tell you that it's not natural—at least not for this scientist. Science is a strong enticement, but so is the partnership of love.

That said, the embers of romance don't seem any easier to keep hot for the adventurer than for others. At least that has been my experience. I explain it this way: Reconciling the lives of adventurous, uncompromising people can be an impossible task. The same could be said in any of a thousand different ways for others. But for me the ordinary things of life got pushed aside to make room for the extraordinary. Sometimes with aching sadness. And so it proved to be for Sara Dalton and me. After my PhD and some teaching stints at the University of Arizona and Rutgers University, we moved to Bowling Green, Kentucky, where I joined the faculty in the Department of Geography and Geology at Western Kentucky University as a tenure-track assistant professor and field researcher. Sara and I had begun as colleagues and lovers in the salt flats of northern Mexico, and we thought we knew each other. But in only four short years, my interests pulled one way, hers another. We parted. Our son, Nathaniel, became more of her life and less of mine, and I will always regret the path of daily fatherhood that I failed to tread.

There was no consolation in that loss, no upside. Just emptiness. I began to wonder if maybe the reason there was so little romance in adventure literature was the paucity of the basic ingredient itself. But three years later, I got a second marvelous chance to mix adventure with love, and I was mindful that not everyone was so lucky. I met the perfect adventuring partner in Narcisa Pricope—a fellow itchy-footed earth scientist who was out to study the effects of climate change on human populations. She was a great beauty, a onetime Romanian gymnast, and to top it off, we had instant, exciting chemistry.

Narcisa and I quickly married. In our minds, we weren't just a boy-girl duo, we were scientific adventurers who wanted to travel everywhere. The formal wedding, with Narcisa's family in attendance, occurred where she was born deep in the mountains of breathtaking Transylvania, a land of pastoral landscapes soaring high above the treeline. I've always felt a yearning for mountains and she grew up in the heart of them. Soon, it was time for my adventuring spouse and me to go on an expedition.

Narcisa was focused on Africa, and her enthusiasm was contagious. She reminded me that mountains weren't the only fragile wildlands ripe for deeper study. So I accompanied her on two expeditions to southern Africa. The first trip was with a large contingent from the University of Florida where we learned the ropes. The second was just the two of us. We set up a research project in Botswana's Chobe National Park and across the border in Namibia's Mamili, Mudumu, and Bwabwata National Parks to study human and animal adaptation to cycles of flood and fire. This vast area of parks and protected areas along the Botswana-Namibia border contains the largest concentrations of elephants in Africa and was an ideal locale for such work. The tree and shrub savannah was prone to fire, and the annual rainy season transformed the Okavango, Kwando, and Chobe Rivers into a vast flooded delta and wetlands, complete with strange *omurambas*, or ancient riverbeds that flowed in the wet season, but only for short distances before the water disappeared again underground. Plus, unlike some national parks, Bwabwata was also home to native people and their villages, but not to urban overdevelopment. The locale was nearly perfect. As you might expect, the park was also rich with wildlife—hundreds of thousands of elephants, along with hippos, cape buffalo, all the big cats, and even wild dogs—enough variety of big animals to keep footbound scientists looking over their shoulders warily. Tourists travel in vans and Range Rovers in African parks, and wildlife learn to ignore them. But we two scientists needed to get away from the well-traveled roads and out of the car, and we lived in the park. Every day spent collecting data, and every night spent inside the flimsy nylon shell of our tent, seemed close to danger.

Working as we did in the bush of southern Africa was often harsh. We had the feeling that everything wanted to kill us. Malaria, sleeping sickness, and other diseases were rife. Animals might smell you, savor the odor, and come to find you in the night. Then again, those who don't smell you are the ones you surprise as you travel upwind— and that could have deadly consequences. Even the plants claw at you and burn your skin as you force your way through the bushes. Bridge crossings over rivers were often nothing more than strings of small logs, lashed together, sagging from the weight of travelers while squint-eyed crocodiles lined the muddy banks, waiting patiently. This was my office. I loved it.

The elephants put me on edge, I admit. African elephants generally were not to be feared by tourists in African parks. They had become habituated to safari vehicles and the travelers inside them. In the small town of Kasane, we even saw them eating in the town dump as the light faded one evening. It was a different story, however, away from the familiar tourist haunts, where we were working and often traveling on foot far from a vehicle. Elephants become belligerent when they encounter people in unexpected places. And a pissed-off elephant or worse, a herd of pissed-off elephants, was a significant problem.

The potential was so serious that while we were with the University of Florida group, the Park Service provided us with two armed guards who went with us into the bush every day. Not only did we feel safer, we enjoyed their easygoing company and became friends. Both were family men and would teasingly ask Narcisa and me when we were going to have children. We felt secure, protected by their oiled rifles and knowledge of the park. When elephants or other animals menaced us, they always got us out.

Then we took a side trip to Botswana to collect data for a few weeks, and when we returned we were dumbfounded to learn that the two rangers had been killed—trampled by elephants. They apparently fought back with rifle fire but were unable to stop the attack. That left us sympathizing with the hard-eyed view of native people, and not tourists, about the dangers of the continent's largest beasts. Elephants were to be feared, and I confess we came to loathe them.

Narcisa and I returned to work in elephant country, now alone, armed with only a GPS and a couple of instruments, a notebook, and the horrifying knowledge of what happened to these two rangers. It was not a comfortable circumstance.

One time, we squandered our daylight hours at park headquarters, waiting in vain for a meeting with someone who we later learned took the day off on a whim. We found ourselves in our pickup truck, driving back into the bush quite late in the direction of where we wanted to camp. As twilight approached, I steered through the maze of sandy tracks, which was all we had for roads out there. I turned this way, and that—feeling my way like a homeward-bound salmon. At last, we came upon some landmarks that told us we were heading in the right direction, near where we wanted to collect data in the morning. Then, rounding a corner, we came upon a terrible sight—a dead baby elephant, nearly headless, lying in a sandy wash near a water hole. Inexplicably, much of the head had been scavenged. I felt the hair stand up on my neck. Elephants live in complex social groups, and matriarchs who lead these herds are ferociously protective of young—their own and others in their group. Might we be mistaken by one of these furious beasts as killers? After all, Africa's elephants were likely to have nightmarish memories of encounters with poachers. How could we tell them, no, we are only harmless scientists? We kept driving, hoping we wouldn't have to try.

We shortly came upon a small tent encampment established by Africans. We stopped to warn them of the danger from elephants, but for all I knew, they may have been the ones who killed the baby. We could see only a few pitiful, dirty women and a man with his hands cut off—refugees from Angola or maybe Zimbabwe. If others were nearby, they were hiding. These parks served as human refuges from the brutal wars that tore apart Africa. Our warnings did not spark alarm, and we were unsure whether we'd been understood. Perhaps it was the case that they had seen, and endured, so much worse. We drove on.

In the warm light of sunset, herds of antelope and gracefully grazing giraffes reminded us of the pastoral beauty of wild Africa. But fresh elephant sign was everywhere—trees ripped from the ground and stripped of bark, muddy wallows like bomb craters. We remained on edge. Were we driving toward an angry mother elephant, or away from her? Finally, in the savannah darkness we knew we could go no further and we picked a campsite next to a pair of scrawny trees. Maybe they would offer a little camouflage from elephants. Besides, there were no better alternatives. We pitched our tent and zipped it closed. We knew it would be an anxious night.

It must have been around midnight when distant screams jolted us awake. The screaming came closer, accompanied by a galloping noise—not hooves, but paws, quick and heavy. We sat still, keenly aware that we were wholly vulnerable and entirely blinded behind the lightweight fabric walls of our tent. Narcisa unzipped the door, grabbed her sleeping bag and bolted for the cab of the truck. I lunged after her, scooping up most of the tent's remaining contents and throwing everything into the back of the truck. Then I turned to face the screams and switched on my headlamp. Twenty feet or so on the other side of the tent, a pair of yellowish eyes glowed from the shadows. I couldn't make out the rest of the creature, although it was too small to be an elephant but still taller than our tent. It froze in the beam of light, motionless and unblinking. Then it lunged and came for me.

I dove into the cramped bed of the truck and slammed the camper top. The animal circled the truck, snorting and snarling. We were sure it was ready to pounce if it found any weakness in our sheet-metal carapace. Most city dwellers, and even a lot of outdoorsy people, never know quite what it's like to be prey. We spend most of our days securely at the top of the food chain, protected by stone walls and guns. Tonight, we were being sized up for dinner.

Lying on the front seat of the truck, Narcisa dared to lift her head. She looked out and identified the prowling animal as a spotted hyena. Well, at least it wasn't a lion, or a pride of lions. But up close it was huge—a lot bigger than I would have thought. It was commonly said that the jaws of a hyena could bite through a two-by-four, which made me wonder what it might do to the door of the truck if it was hungry enough. It paced around us, not going away.

Narcisa had bad news. She could not find the keys to the truck. Neither could I. Soon, we realized they were still in the tent. We might survive the hyena if we stayed put, but now there was likely to be noise and commotion. What if it drew more hyenas? Or elephants? In that case, we would absolutely have to flee. We had seen pictures and listened to stories about elephants attacking a vehicle with people trapped inside. It was nighttime dark in Africa, and we didn't need to be asleep to have nightmares.

I eased open the camper door. The hyena had backed away and was watching us from the cover of brush about fifty feet away. I feared the nearby hyena less than the threat of unseen elephants out there somewhere. I took a folding chair to use as a shield, or a club, and slid to the ground. Narcisa watched the hyena from the cab. I made a dash for the tent, bent down, and reached in. Thankfully the keys were just where I'd stashed them. I stood, spun around and all but dove for the pickup. Narcisa screamed. The hyena lunged. I dove in. The two-by-four-rending jaws clamped down, wrenching my leg violently and tearing off my shoe. But not my foot. I slammed the camper top closed. Safe, scared, and damn lucky. No blood.

We listened. And listened. No elephants. A long, long wait for dawn.

Our Namibian research project was based on the proposition that the African continent would be especially vulnerable to climate change in coming years. Technological advances in food production, common in developed nations, lagged across most areas of the continent. Also, human populations were growing rapidly, and warming temperatures foreshadowed the wider spread of disease, drought, storm, and flood. Combine that with a history of political and ethnic instability, along with the crazy-quilt pattern of national boundaries drawn in European capitals long ago without regard to the sensibilities and tribalism of peoples who lived here, and you would be hard pressed to come up with a formula for easy adjustment to changing environmental conditions. Hard pressed, indeed.

But the world could not turn its back on the continent. At least we did not believe so. For our part, we had chosen to focus on establishing a close-up baseline understanding of this single landscape and the interactions of humans and animals toward adaptation. We would drive a quarter mile at a time down a dirt track and stop. After surveying for dangers, we would walk 350 meters (about one-fifth of a mile) off the road and fix our location precisely by GPS. Following a ritual of sample and measurement, we would record vegetation, surface conditions, and disturbances like the frequent fires that swept the area and the erosion from flooding. In other words, we were creating a spatial map of this environment, one GPS location at a time, day after day.

This series of systematic samplings produced a portrait of the landscape. Periodic revisitation would reveal, in precise detail, subtle and not-so-subtle changes and trend lines. No matter how much data could be acquired from satellites, laboratory scientists were never sure what to make of a landscape until someone trekked into the bush to add firsthand details. In my mind, this "boots in the mud" fieldwork, in conjunction with satellite imagery collected over time, was the only way to truly "see" and "feel" what was happening to our planet and its inhabitants. And without that knowledge, what chance do humans have to develop sound adaptation strategies?

Although my procedures and tools have grown more sophisticated, this methodical data collection, painting by numbers to reveal a landscape, if you will, has remained the basis of my field labors. On a typical expedition day, we might record our suite of data from maybe thirty-five to seventy-five locations, depending on terrain and time. We would later carry all our collected raw information back to the university for analysis and offer it raw to other scientists to digest as they saw fit, When processed, it would then be presented to the scientific community in the form of peer-reviewed journal articles, abstracts, encyclopedia entries, conference presentations, seminars, workshops, and field camps—more than two hundred total such efforts from me alone.

Then, to transform this technical view of what is happening into usable science, we must offer credible answers about what can be done. For the short term, our ability to significantly reduce levels of greenhouse gases—not just slow their emissions, but actually reduce their atmospheric levels—seems impractical if not impossible. It's hard enough, although vitally important, to try to restrain increases in the emissions of these gases. Even so, the inertia of changes now under way in the global climate will continue no matter what efforts we make to mitigate the problem. All signs point to increasing instability in climate and environmental patterns for the foreseeable future, as well as more specific consequences, such as rising sea levels. Thus, farsighted policy makers and researchers are focusing on the more socially realistic and potentially palatable challenge of adapting to our rapidly altering climate while gaining control over the factors that are making things worse.

When scientists and thoughtful social leaders converge to discuss these matters, their calls for action grow increasingly urgent. To name just one, a 2015 study in *Nature Climate Change* estimated that costs associated with flooding in the world's largest coastal cities will soar from $6 billion a year now to $1 trillion by mid-century because of rising oceans and population increases.

Unfortunately, many of the world's vulnerable populations, like those in Africa, are also the least able to invest in adaptation.

Our research in Namibia was focused on a small slice of the larger challenge but in the end served to reinforce the scientific view that our planet is at a critical juncture. Preserving and, where necessary or possible, strengthening resilient ecosystems to survive the relatively abrupt climate transition now under way will provide breathing room for our environment and societies to adapt to continuing change during this century and the next. As we can see and measure already, climate change is intensifying the normal fluctuations in Earth's weather patterns—and that, plus population pressure, adds up to bigger swings in the boom-and-bust cycle. Failure to heed this and act now, whether it takes the form of poor land-use choices, ineffective or inattentive governance, or misguided social resistance, will reduce the odds that we can ride out the first wave of climate change's consequences. If that happens, the impacts on basic food harvests will be felt for decades, or even centuries. You could think of climate change as a harsh series of storms that wash out a road. The drivers who slow down, plan ahead, and carefully pick their way forward will be inconvenienced as a result. But the drivers who blithely race ahead with no concern for the future will suffer far worse.

So, what does adaptation look like? How do we create resilient communities and ecosystems? These questions are of critical importance in this part of Africa and in the many other societies around the world that are wholly or largely dependent on local ecosystems. Famines, for example, occur when local crops fail in societies that have no capacity to obtain food elsewhere. This means that particular attention needs to be given to keeping rivers healthy and flowing. The Colorado River Delta in Mexico and the Aral Sea of Central Asia are tragic examples of what happens when rivers fail, bringing down the societies that depend on them. Today, dozens of rivers worldwide—including some drought-stricken and resource-dependent areas—are threatened by unrestrained urbanization and the demands of agricultural irrigation. Also crucial to maintaining and building resilient ecosystems is sustaining the maximum biological productivity of a given region. Loss of vegetation results in soil erosion, even desertification. Recovery is difficult or impossible. Diminished biodiversity threatens to leave remaining vegetation at ever-greater competitive disadvantage in a climate-altered world.

To achieve even these obvious steps will require greater international cooperation, more ecological refuges and protected corridors between them, and market incentives, even subsidies, for wise land-use decisions.

The obvious problem is that even these necessary laws and policies may not make life better right away. Indeed, things may worsen for many in the short term. But without action, the consequences will be even more catastrophic for generations to come.

The critical question to be addressed in the face of this uncertainty is: How much socio-ecological resilience can we find? What coping mechanisms, economic changes, or legislation would increase this resilience? Clearly, the part of southern Africa we studied has survived many shocks—the blight of slavery during centuries past, the arrogant misrule of colonialism, recent war impacts from Angola and Zimbabwe, independence, AIDS, globalization, forced economic "reform," and so on. Survival itself requires a certain level of resilience there.

Too often, however, coping mechanisms have seemed limited to little more than weary resignation. Farmers we interviewed in Africa would shrug if the rains did not come or if an elephant destroyed much of the season's maize crop. In the twenty-first century, we must resolve to get past this kind of fatalism.

Let me borrow from Charles de Gaulle, the French leader who guided his people through great ordeals in the mid-twentieth century: "History does not teach fatalism. There are moments when the will of a handful of free men breaks through determinism and opens up new roads."

In fieldwork, everything rolls along fine, until it doesn't. Which is why I have a snake tattooed on my leg.

It was another wonderful, bright, panoramic day in the African bush. I was in the company of the woman I loved, my partner in life and in science, and we were walking to a point where we would make another data stop. Wild Africa spread out in front of us. Work? Perhaps. But I would say this was more about living large, feeling free. I thought it would always be the two of us, side by side on the trail. Wherever it led. We could not be better suited as a team. How lucky I was. Our day was winding down and already my thoughts jumped ahead to evening, to camp, to dinner, to sunset. I felt something quiver underfoot and then touch my leg, slimy and "icky." In a nanosecond, my brain sounded "Danger!" and simultaneously I kicked in revulsion as savagely as I could. A six-foot-long black mamba, Africa's deadliest and fastest snake, went spiraling through the air right in front of Narcisa's face.

We raced to reach the predetermined GPS location for our data check, scrambled to enter the data, and dashed wildly back to the truck via an indirect route. No doubt we were even more careless where we stepped running than walking, but a black mamba—so named for its ink-colored interior mouth—ignited the "flight" instinct in a way impossible to resist. We fled.

It was funny, though—it never crossed our minds to go straight to the truck and ignore the data point. We were data collecting machines, Narcisa and me. That afternoon and evening we continued making our measurements and marking our precise positions until it got dark—nervous, even squeamish, but we kept on. Don't get me wrong, I was plenty worried we'd meet another snake. But in my heart, I believe that adversity provides a reason to appreciate life rather than fear its end.

One must also honor karma. First chance I had, I made good on an old promise to myself. To make money in college, I worked in south Georgia in cotton fields that teemed with rattlesnakes. To deal with the constant fear, I prayed to the heavens that if I ever stepped on a deadly snake and wasn't bitten, I'd memorialize whatever mystical blend of luck and fate spared me by getting a tattoo. Snakes, you see, have always given me the creeps. But I couldn't get a tattoo in this region of Africa because of the AIDS epidemic. Nor in Nepal the following year. Eventually I got the tattoo in Peru after a couple of bizarre climbing falls that made me worry about my luck and karma. When you make a vow, you should always fulfill it.

After four months, our work was done. Narcisa and I returned to the United States to assemble and analyze the data we had collected. We produced peer-reviewed scientific papers, met with policy makers in Africa, and presented our findings at the American Association for the Advancement of Science and other conferences to share our work with the community of environmental and climate-change scientists. Narcisa had gotten what she needed for her dissertation, so now it was my turn to set forth a plan for our next adventure. Soon we had tickets for Kathmandu.

I had earned a yearlong Fulbright Senior Researcher Award and as such I would be part of the official US government contingent in Nepal—complete with diplomatic plates on our chauffeur-driven Land Rover. That was a real step up. I was going to teach Nepali graduate students the techniques of satellite analysis and GIS, or geographic information systems—the contemporary process for integrating, storing, and displaying all types of geographic data for analysis according to location. I was going to take them into the field to collect a suite of geo-scientific data for expeditions of fifteen to thirty days. These were budding scientists from the Department of Botany at Nepal's national Tribhuvan University. They knew plenty about plants. I hoped to help them understand what to do with that knowledge for the future benefit of Nepal. When young scientists yearn to protect the places where they grew up and that they love, then "conservation science" has a special meaning. So I ended up learning as well as teaching thanks to these wonderful new friends and future research partners.

We boarded our flight in Atlanta with a massive overweight collection of packs, duffels, and equipment. I had to wear my hot, heavy climbing boots on the fifty-hour series of flights because there was no room to pack them. We took a weeklong layover in Korea to explore the country a little and get used to the time-zone change before departing for Nepal. I know how important first impressions are and I didn't want to arrive groggy. Thankfully, our arrival in Nepal was processed smoothly—we had a special yearlong visa already provided by the embassy, so we breezed through customs, again a step up in experience. After an introduction at the Fulbright office, where I learned how the logistics of our day-to-day life would be handled, and after receiving a massive stack of Nepalese money—our first month's living-expense funds—we headed to our house.

This entire experience was fairly surreal. I've always been poor and traveled like it. Now I was learning how the other half traveled. Pretty comfortably, actually. Our house really cemented the feeling— we lived in a walled compound with massive trees and a gatekeeper. We shared this parklike property in the middle of the city with two other houses—one occupied by a colonel in the Nepali Army and the other by the owner of Buddha Airlines. Our house rose four stories and was overflowing with bedrooms, two offices, and a massive kitchen—complete with our own cook and housekeeper. We enjoyed a large roof garden, and an independent power supply with Internet hookup—a very posh setup indeed. Kathmandu was dependent on hydroelectric power and an antiquated grid. For extended intervals, the country suffered rolling blackouts. During the driest months when the rivers were sluggish, power was supplied for only two, or maybe four, hours out of twenty-four, often late at night. So having a battery storage unit and an independent rig to supply power was critical to our ability to work when we were home. I also learned the great value of portable solar systems during this time.

Nepal presented a research conundrum. People have lived here for many centuries, and their impacts on the landscape have been pervasive. Little productive land was untouched or anywhere near pristine. Without a baseline of prior data to rely on, how could scientists take an accurate measure of the consequences of contemporary climate change? It seemed to us that this fundamental question could not be ignored, or fudged. In almost every way, the people of Nepal lived close to the margins—including in the production of food and in the reliable, year-round availability of water. Technological or economic resources to cushion the country against environmental disruption were either nonexistent or in short supply. Our answer to the problem, and the reason for my Fulbright, was to teach our scientific methods, tools, and rationale to the Masters of Botany students of Tribhuvan University. Better than any outsider, they understood their country's environment, heritage, values, culture, and politics.

This kind of "seeding" of new generations of young people to expand and strengthen the cadre of the world's environmental scientists has been a founding goal of the American Climber Science Program. In Nepal, I led groups of four to twenty-four on field treks, depending on the remoteness of our destination. I was accustomed to the chatty, energetic world of eager students, but I had never met young men and women who talked as much as these budding Nepali students. Their curiosity and nonstop questions enlivened our days as we tromped over the countryside, collecting environmental data.

During our evenings, the topic changed from science and the environment to matters of the heart. Nepalese culture is very conservative. In the university there are equal numbers of female and male students—a purposeful equality that stands in stark contrast to much of the world. But these graduate students knew nothing of kissing or expressing affection, not even holding hands, except what they may have learned secondhand. So the conversations were about love. Their questions were eager and just as nonstop as with daytime science. They were not directed at me, however. Both young men and young women turned to Narcisa for these "love lessons": "How do you tell someone you like them? How do you ask someone out? How do you know if you like someone?"

They were nervous, and for good reason. Love-based relationships were becoming potential alternatives to the tradition of arranged marriage. If they could only understand and master the process. Imagine. Haven't all of us in the so-called developed world listened to our hearts and wondered if we were hearing the truth? Or if our hearts even knew what they were talking about? Here we were, sitting with people in their mid- and late twenties who knew almost nothing of the language of the heart.

It wasn't easy, but Narcisa warmed to the inquisition. She advised them to find their own lives. And that alone seemed a ticket to emotional freedom. Several years later, I followed from afar on Facebook as a surprising number of these students followed the model they saw with Narcisa and me. They married and continued their science work as couples.

One advantage of fieldwork in Nepal was the absence of elephants and black mambas. I wished I could say the same about land leeches. These cursed creatures, seldom mentioned in cheery travel articles about Nepal, were abundant in the countryside during the rainy season and, alas, I had no karmic power to avoid them. These oversized, wormlike bloodsucker parasites made misery of the days all during the rainy season. Gooey as snot and about as attractive, they dropped from bushes and branches that you could not avoid. They latched on to skin and dispensed an anti-clotting agent so that when you pulled the bastards off, you bled and bled. Most of the time, you never saw or felt them until it was too late. By the end of the day, you ended up with blood-soaked socks and dull aches. Not once did I think of getting a leech tattoo. Yet these vampire creatures, sore feet, questionable food, lousy weather, and long hours did little to dampen my spirits.

That was because Kathmandu felt so welcoming. The raw smell from sewage in the river running through town might make you gag, but there were no hyenas at our heels and no wild elephants in our nightmares.

A cynic could describe Kathmandu as dirty, smelly, crowded, and chaotic. But we preferred to think of it as a lovely and colorful place to live. Seven World Heritage sites were within an hour's drive, a greater concentration than anywhere else on the planet—breathtaking collections of ancient temples from the region's cultural and religious foundations, some going back 2,500 years. In the face of such ancient wonders, daily hassles receded in importance.

From my journal in Nepal:

> We just got back from a two week backpacking trip—where we climbed 54,000 feet total according to the GPS. Yes, you read it right—54,000!—we measured it on two GPSs and adding it up on the map, it all agrees. We hiked a total of 150 km (90 miles) over the 11 days and went from 1400 to 4700 meters several times (5000 to over 15,000 feet!) and climbed and descended at least 1000 meters (3000 feet) every day. It is amazing how easy it is when you have food and a warm fire and bed waiting for you every night.

During this year with Tribhuvan University students, I walked more than 1,000 linear miles and, along the way, climbed over fifty miles vertically. We collected baseline information about the impacts of fire, grazing, and warming temperatures on Nepal's vulnerable environment and its threatened biodiversity. Several students did their thesis work from these expeditions and published the results, and two of them came back to study in the United States with us.

Always, the mountains loomed. They were never far away and never out of my thoughts. I could *feel* them—their mystery, their power, their danger. The Himalayas kept calling. And, alas, they proved the fragility of love. I would not have guessed that Narcisa's advice to students about finding their own lives would guide us apart. It was Mount Everest that did it. A warm fire and bed every night were not my destiny.

It happened this way. I was making friends in Nepal, working with Nepali students and rubbing shoulders with the culture of climbers who congregated in Kathmandu. Now and then, Narcisa and I took advantage of an opportunity to sneak in a quick climb of smaller peaks. Then, it happened. In between field treks with graduate students, I found myself sitting in the office of a mountaineering specialist and expedition organizer in Kathmandu. He was Sujan Bhattarai, one of a group of brothers who own a family guiding company called Himalayan Ecstasy. He had assisted with logistics for my treks with students. I was pleased to hear him say he respected what Narcisa and I were doing to groom a new generation of Nepali scientists. We talked about it often. These were the kind of comfortable conversations I'd had with other mountain-loving Nepalis. Then it became something else. As we became better friends, our conversations wandered more widely. We spoke of the great mountains and their scientific promise. We agreed about the urgency of climate-change research. We talked about our lives and the wonderful countryside of Nepal. Then Sujan looked at me, paused, and asked: Did I want to join an Everest expedition in the spring of next year?

His words hit like a thunderbolt.

Sure. Absolutely. Of course. Are you kidding? Gulp.

All I would have to pay was his costs—a fraction of the normal price. Something that was normally reserved for the very wealthy was suddenly in reach.

Everest. Sagarmāthā. Chomolungma. No matter which language you speak, it is the tallest mountain in the world.

There it was, ringing in my ears: The opportunity to attempt the great mountain itself. The opportunity of a lifetime.

When I was fourteen, I made a bucket list. Only I didn't call it a bucket list. I called it a list of the three most badass things a man could do: I would compete in Alaska's Iditarod sled dog race, run an Ironman triathlon, and climb to the summit of Mount Everest. A picture of Everest adorns the wall of my parents' home. Well, by this time in life, I had pretty much given up on the Iditarod—massive kennels of racing dogs were an extreme complication that I could not embrace. The triathlon still remains a distant, abstract idea. But the challenge of climbing Everest burned in me. Now, this crowning jewel of boyhood fantasies was going to become real.

Naturally, Sujan offered Narcisa a place on the Everest team, too. I figured we would climb as a pair and strengthen the bond that held us together. She would be the first Romanian woman to summit the mountain. What could be more wonderful, really? We had shared so much, and now this capstone. We would hold each other in an embrace on the top of the world. Someday we'd put that picture on the wall of our house.

But I was wrong. I missed the signal somewhere. She turned down the chance. In the end she did not share my zeal for high-altitude mountaineering, and she knew that you had to have a deep, gut-level zeal to tackle Everest. Narcisa declined the chance in order to refocus on Africa. Neither of us said so exactly, but we knew that we were finished as a couple, that following the path of our own lives had aimed us in different directions.

When I departed that spring for Everest, Narcisa flew to visit her family in the Transylvanian mountains of Romania. All that remained of our fairy tale was the retelling.

I wondered.

Do I curse my bad luck for losing such a dear companion as Narcisa, and Sara before her?

Or do I say thanks for the very good luck to have shared parts of my life with them?

Interlude

Sunsets

There was another way to answer the "why" question. It had nothing to do with danger or protecting the world. There was no risk involved and no tangible gain. No money was involved, either. Didn't cost a penny. Nor was it a trivial thing. It had to do with a way of looking at the world.

Why climb? I could answer with a question of my own: What makes a great sunset?

For as long as I can remember, I've been transfixed by sunsets. I've sought them wherever I traveled. I've collected them. Sunsets are a pathway to the marvels of nature. I've long savored them. Studied them. You might say that I've become something of an expert on sunsets—the science of sunsets, the aesthetics of sunsets, and sunsets as symbols of what was so wondrous and freely available in nature.

The artistic value of good sunsets compares with the greatest paintings of the world. Yet they are fleeting and in motion, not unlike life itself. Each is one-of-a-kind. Sunsets exist, of course. But they exist chiefly as experiences.

I can tell you about my vast collection of sunsets. But I cannot show a single one. They reside in my memories alone. They are connected to sharp recollections of where I was at the time, who was with me, why, and how we felt—the ancillary details that enrich our moments.

Perhaps when I am old and my bones ache and my muscles are tired, someone will ask, "John, what makes you get out of bed each morning?"

I will say, "So I can see this evening's sunset."

Sunsets are caused by the refraction of light as it travels through the atmosphere across a longer and longer path as the sun drops low in the sky. This refraction scatters light according to wavelength, filtering out blues and greens for the sake of oranges and reds. Water and dust in the air adjust colors and intensity in infinite variety. Volcanic eruptions can exaggerate sunsets for years to follow.

I am a scientist and a student always, but a teacher, too. So gather around.

The most important part of a sunset is the cloud. A perfectly flat blue sky will not produce a great sunset. We need the texture and depth that clouds provide, as well as the water droplets of which clouds are made to better scatter the light.

A favorite sunset in my collection occurred over a vast estuary on the Yucatán Peninsula of Mexico. My brother and I were speeding back to a village in a small boat, trying to outrace darkness after a day spent watching sea birds on a small island reserve. Mangroves blocked the horizon. Overhead, clouds stacked up in big geometric rows. As the boat skimmed along, we leaned back on the benches and watched the light show play out, starting with brilliant orange-yellows and fading to dusky purple. We reached the dock just as the last rays blinked out of the sky. It was like the grand rondo of a symphony.

Even now when afternoon shadows lengthen and I glance up at the afternoon clouds, I'm apt to recall that astonishing warm tropical nightfall.

Next ingredient for a great sunset: a foreground that provides an interesting contrast to the overhead colors and shapes. The Arc de

Triomphe is a wonderful frame for a sunset. But even better is something of Earth itself, underscoring the heavenly aspect of the sky above.

I think of another boat trip, this time in the jungles of Colombia along one of tributaries of the Amazon. Again it was growing late. The exotic jungle noises seemed to become louder and ever more spooky in shadow light. The unbroken walls of the jungle loomed around us. Above, sunset touched the soaring tower of a nearby thunderstorm, which pulsed with lightning. The jungle darkened and the storm light exaggerated the exoticness engulfing us—this realm of the caiman, the piranha, the toucan, the snake, the spider, and the others who call Amazonia home. The Hale Bopp comet emerged in the darkening night and provided an ethereal streak across the sky. As we moved along the river, the storm advanced our way as if in chase.

So much happened in those moments, yet nothing really happened except that nature put on a show and then winked off the lights.

No matter where you happen to be, the people with you and the mood of the moment and the occasion can transform a good sunset into a truly great one. Sunsets when you feel at peace and one with the world tend to be among the richest.

I am not alone in my near-mystical fascination with sunsets. There is a story about the World War II summit conference between Prime Minister Winston Churchill of Britain and President Franklin Roosevelt in Morocco in 1943. After the formal session, Churchill insisted the pair take a four-hour drive to Marrakesh, where the Prime Minister arranged to have the polio-paralyzed Roosevelt carried by two men up winding stairs to the roof of a villa. Why? To watch the sunset flare over the distant, snow-topped Atlas Mountains. Churchill was so moved, he had his palette and easel brought up and painted the scene—the only painting he made during the war. In 2008, the twenty-by-twenty-four-inch painting sold for $350,000.

My personal collection includes a very peaceful end-of-the-day sunset as seen from the ruins of a lighthouse on Turneffe Island—a lonely atoll off the coast of Belize in the Caribbean—alongside my brother, Joe, on a trip when he was learning to scuba dive. And there are many in my collection from the Andes of Peru. When climbing, I aim the door of my tent to the west so I can watch the refracted sunsets spray wild colors over the pure white of glaciers—a spectacular effect known chiefly to mountaineers. Every Fourth of July in past years I have been high in the mountains and watched nature provide stunning fireworks for me. Most vividly I recall evenings after a day of rock climbing in the Catalina Mountains overlooking Tucson, where small thunderstorms throbbed like strobe lights across seemingly endless vistas. The cauliflower clouds registered the dissipating heat of the desert, turning from hot-yellow sharp-edged explosions of water vapor, to cooler smudges of orange, to indistinct purples of old bruises—all while pulsing with bright white flashes and bellowing peals of thunder.

I don't mean to be glib in talking about the extreme effort of climbing in the same context as the effortless watching of sunsets. But the two are flip sides of environmental awareness. I am drawn to climb mountains because nature calls me, and I am drawn to nature because of its wild beauty.

The more sunsets I see, the more keenly I appreciate them. In their glow, I have shared triumph and disappointment with my closest friends. In the ephemeral moments of sunsets, I've kissed lovers and squeezed them tight. Alone in the company of sunsets, I have faced my own mortality and I've redoubled my determination to live with all the vigor in me. Not once, have I seen a sunset of regret.

Chapter Seven

Everest

In March 2010, our small expedition departed Kathmandu in a four-wheel-drive Toyota Land Cruiser—the stalwart vehicle of choice that's gotten me wherever I needed to go, from Bhutan to Zimbabwe. We traveled the crowded and narrow two-lane Araniko Highway, sometimes called the "Highway from Hell" on account of incessant traffic, seemingly endless deep-gorge switchbacks, and steep fall-offs. "One mistake, game over" is a saying among those who ply the route. Tibet was just ninety miles away, although it seemed much farther. Our gear, a mountain of duffels, backpacks, fuel tanks, and crates of food, followed in a weatherbeaten cargo lorry.

Our group was composed of three Western climbers and a team of Sherpas, including my friend Sujan's two brothers, Dipen and Anil Bhattarai—with Anil as the sirdar, or overall coordinator, of the climb. I enjoyed the company of these brothers and felt my friendship deepening with the Bhattarai mountain men. We were going to attempt Everest from its north side, in Tibet, the North Col route, not the now-standard southern approach in Nepal, where I would be in 2014. Here, we would start out following in the footsteps of George Mallory and the first Westerners on Everest—the most storied geography in all mountaineering.

I found myself looking at the empty space next to me on the teeth-jarring journey through washouts and along cliff faces to the base of the mountain. Where Narcisa had been on all those other trips, nothing. We had been inseparable through tough scrapes and harsh country, side by side nearly every hour of every day for years. No more. Normally, I enjoyed being alone in the outdoors. But here I wasn't just alone, I was lonely to the bone. I missed her so much. I missed our partnership.

My thoughts wandered as our vehicles revved and strained in low gears along the winding, bouncy Himalayan road. Little ideas and words addressed themselves to me, seemingly at random, like bumps on the pitted surface. *Science*, I thought. Could I both climb and gather data at the extremes of altitude? *Home*. It really feels farther away than 8,000 miles—more like another planet. *Weather*. So much of mountaineering depends on the undependable. What awaits us? Would something I couldn't control undo everything? *Me*. I grew up reading the romanticized literature of adventure the way that some kids read the Hardy Boys. Now my chance at Everest was at hand. *Everest*. How would the reality stand up to boyhood flights of fancy? The struggles, the injuries, the many deaths, the failures, the capricious moods of nature—climbing Everest was the stuff of long-ago stories that became a familiar dare and now awaited me just down the road. How would I hold up? Naturally, I had studied the northern route up the mountain and knew how it had turned back or killed climber after climber. But "knowing" when you're sitting on the couch is a world apart from "knowing" when you clamp on your mountaineering boots and crane your neck, up and up, just to catch sight of the summit. Even though superlight oxygen systems and fixed ropes have dramatically simplified the climb, this was still, for me, the route of legend and dauntless adventure. *Fear*. I might fail. Lose my drive. Succumb to the cold, to frostbite. Something in me, something about me, might fall short in a realm where the margins were vanishingly small. *Confidence*. No, I was as prepared as any human could be for the challenge. I would not let myself down.

My reverie ended at the sight of the border, tucked into the narrow "V" of a deep canyon. We drove from Nepal across the cascading Sun Kosi River on the famous Friendship Bridge and were greeted by a uniformed Chinese guard, whose stoicism carried a whiff of menace. The whole atmosphere was now different. On the Tibet side of the river, roads were freshly paved, electricity appeared abundant, architecture modern. It was like leaving one century for another in the span of a bridge. With the modern ambience came a stern, militarized attitude. Gauntlets of guards were positioned to look us over three more times as we moved through immigration. We had hidden our walkie-talkies and our vital GPS handhelds in our pants so they wouldn't be confiscated. It seemed absurd, but no communications equipment was allowed into China, even for mountain climbers. At one point, I stood smiling broadly before a blushing, shy Chinese woman who wore the uniform of a border official. I was worried she would look too close and see the GPS bulging in my pants. But she kept her eyes up and fixed on mine, and finally we cleared the formalities and I walked awkwardly ahead.

The China Tibet Mountaineering Association handled all logistics for climbers—which simplified life for us, in return for a loss of privacy so that the Chinese could guard against random mountaineers wandering around Tibet unsupervised. We drove steadily upward, the high-pitched sound of the straining engine serving as background music. We stopped at the town of Nyalum and then again at Tingri. The latter was higher in elevation than the former, and teams spend a day or two at each, hiking and getting acclimatized before approaching Everest Base Camp. The towns had two clearly delineated sections—a modern concrete area for the Chinese and foreigners, and a dirty, mazelike ancient section where the Tibetans lived. Our enclave barred its gates at night to keep out the packs of dogs that roamed the Tibetan sections. We were warned that visiting those areas would almost certainly result in a mauling. After seeing some of the local children who had been attacked in the past, we took the admonishment to heart.

Teammate Ed Laughton and I were beginning to bond. He was an urban planner and globe-trotting health worker for a nongovernmental organization. I could tell right away that we would become good friends and climbing partners. Our friendship and mutual respect would carry on for years through other adventures. Ed was from England and, like me, had been living in Nepal with his wife—who was a doctor working with the Himalayan Rescue Association in Pheriche, Nepal. Both of us were accustomed to the high altitude of these mountains. The third climber in our team was Kenny Cheng, who lived in Hong Kong and had joined us directly from sea level. He acclimatized at his own pace, while Ed and I ran up the hills together—hills that would be mountains in other contexts. We grew stronger and more confident about the climb as we panted in the thin air.

Our next stop was the famed Rongbuk Valley, with a gun-sight view of the giant mountain itself. No matter how many times you've seen Everest, it takes your breath away. At the far end of the valley, at the very threshold of Everest, we passed the holy Rongbuk Monastery. I had been "baptized" as a Buddhist in Bhutan in 2004 and now felt humbled in the presence of this amazing temple at its 5,000-meter (16,404-foot) elevation, one of the highest permanently occupied sites on Earth.

Just five miles further on a gravel "road" that Tibetans swept clean with heavy brooms, we stepped out of the car. This was Base Camp, with a carpet of shale cleaved into sharp chunks by ice freezing and thawing and not a soft spot of ground for miles. Elevation: 5,200 meters (17,060 feet). Near here, George Mallory's pioneering British expeditions of the 1920s stepped off, and now I was following in those footsteps! Our journey had the feel of a dream being realized.

Already, we were nearly half a mile higher than the tallest mountain in the continental United States. With each breath, we supplied our bodies with only half the oxygen of sea level.

"I am a lucky man," said Edmund Hillary.

That was after he reached the summit. After he returned home. That's when a mountaineer can relax and talk about luck. Down here at Base Camp, before the climb began, luck was not something a mountaineer wanted to rely on—not when Everest loomed so large in your vision that your eyes could take in almost nothing else, jagged, icy, white, wind-blown, steep, cold, deadly. So we sought to bring it about ourselves, in the same way our ancient predecessors had. We participated in a solemn Buddhist Puja, or blessing ceremony. The Puja asks the mountain to be merciful, to spare us. The ceremony was meant to offer our thanks and "well wishes" and respect to the mountain. We brought some of our equipment to receive the blessing. I chose my carabiners, which I figured would form my link to the team, the mountain surface, and ultimately, my success. I included my boots and socks and gloves and goggles, my protection for vulnerable extremities. I also brought my GPS, as you might guess. Science could use a blessing, too. We distributed the equipment around a makeshift altar in the bright sun while Chomolungma herself looked down upon us. The Tibetan name for Everest translated, appropriately enough, to

Mother Goddess of the Winds. The lama sat directly in front of the altar and Kenny and I sat on his left, with Ed taking a place on his right. Anil, our sirdar, closed in with other members of our support team. The lama chanted and read prayers. He rang a bell to accent the chanting, and shook his *dorje*, the Tibetan word for the Buddhist's double-ended prayer "concentrator"—the same thing that I now have tattooed on my right bicep. It was entertaining to watch as he interrupted the solemn ritual to answer his cell phone. Twice. Chinese cell-phone coverage so deep into the remote mountains was impressive.

The altar was covered with food and beverage offerings, and the lama gave each of us a plate of grain, which we then sprinkled over the altar and our gear. The ceremony was mesmerizing, as well as emotionally invigorating. We felt, yes, blessed. And encouraged. When I looked up from the altar, Chomolungma loomed in full-retina, high-definition detail, emphasized by the clarity of the thin, dry air. We were ready now.

High-altitude acclimatization for the extremes we would have to endure meant easing upward until the body did not merely cope with reduced oxygen intake but actually began to accept this condition as the new norm. It was a process that could not be skipped or rushed. A human transported from sea level and deposited on the summit of Everest would be unconscious in only moments and dead within an hour for want of oxygen. But there were some things that acclimatization could not ameliorate. The bite of the wind, for one thing. I generally like wind. But enough can become too much in a short hurry, and that was the case on Everest. At Base Camp, the lashing wind never stopped and there was little to shield us, apart from the tents. At night when the temperature plunged, the cold and wind drained away strength and left us languid. Each climber retreated into himself to listen to those reccurring internal arguments between confidence and doubt. At one moment, the world would seem to shrink to nothing more than one's fleshly self, encased in nylon on ground made of rock shards. The next, the enormity of the quest became overpowering.

An early Base Camp entry from my journal:

> It feels like you have a lead suit on your body every minute. Even getting into your sleeping bag leaves you gasping for breath like you are so close to dying. Most of the day you just lie in the tent

staring at the ceiling. Small tasks to do begin to fill your mind but
you just can't move and after hours of thinking about doing something like putting on lip balm, you slap yourself and get up and do
your chores on your way to eat and drink and then immediately
go back to bed. I was lying in the tent reading a Newsweek in which
they were talking about all of the "torture" techniques that Bush
allowed during his presidency. Unfortunately most of them also
sound like climbing here—drowning, cold exposure, lack of sleep,
hunger, etc. This is a beautiful bleak place that does its best to break
you every minute, every day. Laughing here leads to a coughing fit
that lasts five minutes. Pretty much everything leads to a coughing
fit; which leads to the feeling that you are drowning and makes
you think "can I just catch my breath and please breathe easily or
else I will die." I can barely stand sleeping with myself because I
smell so badly of salt and every other odor you can imagine from
heavy sweating while climbing and going weeks without a shower.

My Nepali friends were in frequent conversations with the other
expeditions preparing to climb. Representing one of the only Nepali-
led outfitting companies, Anil and his team were held in high respect
by other Sherpas—and they told me that about 150 foreigners came
to climb the North Ridge in 2010. Of those, an estimated fifty turned
back in the first weeks. They simply walked away from their dreams
and the tens of thousands of dollars they had invested—usually without a backward glance, or so it seemed. The incessant, unending cold
was too much, the effort of breathing at this altitude and higher exhausted them, the great bulk of Chomolungma scared them. Or they
found they missed their families during the lonely, frigid nights. Home
turned out to be a more important reality than the three vertical miles
of ice and rock and avalanche that awaited them. Only when you truly
engage in such an experience do you find out if you love it—and love it
more than anything else. Love it so much you would risk everything.

    For those climbers who stuck it out, vast mood swings were com-
mon during acclimatizing. I tried to concentrate on down-to-earth
matters, such as equipment. At Base Camp I had time to reconsider
every choice of gear that I would use to get me to higher camps and, I
hoped, the summit. Thus, my choice of toothbrush was no longer trivial. Down versus synthetic insulation in parkas was a tough choice:

light versus heavy; fragile versus durable—extra weight meant less chance of gear failure, unless the load itself became too heavy and would slow me up, in which case the gear triggers human failure. I agonized over everything I carried up to the higher camps. How many layers for a given trip up the mountain? At what cost in weight? I brought a waterproof sleeping bag the size of a small kayak. My high-altitude climbing boots that looked like something from NASA. And my down bodysuit puffed me up like Shaquille O'Neal. All of this hemming and hawing over the gear that would be used for only a few days or, at most, a couple of weeks of extreme conditions. Then again, I told myself, people died on account of a single gear failure, a mistaken plan, a sudden storm that overwhelmed their protective equipment. I repeated the old mantra about how one couldn't overdo preparations. Yet part of me kept wondering if I was doing just that. Sometimes I felt I was growing stronger and weaker at the same time. Finally, like so many climbers before me, I took refuge in fatalism. I would do my best. I put on my war face. I applied the same close-in focus to our conditioning strategy.

Inevitably, though, my thoughts wandered from practical matters at hand to idle daydreams, and even into lapses of moroseness. Narcisa would appear in my forlorn thoughts.

From my journal:

> Now I go to do one of the most important things in my life, and she is gone. Funny how life ends up—in a sad way of course. We still talk and say "I love you" over the sat phone, but her tone and my empty heart speak volumes in a way that cannot be misinterpreted. And so I go to face my mountain alone.

Finally, the team felt ready. We packed and moved up to Advanced Base Camp, or ABC, at over 6,400 meters (20,997 feet) for the next stage of acclimatizing. Harsh wind persisted, but otherwise the weather held—with steady, but light, snowfall passing for good weather here. The route ahead followed the path of the Rongbuk Glacier along a rocky moraine more or less roughed out into the vague contours of a trail by yak travel. It was stiff climbing but not yet technical. Trekking companies sometimes described this as the highest walkable destination in the world. This camp, where the serious mountaineering gets started, was higher than any point in North America, even Denali in Alaska.

The mountain we encountered at this elevation was vastly different from what the 1920s expeditions found. I read the old accounts of Mallory-era climbers slowly hacking their way up the Rongbuk Glacier, encountering deep snow and ice towers. It was but bare rock for us, with only the background sounds of rushing water from glacier melt runoff as remnant ice yielded to sun and temperature.

At ABC, we faced our first crisis. Capillaries in Kenny's eyes burst. He became blinded, probably on account of reduced air pressure and incomplete acclimatization. Fortunately, we were in a position to rush him down the glacial trail without delay, the first stage in what would become a marathon relay for the far-off journey to sea level. He eventually recovered, but the process took two years. Higher on the mountain such a situation could have been fatal. Indeed, later that same spring, a popular and outgoing Scottish climber made the summit but then lost his sight coming down. On the near vertical descent, his affliction slowed his team to a crawl. His fellow climbers began to suffer frostbite and their own mobility came into question. Eventually, it was a choice. Would all perish? Or just one? The injured man knew the answer—and said so. His teammates left him on the mountain and hurried down to save themselves. What could be more horrible—and noble? Telling your mates to leave you behind for their sake? Then sitting, blind and alone in the whipping wind, knowing that you would freeze to death alone in a few short hours?

Kenny's bad luck was a reminder, although we didn't really need one: We were penetrating one of the most hostile environments on Earth. Up here lurked an alphabet soup of conditions to break the spirit and destroy the body—maladies such as HAPE, or high-altitude pulmonary edema, and HACE, or high-altitude cerebral edema. In a vivid, although not life-threatening, example of altitude's impact on the body, I tore a one-inch strip of skin about half an inch deep from a finger at Advanced Base Camp when we were moving large rocks to configure benches and tables. The torn flesh refused to heal even the smallest amount for the entire time I remained on the mountain. Once we returned to Kathmandu two months later, it was better in less than a week.

More than 280 people have died on the mountain, and a majority of their bodies remain there. Often, those who succumb do so on the descent, which becomes more dangerous the higher up the mountain one has climbed. In 2010, we heard that seven climbers perished on the North Col route—six of them *after* reaching the summit—because of cold or altitude-related illness. People were not meant to be up here. Which, of course, was part of the mystique.

I was not by any means immune from this kind of adventurous enticement. But there was more to it. I knew there were answers up there in the high camps. And on the summit. Answers to questions about our changing environment. Everest and the Himalayas stand between China and India—the world's two most populous countries. Regional questions about air pollution, glacier melt, and long-term water supply for Asia loom large. These mountains provide water for nearly 2 billion people. The Indus and Yellow Rivers, and other major rivers, flow from these watersheds. Many countries already have re-search projects in this area. The Italians, for instance, maintained a station in Nepal located a short distance below Everest Base Camp. Few, though, have collected data at the highest altitudes. Addition-ally, the summit of Everest reaches the junction between the tropo-sphere, which encases Earth's life, and the stratosphere, where furious winds sweep pollutants around the globe. Everest is also situated at the mid-latitudes, roughly the same latitude as St. Petersburg, Florida. So lessons learned here could apply to our understanding of the atmo-sphere in the most heavily populated reaches of the globe.

A thought was never far from my consciousness: If I couldn't get up there and bring back this information after a lifetime of preparing myself, who could? Yet doing so, and the future I sought as an alpine climate researcher, would hinge on my ability to climb clearheaded and collect data while making no climbing mistakes, not even one, that would put my life, or a partner's life, in jeopardy. That meant all the way to the top, through the so-called "death zone" at the upper reach of the Earth's surface, and back down. Undertaking serious sci-entific work on a lesser peak ironically would allow a margin of error. I would be excused if science had to be sacrificed to some other exi-gency. But the North Col of Everest and above? Not likely. No room up there for excuses.

In short, I would have two tasks, when either was enough to test the limits of human capacity. Would my view of "science" and "climber" survive the Himalaya? Only one way to find out.

The death zone was generally regarded as above 8,000 meters, or 26,247 feet. At this elevation, the body cannot recover. Not even when supplemented with bottled oxygen. Diminished functions were inevitable and got progressively worse the longer you stayed. The death zone was so named because this is where you begin to die, inexorably. Only fourteen mountains in the world reach these heights—all of them in the Asian ranges of the Himalaya and the Karakoram.

Among my essential scientific equipment was an anthology of Everest writings. I carried it with me and intended to bring it along as high as was practical. These mountaineering stories were the closest thing we had to a written history of changing conditions on the mountain. I'd refer to passages written in the 1920s and subsequent years, describing the size and location of glaciers. I'd put my tent in the same spot, on the ground that was now just rock. Where early climbers looked out upon snowfields, I unzipped my tent to see bare shale and schist.

Advanced Base Camp itself used to sit atop a glacier. In the 1920s, the ice was estimated to be more than 30 meters (100 feet) thick. Now much has melted away. The remaining rock surface had an advantage for climbers. It was warmer to walk and sleep on. But it also meant plenty of maintenance work. Melting snow and ice from above washed through the campsite in chains of creeks and ponds. We had to gouge drainage ditches out of loose rock to protect our tents and gear.

Each reference from earlier expeditions provided me with a data point to begin establishing a more careful map by which science can estimate past conditions and benchmark future changes. I found, at least in these opening days of our climb, that this scientific work provided the perfect motivation to keep me active and hasten acclimatizing when otherwise it was so very tempting to laze around. Every other day, I would climb up approximately 1,000 meters (3,300 feet), and record reference data at intervals, starting by selecting a "ground control point" and marking it with GPS coordinates, then measuring the important variables, such as slope, aspect, vegetation (if any), snow, ice, glacier retreat, and human impacts—just the way I had done in Africa. The higher I went, the fewer variables remained to measure. But the more difficult it was to get there.

I set the goal of 1,000 meters for each of these scientific—and conditioning—sorties because that was approximately the elevation I would need to gain daily at higher elevations and for the final summit push. Roughly, this elevation gain was the equivalent of climbing the Empire State Building twice, if it were made of ice, rock, and unstable snow. I figured that by undertaking that kind of effort as often as possible in the conditioning phase, I would bring myself to tip-top form for the final climb. Acclimatization, as one might guess, was mental as well as physical. In this, our low-budget frugality provided a leg up compared to the more posh expeditions. Those outfitters could offer their climbers toasty, heated group tents at lower camps, far more comfortable setups than the cramped, unheated mountaineering tents in which we slept. They would cook and melt snow for drinking water quickly with a powerful gas stove while we relied on a single burner. But we did not feel sorry for ourselves. We were toughening ourselves. And we'd need it.

Fortunately for my scientific pursuits, acclimatizing was not a steady, one-way process upward. Rather, we followed a yo-yo path—shuttling gear up farther and farther, then retreating to lower camps to recover. That allowed me to cover plenty of the lower mountain and added greatly to my inventory of data.

My plan was to continue the process methodically all the way to the summit. Later, information from these ground control points could be precisely linked to satellite imagery that NASA has been collecting since the 1970s. The combination of my up-close measurements with satellite overviews would provide the best-ever record of the surface, and of surface changes on the mountain over time.

Although like practically everyone else, I was perpetually hacking and coughing, and my torn finger stubbornly refused to heal, I began to feel that I was in the best mountaineering shape of my life, mentally as well as physically. However, if I dared waste so much as thirty seconds congratulating myself on being a badass, I would quickly remember that other climbers never made it home from Everest even though they were more fit, stronger, and free of any distracting imperatives of science. Their remains are up there now, scattered along the route and at the bottoms of cliff faces. Alas, I was not the kind of mountaineer who could leave such thoughts in Kathmandu.

We were ready to move up to Camp 1 on the North Col at about 7,100 meters (23,294 feet). Ed was set to climb with Dipen, the brother of my Nepali friend Sujan. Dipen was particularly strong and uncomplaining, as well as a seasoned climber and partner in the Bhattarai family mountaineering company Himalayan Ecstasy. We were packing for our trip in the morning, getting the food ready, when I heard, offhand in the Nepali way, that Dipen wasn't feeling well. Ed and I hurried over to talk to him. Not feeling well? He looked like he was dying—ashen and in agony. He described severe pain in his lower abdomen. And when we got him to sit up in the door of his tent, he began puking uncontrollably. Then he just sat, strings of vomit hanging from his mouth, his head slowly bobbing. Our first thought was food poisoning, or perhaps some complication of altitude. He said that he'd been constipated. He pointed to his right side near his belly button. His intestines, I thought. But this had come on quickly, and Dipen seemed to be getting worse by the moment, pale and listless. Worst case? His appendix—but that seemed too catastrophic. We discussed a laxative or antibiotic, but he asked for painkillers. When he said he needed a doctor, we knew he must be in real trouble. For him to admit weakness was almost beyond comprehension.

An official Chinese climbing team had camped nearby, and the team physician came to assist. The diagnosis: a burst appendix, with death likely in less than a day without surgical treatment. We quickly rigged a stretcher and I packaged Dipen in a sleeping bag with a bottle of oxygen for the long descent. He looked awful as seventeen Sherpas set out with him, running in relays, rushing him down the glacier to Base Camp. By then, Dipen was unconscious and I had grave doubts whether he would survive. He was loaded in a vehicle and was taken away in the direction of Kathmandu.

But Dipen was uncommonly strong. We later learned that he recovered and would resume his climbing career. Ultimately, we would be together again on Everest—at Base Camp on the south side in 2014 when the serac collapsed and killed so many.

His sudden illness this time left the remainder of us shellshocked. We found ourselves standing around numb, lost, trying to ignore dark thoughts about omens. We were a small group to begin with. Now we were weakened. Two of our team had to be taken off the mountain with catastrophic medical problems. And we still faced the hardest part of the climb in the toughest conditions on planet Earth.

Dark thoughts. On this side of the Chomolungma, you could not get very far from the painful history. It followed you all the way—the knowledge of the great toll that pioneer climbers paid to open this mountain for the rest of us. Among them, the famed George Mallory, who was last seen near the summit nearly ninety years ago before vanishing. Everest could be a cruel place.

To clear my head and be by myself for a time, I clambered up a scree slope toward the North Col. I looked up at the route ahead. Then I saw a puff of white from an avalanche just below a feature we called the Black Eye. It was directly on the climbing route. The moving cascade of ice crashed over a couple of indistinct dots. People? I prayed not. Maybe the dots were only rocks. I moved farther up the hill, at this altitude a slow process even without a heavy pack. A breathless Sherpa loped down the mountain, asking urgently if I had a radio. No. He stopped long enough to report that two or three climbers had been carried to their deaths in the avalanche.

"Ice had collapsed because it is so ungodly damn hot," he said.

Everest was melting. And shedding its skin of ice and snow in the midday sun. I was too far down, and without crampons or adequate climbing gear to try and join in retrieval of the bodies. So I watched, heartsick, as distant climbers prepared to search for victims, not mount a rescue.

It hit me hard, the realization that the Sherpa knew exactly what happened. It was too damn hot. The climate on Everest was changing and getting warmer, and now the entire headwall on the climbing route was collapsing, ice avalanche by ice avalanche. Elsewhere, glaciers were disintegrating—the sounds of their cracking and groaning echoed through canyons. Climbers were dying. Climate change was killing them.

Then another realization sent chills over me. If Dipen hadn't gotten sick, we might have been right there in the path of the avalanche. The search party would be looking for our bodies. Climbing was inherently risky, but global warming was stacking the odds for the worse.

I shambled back down to camp feeling rock-bottom low, dazed even, not knowing what to say or how to say it. The climbers who died were not good friends, but they were part of the brotherhood of the rope. And that made them my brothers. Later I learned that the climbers caught in the icefall were Hungarians, and that one had survived. A safety line had caught him, and he suffered only a broken arm. Another climber was found alive with a broken hip in the debris at the bottom of the headwall. But he died that night.

Later accounts agreed that the crumbling ice avalanches were without modern precedent on the northern side of Everest. Climbers reported encountering snow avalanches. But there was no record about the ice itself letting go.

The next day, we collected ourselves and turned our focus to our own climb and the task of moving up to Camp 1. This would take us beyond the realm of even the most intrepid trekkers, and into pure mountaineering terrain.

The first part of the route followed the winding East Rongbuk Glacier and presented us with a difficult choice. If we utilized the undulating surface of the wet, melting glacier itself, we would have to rope up and probe our way to avoid deadly crevasses. That would be slow going, indeed. The other option was to sidehill along the scree-covered edge of the glacier. We chose the scree as the lesser of two evils.

I hated every step on this loose and unstable rock. My lungs screamed. Step, breathe, step, breathe—boring, boring, boring. It seemed to go on forever. The grade was perfectly unpleasant—too steep to be easy going, but not steep enough to be mentally challenging. With my head down, I watched my boots shuffle through the sharp, broken sea of rock. When I took the chance to look up, the face of the North Col headwall filled my view, a 60° upslope of broken, choppy ice that appeared almost vertical. Off to my side, I was confronted with the unpleasant sight of climate change at work—this mighty glacier dissolving in the heat, rapidly, even at this high altitude. Fast-moving rivulets of meltwater collected into creeks and then into small rivers that laced across the surface. When we were forced by the route to cross the glacier, it was like stepping onto soft taffy.

The day was already scorching. We baked in the furnace of the sun. I struggled to peel off layers of clothes. Then reflected rays from the snow and ice seared exposed skin, and I could feel myself turning crispy. The air was so still and hot, I could smell the sour odor of my own body. Slowly the sun dropped and long shadows began to catch us. The afternoon wind kicked up and brought a chill, then cold. I stopped and re-dressed. I was good and wet from the glacier melt and perspiration—and even with all my gear back on, I shivered.

Climbers ahead of us were already zipped in their tents by the time we reached the col—a French term common in mountaineering describing the low point on a ridge. We heard their dry, rasping painful coughs. They were probably feeling sorry for themselves, too.

Ed had stepped up to do the cooking for this part of the climb, and I was grateful. We gulped down tea and soup. A man my size could lose ten to twelve pounds of body weight during a day's hard climb on account of water vapor loss from sweating and heavy breathing. The failure to be diligent, even obsessive, about replenishing fluids risks bringing on everything from cramps to kidney failure. As we drank, my deep breathing slowly, very slowly, replenished my body's depleted oxygen. I was becoming human again.

At about 7:30 p.m., the coughing faded away as climbers lapsed into sleep. I could hear the unmistakable sandpaper sound of dry snow falling against the tent, interspersed with tent-rattling wind bursts that steadily increased, whipping and howling and tearing at our shelter. I was glad we had Ed's tent—supplied by his British sponsor Vango. It was a Quonset-hut design and seemed very sturdy. We knew we would need good shelter; there were still weeks left on our journey. We had a long way to go.

We remained at Camp 1 for a week of acclimatizing. It was a stormy interval, and partway through, we made a gear haul up to Camp 2 at 7,600 meters (24,934 feet). The higher we climbed, the worse the snow and wind became. This section of the climb was justifiably known for harsh weather, and we took it on the chin. By noon, we moved purely by feel in whiteout conditions. I couldn't see anything of Ed although he was just a few feet away. We receded into ourselves, disappearing into private worlds of exertion. Climbing became automatic.

Back in the United States, contemporary self-help literature is awash in books about meditation and mindfulness as a means to achieve harmony with the present. This was another way to achieve this same state. If you wanted to redirect your thinking away from yesterday without worry about tomorrow, just take on a pitch of Mount Everest in a storm. If you gave so much as an instant's worry about your credit-card balance up here, you just might take that one errant step that would send you cartwheeling down the mountain. That was living wholly in the present.

Ed and I climbed on a rope from anchor to anchor. Not only were these anchors our protection against falling, they provided firm touchstones to reality. We stumbled forward and the pitches grew steeper still. I managed to take a couple of data samples, but the task was largely impractical. The incessant wind hounded us. If I turned to face it, my facemask froze and choked me. Conditions like this were the reason we had obsessed over our gear earlier. Being poorly equipped in such circumstances could have ended the discussion, permanently.

Despite my confidence and my conditioning, I started running out of gas as this day wound down. After we dropped off our loads at Camp 2, I dug deep for the strength and resolve to descend back to Camp 1. We found it largely deserted. The snow and wind had driven most of the other climbers to retreat. With the storm still lashing us, we crawled into the tent and Ed lit the stove to boil our first pot of drinking water. Then he collapsed. I did the same. We napped and took turns with cooking chores. Although a tedious exercise, cooking focused my thoughts on something tangible. I rather enjoyed the process—all except for the standard discomfort that an oversized man feels hunched over in a mountain tent watching a stove and waiting for the snow to melt.

Our menu was prepackaged Indian food. It did not taste right, but the need to eat was greater than our desire for something better. So we gagged it down. Sure enough, I paid the price with a full-on stomachache. I dozed, but with my guts roiling, I found it impossible to sleep for long. It grew colder outside and quieter. The storm had broken, and that meant no blanket of clouds to hold heat. Colder still.

Coming out of a foggy snooze, I came close to making a huge mistake. My throat was parched and my mouth felt like it was coated in sand, so I reached down for my water bottle. By mistake I grabbed the wrong bottle. Stepping outside to pee was not something one did at Everest's high camps. So what I had unknowingly uncapped was the pee bottle and I was about to take a swig.

The thing about mountaineering was that it stripped away the extraneous "things" in life and reduced matters to the essential. Here, minimalism was not some trendy idea but the essential fact of life. Back home, things piled up in a clutter. But here, if something wasn't important enough to carry on my back to the top of the world, it didn't come. I needed a water bottle to prevent dehydration. I needed a pee bottle because it would be a terrible waste of energy to suit up and venture out for something so simple as emptying the bladder. I just needed the presence of mind to grab the correct bottle.

I caught my mistake. Then I found myself wondering. Did the fact I came close to drinking my own urine mean the altitude was getting to me? Or did the fact that I checked myself mean that it wasn't? Probably both. With that ambivalent answer, I dozed off. My stomach was improving.

In the morning I felt better and we descended to Advanced Base Camp to recuperate. Then we got sick, for real sick—deathly sick. I should have stopped eating when blood had spurted out of the under-cooked chicken on Ed's plate. But we were famished from the descent. A plate of hot food with meat was hard to turn down. After dinner, the pain started and soon I felt like a mule was kicking me in the stomach. I rolled around in the tent, doubled up. I couldn't sleep, and I was sure my dry heaves were going to turn into the real thing at any moment. About midnight, it started snowing, and the storm grew more intense.

I counted on feeling better in the morning so we could plan our next upward move. But I felt worse. I drank a bit of tea and then vomited. Ed was feeling equally horrible. Neither of us could eat breakfast or lunch. Instead we just lay in our tents. My occasional companion, self-pity, dropped by. I told him to make himself comfortable. I had a throbbing sinus headache in addition to a rumbling gut.

I slept fitfully until about 11:00 a.m. and then got up for a while because being up felt half a notch better than lying down, and it was painfully hot in the tent. I managed to put out the solar panels to trickle-charge the GPS and iPhone and let my sleeping bag air out between naps. I swallowed some tea and then slept again until 4:00 p.m., this time more deeply. Then put on earphones and listened to a Bernard Cornwell audio book about war in the age of Napoleon. It began to snow again.

I thought about the obstacles we had encountered. Then I remembered the motivational observations of Randy Pauch, the professor at Carnegie Mellon University who wrote a best-selling inspirational book after learning he was dying of cancer. "The brick walls are there for a reason. The brick walls are not there to keep us out. The brick walls are there to give us a chance to show how badly we want something. Because the brick walls are there to stop the people who don't want it badly enough."

I was too weak at this moment to surmount brick walls. But to prove my determination—at least prove it to myself—I gulped fluids until I couldn't bear more. Then I drank more. Dehydration loomed as my top worry. Food poisoning was usually temporary. But the explosive diarrhea that accompanied this bout of food poisoning was enough to take me out of the climb if I failed to stay hydrated. I didn't keep track of how much I actually drank, but it was a good deal more than was pleasant. To check the results, I pinched the skin on the backs of my hands to make sure it was supple and pulled back into shape, a sign of proper hydration. Before long, I told myself, I'd be ready for brick walls again.

Ed, too, was working to recover. He and I took the chance to walk down to Base Camp and then to the Rongbuk Monastery with Anil. It was our good fortune to enjoy a more intimate visit with the lama who had conducted our Puja blessing ceremony at the beginning of the expedition. Anil was well respected and frequently got us uncommon access. The lama welcomed us into the very spartan living quarters assigned to the temple's religious leaders. His sister, a nun at the monastery, served us tea. In soft voices, we talked with the lama for more than an hour, with Anil translating. As we departed, Ed and I shared the uplifting feeling of having enjoyed a special and deeply spiritual moment on the mountain.

So, how long does it take to climb Everest? It was often the first question people asked me. The answer was not straightforward. Once everything was in place and our lungs, blood, muscles, bowels, sinuses, attitudes, and gear were ready, it might take average, strong climbers six days, weather permitting.

But that was after investing weeks of nonstop effort to prepare for the final push. Anything less would be reckless. So that time must be considered part of the "climb." Add to that the long interval getting ready at home. The time in transit. The time getting home and readjusting. Two months in total. It was a wonder so many people found enough room in their lives for the challenge.

Even though I was feeling stronger, I needed more time now to recover. I spent the interval at Base Camp catching up on science. It became a bittersweet exercise. On the one hand, I was living my own pinch-me dream of being a climber-scientist bound for the top of Everest. I had a strong partner, a reason beyond ego for the effort, and of course, I had my war face at the ready. On the other hand, the more I trudged up the slopes to measure and sample around the great Rongbuk Glacier, the sadder I became. People were still alive who could remember when the glacier extended all the way down to Base Camp at 5,200 meters (17,060 feet). Now I had to walk several miles to about 5,600 meters (18,372 feet) to find any ice, and then it was not really what would be described as a glacier. It was a nice enough trek along the river that came gushing out of the receding glacier, a cascade of whitewater rapids connecting a series of small lakes and pools. Everest, towering in the background, made it a breathtaking vista—so long as you didn't think about how fast changes were occurring up here or wonder how the people and animals downstream would meet the challenges to come.

The "real" glacier, like the one in the old photographs of decades past, had receded all the way up to over 7,000 meters (22,966 feet), the loss of miles and miles of ice. In a word, the glacier was dying. It was also becoming more difficult to study—burying itself under the rock as it melted. Shoe-leather fieldwork seemed all the more vital in these conditions, and I spent as much time as I could recording observations and fixing precise locations.

This took me away from the normal paths of human travel, and I was rewarded by one of Everest's rarest phenomena—an encounter with wild animals. I was measuring ice when ten musk deer approached, sweet-looking animals with kangaroo faces. I was alone on a scree ridge just above the glacier. Rather than yield this one reliable trail to me and risk the unsure footing elsewhere, they approached head-on. Then, just beyond my reach, they skipped and jogged around me, and carried on their way. Animals were incredibly scarce on Everest, and I was lucky to share a moment with them in their home.

Finally, Ed and I were ready.

My last journal entry before we headed toward the summit:

I read about Tasker and Boardman's deaths in my (Everest History) book and then the next section was written by Tasker's girlfriend as she and Boardman's wife traveled to Everest to see where they died and mourn them. It was sharp and poignant and I remembered when Narcisa used to feel that way about me, when love dominated our lives. It is so sad how it shriveled up and passed away. I have loved many women before, but never with such a reciprocated intensity. Now I go to do one of the most important things in my life, and she is gone. . . . My parents and family love me and that will give me strength. But in the end, it is my legs and my lungs and my soul that will be driven by my will. I pray it doesn't ever fail . . .

Interlude

The Stuff

What does it take to climb Mount Everest? After how long it takes, this is usually the second question people ask. Taken from my notebook, here are partial lists of basic personal gear and camp equipment. I've included a sampler of just some of the scientific equipment essential to our work:

Clothes and Boots
Your clothing should be kept dry using waterproof stuff
    sacks or large plastic bags
3 polypropylene T-shirts
2 long-sleeve polypropylene shirts, medium weight
1 polar-fleece pullover, medium weight
1 polar-fleece jacket
Gore-Tex jacket with hood
Lightweight down jacket
Synthetic underwear
1 pair walking shorts
1 pair walking long pants for trekking and around camp
2 pair lightweight thermal bottoms
1 pair expedition-weight thermal bottoms
1 pair insulated or polar-fleece pants
1 pair Gore-Tex pants with full side zips

For high altitude use, 1 very warm down jacket with hood
and 1 pair thick down pants—or a down suit (can be
purchased in Kathmandu for a fraction of the cost)
1 pair lightweight poly-liner gloves
1 pair heavy insulated gloves
1 pair Gore-Tex down over-mitts
Warm hat
Windproof balaclava
Face mask
Ball cap or sun hat
Glacier sunglasses with side shields
1 pair ski goggles
2 headlamps with extra batteries and bulbs
Bandana
1 pair Millet One Sport Everest boots or equivalent
1 pair sturdy leather walking boots with good ankle support
for the trek to base camp
1 pair running shoes and/or sandals for Kathmandu and in
camp
1 pair down booties (optional)
3 pair medium-heavy poly or wool socks
3 pair liner socks, polypropylene or wool
3 pair lightweight trekking socks, poly or wool

Sleeping
For high altitude, 1 down sleeping bag (rated to −40°F).
In the high camp, you can sleep in your down clothing
inside your sleeping bag;
1 additional sleeping bag for base camp (good to −10°F)
At least 3 closed-cell foam pads for use in base camp and
high altitude
1 Therm-a-Rest mattress or equivalent, plus repair kit
Waterproof stuff sacks for sleeping bags

Backpacks and Travel Bags
1 medium pack (70 liters)
Day pack for trekking

2 large (120 L / 7,500 cubic inch) heavy-duty duffle bags
Small padlocks for duffel kit bags

Climbing
Alpine climbing harness
20 feet of 6 mm climber's accessory cord
2 large mitten-sized ascenders and arm-length leashes
Locking and regular carabiners
Pickets, rope, and assorted lead climbing gear
Ice ax with leash
Crampons (must fit boots perfectly), steel crampons with
    anti-balling plates

Miscellaneous
Battery-powered alarm clock or watch
Camera with extra memory cards and extra batteries
Nylon stuff sacks for food and gear storage, large Ziplocs are
    useful also
3 water bottles (wide-mouth Nalgene, insulated)
1 pee bottle, wide-mouth Nalgene—different color from
    water bottles
1 plastic cup and spoon
1 small folding knife
High-altitude eating utensils
4 large trash bags
Passport, 2 extra passport photos
Separate photocopies of passport and relevant visa pages
Proof of insurance
Cash for purchasing Nepalese visa at Kathmandu airport,
    Tibet visa, restaurants and hotels, for gratuities, snacks,
    and to purchase your own drinks and gifts
Credit cards, bank/ATM cards
Female or male hygiene supplies
Lip sunblock
Skin sunblock (minimum factor 30)
Toothpaste and toothbrush
Soap or hand sanitizer gel

Small towel

Hand wipes

Small personal first-aid kit

1 skin-blister repair kit

1 small bottle anti-diarrhea pills

1 small bottle anti-headache pills

1 small bottle cough and cold medicine

1 small bottle Diamox (acetazolamide)
    for altitude sickness

1 small bottle antibiotic: Ciprofloxacin, etc.

1 set earplugs

Extra prescription glasses, or contact lens supplies

Special energy or snack foods such as PowerBars, GUs,
    Honeystingers, etc.

1 small roll of repair tape

1 sewing repair kit

1 cigarette lighter

2 small boxes matches

Paperback books, playing cards, iPod/iPhone/iPad with
    music and books, etc.

Solar chargers

Travel clothes for base camp and in town

Group Equipment

Two-way "walkie-talkie" radios

Satellite telephone

High-altitude tents (2–3 person)

High-altitude stoves, canisters of butane/propane high-
    altitude mix stove fuel

Snow shovel

Complete base-camp kitchen equipment and dining set,
    plus pot sets for high-altitude stoves

Large eating tent

Cooking tent

Base camp food and drinks (local origin)

Trash bags for environmental cleanup

High-altitude medical kit

Sampler of American Climber Science Program gear

Multiparameter water-quality instrument (measures
   dissolved oxygen, pH, conductivity, temperature, etc.)

Vials for water samples (usually several hundred for an entire
   expedition)

Quartz snow-monitoring filters

Syringes and filter holders

Snow-sample vials and Ziploc bags

Weather station for measuring temperature, relative
   humidity, CO_2, etc.

Spectroradiometer set-up for measuring incoming solar
   radiation and the proportion reflected back into the
   atmosphere

GPS handheld and backup

High-resolution digital camera (documentation of
   everything)

Clinometer

Compass

Soil-sample bags

50 ml plastic centrifuge tubes

Chloroform

Soil corer

Spoons and scoopulas for weighing soil

Laser range finder, handheld

Rite in the Rain notebooks and pens

Plastic insect collecting jars

Flagging tape

Petri dishes

Vacuum flasks and syringes for gas-exchange measurements

Handheld 12-power magnifying lens

Plant press (depending on location)

Chapter Eight

Top of the World

We moved up to Advanced Base Camp for the final time. No more preparation. On May 20, we set out for the summit. The forecast called for clear weather on top of the mountain on May 23. Every other day was predicted to be windy and stormy. Because the mountain penetrates the stratosphere, winds greater than one hundred miles an hour were typical for nearly the entire year on the summit. Such tempests were enough to lift climbers off their feet and hurl them into the void. A single day with the promise of fair weather was a very narrow window. But at least we had a window to anticipate, and such razor-thin margins were typical of Everest.

We ate as much as we could stuff into our stomachs. I took a couple of hours to dress, carefully pack, then double and triple check. I'd already cached my down suit and other extreme gear up at Camp 1, and other items all the way up to Camp 2, during earlier gear hauls, so I unzipped the tent and stepped into the bright sun and fluky winds wearing just a light Gore-Tex jacket and pants. This outfit was my best defense against sunburn or overheating from exertion, my chief concerns at this opening-day stage. Normally, my massive Millet One Sport boots felt like twenty pounds of deadweight on each foot, but now thanks to adrenaline, I didn't notice. My pack weighed about forty-five pounds, I guessed. But it, too, seemed featherweight in the moment of excitement. The pack contained various climbing gear and also included a heavyweight sleeping bag, my two handheld GPS devices, some extra layers of clothes for when the sun dropped later on in the day, a pair of headlamps, trail food and water, and of course, my trusty iPhone. Even though I received no cell signal on the mountain, it held digital books for me to read and served as my diary. Fitted into my climbing harness and holding maybe the most important tool of all, my Black Diamond Venom hybrid ice ax, I looked up, sucked in a deep breath, and took my first step to the top. It was midmorning.

Because we had made this climb before, there was no need to choose routes. We aimed straight into the steep scree, where we slipped and slid and tried to concentrate on not making that one misstep that would cost us a twisted ankle—and any chance of the summit. At intervals, I marked ground reference data by longitude and latitude, and recorded conditions for our later analysis.

We climbed. Our route led toward a cliff, which rained down sheets of crumbling rock. The route flattened some as we moved onto the translucent East Rongbuk Glacier, which snaked up its own canyon for miles toward the North Col headwall—that steep face that served as the springboard to Mount Everest. Small, twelve-inch-wide crevasses presented themselves every once in a while on the surface of the glacier, but they were narrow enough that we could hop across— while glancing down into the blue-black darkness below.

Steadily upward. We knew the headwall to be more challenging and steeper than it looked from afar. First we followed a zigzag route up the lower snow ramps and then surmounted a pitch of steep ice. On this day for which we had labored so long, we indulged ourselves by stopping now and then to savor the astounding panorama. Fast-moving clouds seemed almost within reach—long, torn streamers of ice crystals riding furious winds in an ever-changing pattern of clean white against the 3D cobalt-blue sky for which the high Himalaya is famous. It was hypnotizing, and we had to remind ourselves not to dally. Ed and I both felt strong. Our spirits, already high, seemed to rise with the elevation. We smiled and raced upward, keeping pace with the fastest Sherpas. Because of the forecast for only a single favorable day ahead on the summit, the climbers for the entire season— that is, those who had made it this far—were all on the move at the same time. It was a busy mountain today.

We topped the wall and reached the North Col in early afternoon, the sun providing a warm welcome to 7,000 meters (22,966 feet). Intermittently, the mellow pleasantness we enjoyed was interrupted by blasts of wind sweeping down from the summit. With the winds came shocking cold that momentarily froze us in place.

Our poor tent was in terrible shape. Because of the bloody under-cooked chicken and the food poisoning, we'd had to leave it up here and were just now getting back to it. The wind and snow had beaten it into a mangle of nylon and alloy metal. We reshaped it and scooped snow from the inside. Our gear seemed to have survived, but the cached epi-gas canisters for cooking were buried in solid ice, the result of the daily thawing from the sun's warmth followed by the freezing cold of night. I worked slowly with just the tip of my ice ax to chip them loose—they weren't something you wanted to accidentally puncture.

At least we had a repairable tent and our full kit of gear. Ed was talking to an English guide when a blast of wind punched through the camp. They both watched, speechless, as the guide's tent and its con-tents—sleeping bag, pad, clothes, and the rest—sailed over the ledge and down a 6,000-foot cliff.

There were no second chances on a mountain like this. No extra gear to outfit the guide. Simply no spare time for him to retreat and re-outfit himself. His climb was over.

Ferocious gusts continued into evening, enough to make me wince and wonder about the vulnerability of our own camp. We ate dinner but never fully relaxed, bracing ourselves against the next burst. Sleep was fitful. Wind-driven snow worked its way through the tiniest opening, and by morning, we were buried by a snowbank in-side the tent, with the walls encased in a thick coating of hoarfrost from our breath.

We heated water and drank tea and nourished ourselves with a PowerBar. The climb ahead to Camp 2 was also familiar, so we again allowed ourselves a relaxed start. It was cold and clear. Higher up the mountain, however, we could see that lashing winds made for white-out conditions on the summit approach. We asked ourselves, what were the odds the weather forecasters would be correct about a single day of opportunity? Well, we wouldn't find out down here.

At first, we picked our way through steep snow. But not for long. We reached a ridgeline where wind had blown the route clear and we climbed still higher up on exposed, half-rotten rock. But it wasn't just the wind that did this. Warmer temperatures had reduced ice and heavy snowfields all over the mountain. I began to seriously wonder if I could make the climb without crampons. In the past, the ice and layer-cake snow would have been unnecessarily risky, not to mention slow going, without the added footing that crampons provided. But now? Hummm. I decided to keep my crampons packed away and see. I would become my own scientific experiment. Had global warming made it possible to now climb to the highest place on Earth in regular mountaineering boots without crampons? What a terrible signpost for the future.

I was curious about something else. If George Mallory had summited Everest before he disappeared, he would have done it without crampons. Even though his hobnailed boots had a better grip than my smoother boots, and conditions on the mountain were radically different, this would be a climate-change experiment that might bring me closer to experiencing Everest as he did.

Step. Breath. Step. Breath. Like many climbers who attempted this route, Mallory was in my thoughts. Step. Breath. Did he make it? Step. Breath. How close did he come? Step. Breath. Breath. Will we ever know for sure?

We do know that Mallory is one of only three mountaineering greats universally identified by one name alone—the others being Hillary, as in Sir Edmund, and Tenzing, as in Tenzing Norgay, the great Sherpa. A British schoolteacher and World War I soldier, Mallory participated in the 1921 British reconnaissance expedition that provided the first usable maps of the massif. Mallory was with the group that climbed above the Tibetan plateau and onto the slopes of Everest for the first time. What a great exploratory moment. He returned with the 1922 expedition that unsuccessfully sought the summit, and then again in 1924. On June 8 of that year, he and his partner, Andrew Irvine, were seen about 240 vertical meters (800 feet) below the summit and moving up. That was the last sighting of them alive, and it left behind one of mountaineering's greatest mysteries: Did they actually beat Hillary to the top by twenty-nine years?

In 1999, a research expedition set out to look for the bodies of the missing men and any evidence of their final climb. At 8,200 meters (26,755 feet) on the north wall, Mallory's remains were found, face down, frozen and preserved for seventy-five years. He had injuries consistent with a fall. The camera that the duo had taken with them was not found, nor were the remains of Irvine.

These days, climbers have it so much easier on Everest. Our equipment is far more refined, for one thing. But the real difference is that we can rely on a route already well known and prepared. I'm with other contemporary mountaineers in viewing Mallory and the other Himalayan pioneers with speechless admiration. I think we all ask ourselves, could we have kept up with them?

When my mind was not wandering back to those early days on the mountain, I found myself pondering the disparities among contemporary Everest climbers. The promise of favorable weather on May 23 meant that almost everybody with summit ambitions had to advance. That exposed vast differences in abilities and acclimatization. Some people moved quickly, steadily, and with purpose up the mountain. Others dragged along, dazed and sometimes almost motionless. The slowest of these zombie-like stragglers did not reach Camp 2 until 9:00 p.m., exhausted. I felt that my own movements were deliberate, bordering even on sluggish in the oxygen-deprived environment. I stopped often en route to take samples and measurements of pockets of snow where it still existed. Still, I reached Camp 2 early in the afternoon. I couldn't help wondering, and worrying, about those down below who lagged so far behind.

We enjoyed the afternoon and evening at 7,600 meters (24,750 feet). Intermittent squalls howled through camp but, hey, this was Everest. Otherwise the prevailing wind was gentle, for which we were grateful. This exposed campsite was notorious for unrelenting gales of forty to fifty miles an hour. And nothing saps the body like incessant, cold wind—weakening climbers just when they need to preserve their strength.

In the crystalline visibility of Everest's thin, dry air, our view was spectacular. Each step had opened more of the world to us. Now, we looked thousands of feet below toward where the storied Rongbuk Glacier made a sweeping left-hand turn. Beyond that and for many miles on either side, peaks as sharp as spear points reached into the sky. The distant horizon was defined by the rugged brown terrain of the Tibetan plateau. We were higher here than at any point in the Western Hemisphere—indeed, higher than anywhere on Earth outside of Asia. Yet this was only Camp 2.

Nothing of those distant scenes, no matter how moving, could match what loomed above. Crane your neck. Higher. There—the steep, implacable upthrust of Everest itself.

We retired to our tent to begin melting snow and preparing for tomorrow. Light snow began to fall. We worried about whether we should be worried about the weather. What was happening up higher? From here on, we faced new terrain, known to others but not to us. At some point, our concerns yielded to fatigue and we slept fitfully.

Ed and I awoke and, again, the inside of the tent was coated with thick hoarfrost—evidence of just how much moisture we lost by breathing. If we accidentally bumped the walls, we triggered our own indoor ice storm. That wasn't the only reason to move carefully inside this tent, however. We were pitched on a tiny, uneven tent platform scraped out of the gray, dirty scree that composed much of Everest. It was such a small space on this steep terrain that the farthest portion of our tent dangled into space.

We unzipped the tent and stepped carefully outside, and we took our time once more in packing up. Camp 3 was close enough above us that we felt little need to hurry. Good thing. Our precarious location meant that to organize ourselves and pack up, we had to hop and clamber around rocks, ropes, gear, and the debris left behind by climbers in years past–a good place to go slow and move with caution. When we shouldered our packs and set out, I went without crampons once again. It was now a goal instead of just an idea. We surmounted two nearly vertical sections of rock without incident and traversed around headwalls that were too steep to climb easily. Our worries about the weather did not pan out. Last night's storm had deposited only a little bit of snow, so mostly the route took us over marble-size loose scree the dirty color of gunpowder. This was not very aesthetic or graceful climbing. The thinning air made it tedious, and it grew more tiresome as we went higher.

We began catching and passing climbers who had left earlier. People were becoming spread out along the route. One of the oddities about this lonely business of Himalayan mountaineering was finding yourself in traffic jams. Earlier, on the climb up to the North Col, fixed ladders across a pair of wide and deep crevasses created a serious bottleneck. The second was particularly eerie—spanning a crevasse at the very edge of a cliff. I hurried across and felt wind gusting from beneath, the cold breath of Everest. Ed politely deferred to others and wound up thirty minutes behind me as he was blocked by four people descending and five climbing. There was no time for, or interest in, small talk in such circumstances. When we passed climbers, no one spoke. That would be energy wasted. No offense meant or taken, everyone understood. We were alone together up here. Each of us knew the odds—5 percent of us would perish in the coming hours. That was the history of climbing on the north side. These were the hard data that none of us could escape.

Sometimes, though, the impersonal seemed a little extreme for my liking, and occasionally dangerous. Above me on one pitch, a stranger stopped and blocked the path. I waited. Then his knee buckled and he toppled upside down onto me, and I caught him like a baby in my arms and set him on his feet. Neither he nor his partner offered thanks or even said hello. I'm not sure they even noticed me in their delirium. Worse were the rocks and cast-off gear that climbers sent bounding down the mountain without seeming to spare a thought for anyone below, an unhappy occurrence that became commonplace on a day like this, when so many people were racing against the weather.

Incrementally and unavoidably, even the routine was becoming more difficult. There was no marker, but at 8,000 meters, or 26,247 feet, we entered the death zone. One step. Three breaths. Another step. Three breaths. Every ten steps, a rest. Repeat. And so on. No wonder so few people relish this kind of high-altitude mountaineering. Step. Three breaths. Ten seconds. We passed other climbers. They looked like zombies. They moved in agonizing slow motion. Three breaths. Close my eyes. Fifteen seconds. Agony? Not really. In fact, I was feeling pretty good. No complaints. Coughing a little. Nothing serious. Step, breath, breath, breath, step. The towering visage of Everest's summit pyramid drew me onward. I put on my oxygen mask and set the regulator at one liter per minute—a rate that amounted to just sipping supplemental O_2. This was a significantly lower flow than Hillary and even more contemporary climbers relied upon. But mountaineering-grade bottles of pure oxygen were expensive, and I had only one. It would have to do.

I have talked to other climbers, strong climbers, who have climbed Himalayan giants without oxygen. To me, many of them speak like brain-damaged boxers who traded some of their cognitive function for the attempt at fame. I wanted nothing to do with such risk. My brain was my strength.

Despite the altitude, the sun was starting to torch us. I unzipped my down climbing suit, exposing nearly bare legs and arms to offload some heat. This invited the misery of sunburn. I would have to worry about that later. Three breaths. Cough. A couple more. My definition of joy is to feel strong enough to know that I'm unstoppable. By that crude measure, these were joyous hours. Cough, cough. My data collection became automatic—stop, mark the location with my GPS, note the few variables, which thankfully grew fewer with elevation, record the scene with pictures, and move on. I passed a climber who looked like he was dying. I reminded myself that I was dying, too. We were all dying now. None of us would get stronger, none of us would recover until we turned around and descended.

The afternoon sun was still sizzling when we reached Camp 3 at 8,300 meters (27,390 feet). It had taken us five hours, a short day. Never had altitude seemed so . . . well, so high. The view below evoked the unreal sensation of Earth as seen from outer space. We were very conscious of breathing in the reduced oxygen up here. There was no such thing as catching one's breath. All you could do was keep trying. Still, relatively speaking, Ed and I felt strong. Our weather seemed to be holding. Good omens.

We dug into the loose rock to create a tiny, roughly level patch and pitched our three-person tent. Ed and I and the two Sherpas climbing with us, Mingma and Ang Kami, crowded in. This was really more a curtained way-stop than a full camp. We wouldn't be staying long. So while we could, we rested, snacked, melted snow, and gulped water. But never truly relaxed. Buried in my puffy sleeping bag, I simmered with excitement. From the doorway, I could view the summit of Everest itself, seemingly only a few short steps away. I could study the route and plan my path. I began to really believe . . .

Camp 3 was located just below one of Everest's most notable features, a distinctive layer of sandstone called the "Yellow Band." The color wouldn't mean much to us, however. We planned to be passing over it in the dark—our last night high on the mountain. We agreed to depart for the summit at 9:30 p.m. Most other groups crammed together here at Camp 3 would be heading up at 8:30 p.m. From what we had seen, most of these climbers were slower than us. We hoped to avoid getting tangled with them at a difficult bottleneck, or suffer as they rained loose rocks down from a steep pitch above. So we would give them a head start to let them get onto the easier North Ridge before we started behind them. We figured on catching them higher up, where the route was wider, and we could pass without trouble. We knew we would be moving fast enough to make the summit in good time. Even with our mountaineers' nagging coughs, we felt good and confident, and ready for this last step.

You get only one chance. Mine was now.

Three groups packed up and trudged slowly upward ahead of us, each according to its own schedule. The weather remained clear. Stars seemed almost within reach and illuminated the mountain in film-noir-style black-and-white. It was truly cold, maybe forty below or more. I couldn't tell for sure. My thermometer had bottomed out at minus thirty.

Up here with reduced oxygen and deepening cold, every movement was a struggle. And each struggle was wholly absorbing. Nothing was casual. I was shocked to watch myself and see how slowly and painfully I moved just to pull on my boots. Whatever instructions my brain delivered, my body responded only in slow motion. I had to wonder if I'd ever get going. For sure, I didn't want to fall behind here at the very beginning of the attempt, but there did not seem any way to accelerate the process. We had planned our timing so that if the weather held, if the climb went as we hoped, if our strength did not fail, we would reach the summit at daybreak. If.

Ed set out five minutes before me with both Sherpas. He had gotten his boots on faster and he was cold. At a little after 9:30 p.m., I followed, alone. Once again, no crampons for me. Ed and the Sherpas were climbing strongly. I came up in accordion fashion—catching up to them, then falling behind as I stopped to mark ground reference points and record my data in the darkness. Behind us, a large group of climbers prepared to follow.

I reached the Yellow Band without trouble, ascending a gully and then surmounting a vertical section of rock. Next came a traverse over to another section of the band, where the rock was loose-as-hell sandstone. I had to concentrate to keep from slipping.

The hour was perhaps 10:00 p.m., or maybe 11:00 p.m. I trudged up a long snow ramp. Without crampons, I had to take extra care to securely set my footing. The section steepened, and my progress slowed. Then, in what felt like a sudden miracle, I was up and onto the Northeast Ridge. It cut into the sky like no other knife-edge ridge I've known—rising all the way to the summit, but only thirty feet or so wide, dropping away for many thousands of feet on either side. A veritable tightrope of rock and wind-blown snow. Everest, and I finally mean the very top of Everest, loomed so very close in the night light.

This was a wonderful place and probably the happiest and most exciting part of the entire climb. With the summit now realistically within reach, I advanced euphorically at a walk. Yes, for a spell, it was a walk on relatively level ground. After maybe 100 meters (330 feet), the beam of my headlamp caught sight of a small overhanging cave off to the side, supplied with oxygen bottles and two sleeping bags.

"That's smart," I thought, "someone put these here for an emergency."

But at nearly 8,500 meters (27,887 feet), there are no emergencies that can be solved with sleeping bags. Looking closer, first I saw a boot, and then the dead body, and the "bags" were his down clothes. As with most of the bodies seen here in the death zone, he had curled up in the fetal position before he died and was frozen in that pose. He had fallen over and his head now lay lower than his boots, which were still fitted with crampons. My skin crawled when Anil later told us that used mountaineering equipment in Kathmandu was sometimes salvaged from the dead. Under this climber's remains was another body buried in the wispy snow. The lower body was an Indian man referred to as "Green Boots," who had died during a disastrous 1996 climbing season.

In an eyeblink of realization, my exhilaration turned to despair—an unholy stew of sadness for these two unfortunate men and a feeling of personal vulnerability for myself and my fellow climbers now on Everest. Imagine being known only by the color of your boots, left dead and frozen on a great mountain, visited by shambling passersby a few times each year. Imagine dying so high up that retrieval of your remains is not practical. Imagine that your frozen remains are listed in guidebooks as a trail marker. Imagine the gear you so painstakingly assembled pillaged from your carcass for the Thamel tourist markets.

I trudged on, numb. Then the ridge swept upward and climbing resumed. My thoughts turned to the major obstacles before the summit: the rock outcroppings known as the "Steps." The First Step straddles the ridge like an imposing castle fortification. The route to

AFRICA: Botswana giraffes at sunset along the Chobe River. The river is the lifeblood of the region, and animals congregate along its entire length. [CREDIT: JOHN ALL]

Crossing a flooded log bridge in Namibia—hippos and crocodiles lurked just underneath, waiting for the bridge to fail. The lack of infrastructure and constant physical threats make research for us, and life for locals, exceedingly difficult. [CREDIT: JOHN ALL]

COSTA RICA: This rope bridge was our first sign of civilization after crossing the Talamancas. It is amazing how the simplest human construct redefines the rain forest. [CREDIT: JOHN ALL]

Our first view of the Talamanca mountains as we crossed Costa Rica. The morning mists quickly burned away as the tropical sun slowly began to bake the countryside. [CREDIT: JOHN ALL]

DENALI: Climbing here presents its own set of challenges, but being able to compare environmental responses to climate change from the tropics to the poles is invaluable. [CREDIT: JOHN ALL]

EVEREST—TIBET 2010: Base Camp. This lonely basin was our home for two months as our bodies grew used to the altitude and as I collected data. The harsh, windy environment tested our spirits as Everest loomed above, waiting for us. [CREDIT: JOHN ALL]

Climbing toward Advanced Base Camp in Tibet, the mountain wears us down just as it does the rock and ice that mantle it. But now the ice is disappearing in an unprecedented fashion as temperatures soar. [CREDIT: JOHN ALL]

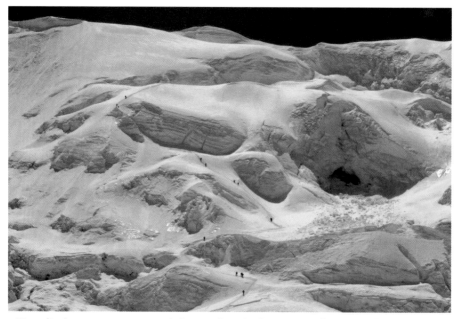

Tiny climbers move up toward the North Col. The massive "black eye" to the right is the site of the avalanche that I watched hit two climbers in 2010. This is an extreme example of the mountain melting away and collapsing. [CREDIT: JOHN ALL]

PERU: Every year the appearance of the mountains changes in the Peruvian Andes, and so as we approach the summit of Chopicalqui, we have to pick out a fresh route. Every climb becomes a first ascent as the landscape slowly melts beneath our feet. [CREDIT: JOHN ALL]

Pondering the route and enjoying the view as we prepare to climb Alpamayo. Climbing to this col in 2011 was a near disaster as I had to help rescue part of our team. In 2012 when this photo was taken, conditions were perfect and we climbed the mountain in only 3 hours. [CREDIT: JOHN ALL]

Tents are more than a physical refuge in the mountains—they allow a mental break from the rigors of the environment. They allow us to relax and contemplate our place in the cosmos and to examine why we are in the mountains. In a tent, we are free to live in the moment without fear of avalanche or crevasse. A moment paused that allows for reflection. [CREDIT: CLINTON LEWIS]

I'm collecting snow on the summit of Urus Este (5423 m, 17,782 ft.) and enjoying a warm, sunny day on the glacier. My pack bulges with samples and typically weighs 65 or more pounds by the time I reach Base Camp. [CREDIT: JOHN ALL]

NEPAL 2014: Our prayer flags and the location of our puja at Everest Base Camp. I, and most Nepalis, would never consider climbing a major mountain in the Himalaya without a puja. The mountains are too harsh and conditions are too capricious. [CREDIT: JOHN ALL]

This image was taken mere minutes before the serac broke away and plunged down onto these climbers. As they struggled to fix the ladder and resume climbing, the ice swept them to their deaths. Most of the people in this image died. [CREDIT: JOHN ALL]

HIMLUNG: My camp at 6000 meters on Himlung. I crawled back to this tent and spent the longest 19 hours of my life waiting for a helicopter to retrieve me—hopefully before I succumbed to my injuries. [CREDIT: JOHN ALL]

SUNSETS: It's all in the clouds....

[CREDIT: JOHN ALL]

surmount it, fortunately, was easier than it first appeared. I moved around to the right and then climbed a crumbly, outward-sloping section of rock. In the United States, rock climbs are rated from 5.0 (easy), in an ascending scale, 5.1, 5.2, 5.3, and so on, to 5.15 (not for mortals). This climb up the First Step was perhaps 5.3, similar to climbing a ladder missing an occasional rung. However, this was Everest, where technical numbers did not account for reduced oxygen, darkness, cold, or the thick down clothing climbers had to wear. On the other hand, I wasn't burdened with crampons, which are a liability on rock like this.

I made it to the top of the First Step without incident. In the end, I figured it was a relief to focus on a technical climbing challenge instead of dwelling on the abandoned dead in this icy graveyard.

Following another fairly direct stretch upward on the ridge, I reached the Second Step. This would qualify as a much more challenging 5.9 climb, at least for a short way. But a permanent aluminum ladder has been fixed to the vertical rock and made everything except the approach fairly straightforward. Getting to the ladder required entering a small alcove, then wedging my boots in a crack, and then heaving myself onto a flat boulder surface above. At this point, I held back a wave of vertigo. Looking down about ten feet, I saw another body, this one still tied onto a rope. Reflective strips on the climber's motionless boots and clothes glowed in the beam of my headlamp.

I followed a snow chute upward to another section of the Second Step. I passed two climbers who were stationary and changing an oxygen cylinder. They dropped the used one without regard for who might be below and it bounced down like a missile.

It is possible that this was where Mallory and Andrew Irvine made their fatal slip. Possibly together, they plunged over the edge of the ridge and down the cliff. Mallory's body was found nearly 300 meters (1,000 feet) below, leaving unsolved the mystery of whether the two were going up or down when they perished. These days, thanks to a Chinese team that brought the Olympic flame to the top of Everest— along with a new fixed ladder put up by the climber Russell Brice, the danger has been reduced. But many other bodies remain in the vicinity and speak to the horror of trying to climb overhung, loose rock at 8,600 meters (28,215 feet) when exhausted.

Beyond the ridge, the route meandered upward and narrowed as it fed into another snow slope. Epic cliffs fell away on both sides. Then

the broken rock face of the Third Step blocked the path. How to surmount it was not clear as I came closer. But a climber sat resting in
front of the rock face, and I approached to ask. It slowly entered my
altitude-addled mind that sitting alone in the dark was most unusual.
As I got closer I saw that he was lying sideways in the snow, in the
fetal position. Dead. Worse, the easy way to continue would have been
to step over his frozen remains and move to the left. No footprints
led that way, although other climbers had circled the body and left
fresh footprints. My God, rubberneckers. Later, I learned the story
from Anil, who had climbed with the dead man a few years before.
The climber had summited without problem and proudly radioed the
news to his girlfriend waiting at Base Camp. He was on his way down
when he sent the others ahead and stopped to rest for a few minutes—
to savor the view and the feeling of triumph. He was never seen alive
again. The body was found the following year pretty much as it now
rested—undignified and deserted. I could not imagine the utter grief
that wracked his girlfriend after she had waited, and waited, and
waited, to celebrate his triumph.

I followed a frayed-looking rope up the face of the rock. It was
only 5.5 or 5.6 in difficulty, but it was composed of broken limestone.
The loose rock seemed to be held together by nothing but ice. So close
to the top. I wondered if it would break apart in my hands or underfoot. Looking down for a foothold and seeing that body was especially
unnerving. But it turned out to be the correct route. Once on top of
this Third Step, I was on the actual summit pyramid. So many climbers would have given everything to reach this point. Scores of them
gave everything just trying.

Looking east, I was startled to see the sun beginning to lighten
the distant sky. Then, a faint pencil line of orange emerged along the
cloudless horizon. It was going to be a spectacular, fair-weather morning. Our prayers back at the Base Camp Puja were being answered.
Now with each step, the mountain assumed the daybreak blush of reds
and oranges instead of nighttime's eerie black-and-white. I kept looking back and waiting for the sun to light up some part of Tibet. But I
stood so high that the sun hit here long before reaching down to the
surrounding landscape. I have been on other peaks at dawn. But Chomolungma was so dominant in this scene that it spoke the language of
the Earth itself. One by one, the high peaks around me—some of the

tallest in the world—caught the sun and flamed into view. Only the occupants of the Space Station and maybe a few long-distance pilots had a chance to witness dawn before I did.

I resumed my climb. Ahead was a rocky snowfield, more rock than snow. I approached a climber resting in the fragile morning glow. But I wasn't tricked this time, especially when I saw that he was sprawled on his back with his head facing down the slope. It looked as if he had been sitting and facing away from the trail, studying the unreal beauty of the Earth spread out before him, when he just faded and pitched backward down the slope. This body was the worst of them all. The climber's arms were outraised and his upside-down face aimed directly at anyone climbing up the route, only a few feet away. Closer, and I could see that his skin was bleached and dried, and his eyes were pecked out by birds—which surprised me at this altitude. Too late, I turned away. The nightmare image will never go away.

I was told that nine frozen bodies remain within ten feet of this Northeast Ridge route used by climbers. Many others lie farther afield—scores, in fact. All are preserved as Mallory was, frozen and desiccated but remaining unmistakably human. Bodies can't be removed because helicopters max out at 6,000 meters (19,685 feet) and the deadweight of a body would require a team of ten Sherpas, near death themselves, to sacrifice their summit to retrieve the body. The rumor was that during the 2008 Olympic torch climb, in order to get the torch to the summit on time in spite of the weather, numerous Chinese Sherpas died. The Chinese government was embarrassed about the incident, so it closed the route and had other Sherpas go up and throw the bodies off the ridge into the depths below. How achingly sad that so many people were destined to remain in this hostile place, exposed, stripped of both life and dignity, abandoned where they fell.

Perhaps other climbers wondered, as I did: What were their stories? Who loved them? Who did they leave behind? Why did they come? Why did they give up? What might have made the difference in those final moments between surviving and falling over backward, or curling up into the fetal position?

Humans tolerate only the narrowest range of environmental variables; the dead of Everest proved that.

I couldn't put the scenes of the corpses out of mind. I have always talked about trying to live in the present, and live fully. Being *here*—here in the moment—is a tenet of Buddhism. Walking among the bodies of those who perished strengthened my resolve to do better if I survived. I hoped these climbers died up here without dwelling on regrets. I will think of them, these dead, as I remember to tell the important people in my life that I love them. I will remember how fragile and capricious life can be and tell the people I hold dear how very much their support counts. The mountains have taught me this lesson over and over again.

A few of the newly dead on this mountain were people I knew. At Base Camp, they talked about home, about ambitions and the happy celebrations awaiting them on their return. Up here, the dead speak to me about what to cherish in life, while we still have it in our grasp.

Something else. The corpses on Everest become telltale signposts that I am dying, too. Everyone up here is dying. I feel as if the billions of cells in my body are slowly—or not so slowly—calling it quits. I am a snowman, melting in the rising morning sun. It doesn't happen all at once, but slowly the snowman succumbs. One ten-minute rest, just a simple, blessed rest, becomes a forever rest. No one who has fought this hard to get this high means to die.

The sky was growing lighter. With it, the vertical scale and angle of this summit pyramid came into focus. Think of New York City's Chrysler Building and imagine climbing a corner edge, slick with hard snow. I questioned my decision not to wear crampons as the slope steepened to 60° for a short section, feeling nearly vertical in the thin air. It was very slow work to kick a solid foothold into the windblown, icy snow. And I was too weary to use my ax to chop steps for myself. But I was stubborn. A rope had been anchored above, and I pulled myself up arm over arm—using it like Batman in a huge effort. The grade eased off, and I aimed for an undulating series of snow ridges. The top of the summit pyramid rose ahead. Odd, wasn't it? To think that ancient limestone began as sediment on the sea floor. It was now atop the world. Marine fossils could be found here. Environmental change is Earth's old acquaintance.

Just a few more feet to climb. The route was not particularly difficult, but neither was it a straight shot. For most of the year, the frigid, violent weather sweeping across this terrain was unimaginable.

Whatever pathway existed reflected only this moment on this day, only this creeping dawn—not yesterday's nor tomorrow's. The wind and the snow would reconfigure it, again and again. I wandered to the left, to the right and back a bit, linking up the weaknesses in the mountain's defenses, connecting ramps to ledges. Step. Breath, breath, breath. I made my way higher, my throat growing raw, my footsteps lumbering. My boots were as heavy as cement sacks. I wanted to finish. To get to the top. And to get off the top and out of here. If you were to draw it on a napkin, the route became something like a big, reverse "Z" along a ledge that connected, higher up, to a ramp and then, higher and steeper still, to the final approach.

Rocks rained down around me. Climbers above were struggling to make their way down and not being considerate of others. We converged. I was going to complain about their careless disregard. But I saw that one of their team was clearly dying and the others were trying to get him down the mountain as quickly as possible. I said nothing to them. Inside, I whispered a prayer for the failing man.

On the gentle ridge above this final obstacle, I met up with Ed. I had stopped to take yet more measurements of slope and snow conditions and he appeared right in front of me. He was coming down, not going up—he had reached the summit, he was homeward bound! He was elated. So was I. He earned it! Great going, mate. We chatted briefly. Ed was cold and spent and wanted to get down as fast as he could, but nothing could erase his smile of fulfillment. He wished me luck and we parted.

My pensive mood brought on by the bodies vanished. Ed's success provided the boost I needed. Mountains were notorious for inducing mood swings in climbers, and this one came on in full force, just at the right moment.

Step. Breath, breath, breath. Down a small undulation on the ridge. Step. Then up the other side. The snow was losing its rosy complexion and becoming whiter and brighter.

I was approaching 8,800 meters (28,871 feet). Above me I saw people, and a string of Buddhist prayer flags, stretched tight and snapping in the unending wind. Easy going now. Step. Breath, cough, breath, step. This was great. Cough. Still climbing. Nearer.

Then, no more up. This was as high as you could go with your feet on the ground, 8,850 meters (29,035 feet), according to the National

Geographic Society and GPS technology. China and Nepal agree to disagree about the actual height—is it the height of the snow, or the rock beneath?—but have compromised at 8,848 meters (29,028 feet). As a scientist, I believe the GPS. All the world was downhill now. A surge of euphoria. Breath. Breath. At 6:00 a.m. on May 23, two days shy of my forty-first birthday, I stood on the summit of Everest.

I believe I was the first to reach the top without crampons.

In all ways, I was fortunate. I could have been in a downer mood. But I'd hit the cycle just right. I was exultant. I could have been ill or weak—there was, after all, plenty of reason to feel that way. Instead I was strong. Really strong. I could have been battling hurricane winds or a sudden blizzard, the kind of weather that catches the unlucky and hurls them into the void. But this was the prettiest day ever on the summit. Prettier than any picture I'd ever seen; better than any day ever described to me.

The 360° panorama revealed not a wisp of cloud anywhere. I'd read that on a clear day such as this, a climber could see more than two hundred miles in every direction. This meant I was looking down upon something like 1,200 square miles of untamed Tibet and Nepal. A godlike view from the mountain's throne room. I could see the two base camps—the one in Tibet and the one in Nepal—and long snaky trails of glaciers, the bright sunlit face of Lhotse. I took pictures, and a video. But it was tough. My four batteries, fully charged from solar panels, lasted only thirty seconds each before petering out in the cold. As each in turn left my warm climbing suit, I had to take pictures quickly before the −40°F temperatures drained them. Four quick chances to take photos for a once-in-a-lifetime moment. Even if I made the summit of Everest again, it would never be exactly the same.

The summit itself was not much bigger than a dining-room table and was littered with torn prayer flags, discarded nylon crap, and several Buddhist statues—one of which was in a small glass and steel box for protection. Three ridges converged here, and in between them, the mountain fell away in dramatic downslopes and cliffs. The great, fluted Kangshung Face to the east dropped an astonishing 3,400 uninterrupted meters (11,000 feet), making it one of the most formidable mountain cliffs in the world. Imagine dropping a piece of gear and watching it fall over two vertical miles. Climbers, gasping for breath, steadily arrived to share the space, and just as steadily departed to make room. No solitude here on such a day.

In my continuing euphoria, I resisted the impulse to leave. I wouldn't come this way again—at least not often—and the weather would likely never be this favorable again, even if I did return. I couldn't get enough. I wanted to savor the experience. I felt strong enough to linger, and the sun offered a comforting touch of warmth. All of my training, all that effort, had paid off.

Finally, after about twenty minutes of photos and video and studying the summit, I started a leisurely descent, stepping down the snow. When I reached the first rock outcrop below, somehow my oxygen-deprived mind had the capacity to remind me that my brother, Joe, had asked me to bring home a rock from the summit. And I remembered I wanted to collect samples for some geology work. I stopped and stuffed my pockets with a few smallish rocks and was thankful that my brother's request had remained in my mind as even the science was beginning to fade. Below was a snowfield, and I picked my way down until once more I remembered something. I had forgotten my scientific duty and had not fixed a final ground reference data point at the summit. I'd not made the corresponding measurements. My head was getting cloudy for lack of oxygen. I turned around and headed back up. Step. Gasp. Breath. Cough.

I summited Everest a second time. It was barely 7:00 a.m., but I could see the day was starting to get away from me. Only a couple of stragglers remained on top. The others were heading down for their tents, for hot tea, for food, for warmth, for richer air. But having more space to myself, I resolved to make use of it.

I logged reference points at the very tip-top of the mountain and then went down on the south, or Nepal side, a hundred yards toward the South Summit. I noted more reference information and environmental data and took a few more photos. Then I realized my selfies showed me wearing mask and goggles. I peeled them off and smiled for my camera. My face was miserably sunburned and the images depict me as suffering more than I really was.

After I had gone through my mental checklist and done everything I needed to do, and took every picture three times and soaked in my good fortune to enjoy such a perfect day—once I was truly satisfied that my mission was accomplished—I headed down for the final time.

Now I paid the price for refusing crampons. The snow slopes were difficult and energy consuming without them. I had to dig the edge of my boot into the hard snow and sidestep to safely make progress. I could have stopped at any time to put them on, but I wanted to know if it could be done without them.

I became vaguely aware of how thirsty I was. But the descent down the ridge beckoned me along. I took dozens of pictures of every aspect of the descent, looking away whenever I came upon one of those lonely bodies. I felt it increasingly difficult to turn my head—my neck was sore and stiff. Mental switches seemed to be flipping off as I entered the twelfth consecutive hour of high-altitude mountaineering. I was getting tired as I clambered down the Steps in reverse order, Three, Two, One. From above, these obstacles appeared smaller than they actually were. The Second Step proved to be just big enough to be almost impossible without the new, wonderful ladder. The First Step was easier. Then I picked my way down the ridge. I passed a couple of climbers, but otherwise this part of the mountain seemed deserted now. Homeward-bound climbers were ahead of me on the descent. We had a long way to travel. Later I learned that the large group that had followed us up from Camp 3 had pretty much failed and retreated on account of a series of mistakes. Only four of twenty-two team members made it to the top. The others were retreating and were devastated by their failure on such a perfect day—failure caused by the poor logistics for too many climbers in a single group. The tourist climber is less common on the north side, and far less likely to actually summit because of the difficulties. This was proof.

Up ahead was the daunting geological formation known as the Pinnacles that blocked progress along the North Ridge. I stepped off the ridge where the going was easy and began the steep descent to the Yellow Band. I took some rock samples, but here I started having trouble. The air on Everest was exceedingly dry—less moisture than in a desert. Dehydration was catching up with me. Without giving it considered thought, I'd made a huge error and allocated myself only two liters of water for the climb. I should have consumed a liter per hour—melting snow every few hours on a small epigas stove. I was now about a dozen liters behind. That was a shortfall of more than three gallons. And I had no stove to try melting the –30°F snow to start catching up. I began to imagine my urine going from liquid to gel to dust. Mistakes like this accounted for some of the tragic body count along this route. It came to me in my foggy thoughts that my increasingly sore neck was a consequence of my throat swelling almost shut. Damn.

Faced with a crisis, I naturally felt the urge to move faster and get back to the nearby Camp 3. Water. I needed water. A Coke. Wow. But Mount Everest is the largest scree pile on Earth. The frost-thaw cycle had broken most of the climbable route into loose rock, ranging in size from baseballs to watermelons. Trying to accelerate meant slip-sliding down the crumbly slope halfway out of control and hoping that it wouldn't get worse. That was another way to die. Once again, my size and correspondingly high center of gravity worked against me. I staggered and slid down the route, evermore like a drunk trying to rush home at closing time. I was desperate for water and equally desperate not to lose control. I had depleted my oxygen bottle long ago. A sense of peril consumed me, and my consciousness seemed to slip in and out of focus. I was acutely aware of time passing. Then I lost all awareness of time. An occasional stumble brought home the danger with a start. My mouth felt like a rough, dirty carpet. Finally, I stumbled into Camp 3. I searched for, but could not find, a canister of epigas in the tent. What the hell? We left behind several for just this kind of moment, but someone had helped themselves to our lifeline. Petty theft could easily mean the difference between survival or not at such altitude. Unfortunately, that was why some teams with greater Sherpa support would lock up life-sustaining gear at the highest elevations. One of Everest's dirty secrets.

My thinking was blurry, but it did not obscure the do-or-die choice: Stay and continue what might be a futile search or flee. If I failed to find gas, perhaps some other climbers someday would find me in the fetal position, maybe with my eyes pecked out. Or I could make a run for Camp 2, exactly one-half mile lower in elevation. I'd left an epigas rig in our tent there as well. Surely the entire mountain hadn't been plundered.

I could sense the temperature dropping. The perfect day had to end. I made a run for it. Or, at least, I plodded for it. I struggled just to pull on my pack. Each step down bordered on a stumble. Sixteen straight hours became seventeen. I fought nonstop to keep my balance. Ahead were other climbers, also trying to get down. They were even slower and two of them looked worse than I felt. Unable to walk, they were being helped by their teammates. I gave each of the exhausted ones a small GU Energy Gel packet. One fellow seemed to perk up immediately. I squeezed a packet into my own mouth and hoped it would drain down and lubricate my paralyzed throat. I staggered on.

At a small cliff face, I grabbed the fixed rope and abseiled down clumsily, landing hard and slipping on loose rock. I fell sideways and smashed my back. I lay dazed, looking skyward, running through a mental checklist to see if I was broken. Or where I was broken. My memory seemed to be shutting down—leaving gaps in events now.

I was getting hot in my down suit. I lowered the hood and unzipped my jacket to cool down. It was more than cool outside of my own cocoon—icy daggers penetrating everything. I realized the wind was rising as clouds began to close in. The outside of my jacket continued to blossom with hoarfrost from the water vapor I had breathed away. The brightness of the day suddenly faded. The sky was disappearing into a darkening penumbra of storm clouds. Yes, the perfect day had to end sometime, and that was now.

Later, and I didn't know how much later, I shambled into Camp 2 in a growing snowstorm. I went straight for our tent and found the epigas canister and burner. I filled a pan with icy snow and melted a liter of water. My raw throat screamed as I sipped. Gulping was impossible. Then the stove sputtered once and the flame vanished. Out of gas. I collapsed into my sleeping bag. Pain shot through my back, then I remembered that I'd fallen. When I turned on my side, I found that I'd let my ear freeze when I had lowered my hood—freeze solid. Mistakes were mounting up. Snow began to fall. I lay there, somewhere in between sleep and death.

My mind cleared as the snowy dawn began. I guess I'd awakened. But I was too miserable to rise. A climber can burn 10,000 calories a day. I was starved and there was no food; I was desperately thirsty and without water. All I had was the warmth of this big gunboat of a sleeping bag. My thoughts drifted away. Then wandered back. The only thing that didn't hurt was to close my eyes. And that begged the question.

John, I asked myself, *are you ready to die now?*

Hell, no, I answered to myself. I was wounded. But I was strong. I was a brute. What kind of a man would let the comfort of a sleeping bag kill him? I rolled over, pulled my arm out of its warm shelter and reached for my pack. I started loading up while lying sideways. Just this modest exertion brought on a coughing fit that ripped through my dry, swollen throat. I packed everything up and put on my dark glacier glasses. Except they wouldn't fit. What the heck? I felt the side of my head and my frozen ear had swelled up twice its size. My glasses dug into the overstuffed flesh and pus shot into my hair.

Now I was getting mad. Damn it all. Professor Badass dying all warm and cozy in his sleeping bag with a sore ear? I grabbed my ice ax and set out down the worst terrain of the whole descent. Nothing here but loose, rotten scree glazed with fresh snow from the storm. It was like trying to maneuver down a ramp of greased baseballs in a space-suit without slipping and breaking an ankle. It snowed harder. Before long, I could barely see to take a step. I could hear the whistling of my breath through a constricted throat. It sounded like the war rattle of a crazed baboon.

I relented and broke a pretty serious rule. Desperate for water, I started eating snow. At such extreme sub-zero temperatures, snow could freeze and then scald the tissues in your mouth and throat. It surely did mine no good. And introducing that level of chill into one's body put stress on the temperature regulation system—exactly at the moment when I had no source of nutrition to boost my energy. But dying of thirst was no good option, either. Once I started eating, I didn't stop and my thirst pains eased.

Snow deepened along the route. Inches became feet. Visibility was nearly whiteout. I slipped. With my pack full of sample rocks and gear throwing me off balance, I flipped completely head over heels and just lay there on my back, groaning. Later, a leg slid out from under me, putting me in a split. I toppled over onto my back once more. If there was some new way to stumble, trip, or fall, I found it. Later I learned that the storm killed a number of climbers on this day and brought an end to the mountaineering season on Everest. My one day indeed was the only good day of the spring. Later I could rejoice. I just had to live long enough.

For now, I was coming too close to never seeing later. Stumbling along in my puffy clown suit, falling, gasping. I stopped thinking about hard or not-so-hard sections of the route and focused on the basics, do or die. Above Camp 1 on the North Col is a snow slope one-third of a mile long. While reading Everest history, I came across the story of an early British climber who reported glissading from the top of the snow to the North Col in something like fifteen minutes. Exactly. I needed something fast and easy like that.

I counted on the storm to have deposited enough snow over the ice and rocks so that my glissade would be easy—*glissade* being a fancy mountaineering word for what school kids call sliding. I sat with my feet aimed downslope, grabbed my ice ax in a position to bite into the surface as a brake when necessary and to help steer a little. I wriggled and, yikes, down I plunged, churning up a wake of powder snow behind me. When the angle steepened, I dug my ice ax into the surface until it hit ice or compacted snow and slowed down. At a flat section, the fun ended and I had to stand and stumble forward. I passed a lone climber who had attempted the summit unsuccessfully without supplemental oxygen. He looked awful but said he was happy to have tried. I bade him good-bye and sat down to resume my glissade as soon as the route steepened. I wondered if he could hear my laugh of delight. Probably not. My throat allowed but a few squeaks. That did not spoil the joy, however, of taking a rocket ride on my fanny down the flank of Chomolungma. Down where there was food. Water. A Coke. Friends.

Of course, it was an insane thing to do. The snow slope was barely forty feet wide, give or take, bordered on one side by a cliff and on the other by an even bigger cliff. Going off either edge would have been my final worldly deed. But reduce a man's oxygen for a spell and he'll do any damn thing—and finish up frosted by snow head to foot, probably with a smile on his face.

I was disappointed when the snow slope ended. Nothing is rarer or more precious for a mountaineer than having gravity on your side for even a few minutes. Now I had to wade into the deep snow again and it seemed twice as difficult as before. On the other hand, I was approaching the North Col, where I expected to find water, perhaps food, maybe warmth. I stumbled along for a few hundred feet with those happy thoughts, then stepped into a crevasse. It was hidden under the fresh snow. Luckily, it was not wide enough to swallow all of me. It took just my foot, throwing me off balance and sending me flying in a full flip. Somehow, I didn't break my leg as the force of my fall yanked it out of the crevasse. I stood, tried to gather my wits, and resumed my march toward Camp 1. Two steps later, I managed the same infuriating thing—stepping into a crevasse, falling downslope, cartwheeling and praying I didn't land on my head. I used my ice ax to pick the remainder of my way to the col. I dragged myself up a small wall and then over a hill to Camp 1 itself. I planned on stopping here for an hour or so to melt snow for water. I had left a reserve stove in our tent.

The entire campsite was wrecked. Heavy snow had crushed and buried everything. Our tent was flattened. In fact, all the tents were smashed. I was pretty sure where I could find a snow shovel to clear the tent. But I'd first have to dig a few feet down for the shovel itself. That's what other groggy climbers here and there were trying to do. But in my condition, dehydrated and foodless, it seemed like an impossible task. I turned and headed downhill again.

Conditions were getting weird. The snow raked me with blinding, blizzard force. But the cloud cover overhead was thinning. More sunlight was penetrating, casting a bright haze into the storm. A classic warm and humid greenhouse effect during a blizzard—just about as rotten a circumstance as I could imagine.

I gobbled more snow in vain attempts to meet my body's need. But at least descending the headwall below the North Col, I shouldn't trip any more. The first part of the descent was down a vertical ice wall to a large and open crevasse, which could be crossed only by balancing on a long, bouncy ladder. I didn't think about how icy the fixed ropes would be, and they slipped through my hands and I almost lost my grip, which would have sent me careening down the wall onto the ladder or past it into the crevasse. I hung on for dear life, because dear life was in the balance. I got control, then moved down with greater caution. Three steps, gasp-gasp, rest, eat snow, three steps—down the wall, one hour, more. I reached the glacier.

Once I was on more or less flat ground, I felt like dropping to my knees and kissing it. I have never been so relieved to leave behind the vertical and reach the horizontal. But if I dropped to my knees, I might not be able to stand again. I stumbled ahead and kept repeating to myself: *John, you have been a walker all of your life, don't stop. Keep walking.* The taunt kept me moving.

In between my lectures to myself, I vaguely considered the lingering danger around me—fresh snow on top of a glacier, covering up crevasses. There didn't seem much I could do about it. And others had followed this path on their descent. I kept moving. Fatalism is the province of the worn out and the desperate.

But dark thoughts were momentary, intermittent. I was anticipating finding a familiar face just up ahead. That was something to dwell upon. Back when we descended from the North Col that very first time, one of the richly financed teams positioned a fellow down at the edge of the glacier near here with Thermos bottles of life-giving tea for his climbers. The fellow shared some with us that time. For what seemed like miles now, I'd been anticipating that guy. The thought became a phantasm and it drew me on. I squinted and scanned the landscape. In my head, the Thermos of tea had become a can of Coke. Amazing what daydreams of Coke can do for the weary. I could hardly wait. Where the hell was he, anyway?

I was stumbling some, but not staggering on this easy slope. Onward. Time was a muddle. Step after lumbering, heavy-footed step. Minutes passed, no doubt. But how many minutes? Step, another, breath, three. I didn't look back. I wasn't thinking of the great mountain, the mountain of my boyhood dreams. This spring on Everest had been a most wonderful adventure. But savoring that sweet realization would come later. My success was not a triumph. It was a gift—of nature, of good fortune, maybe a reward for perseverance, maybe the consequence of prayers delivered from the heart, or maybe . . . maybe, what?

And the lessons? Well, the easy answer was that I could walk and think at the same time; climb and pay heed to science. But the larger lesson, the much bigger one, well, that would need some chewing over. We humans, with our busy-busy beehive lives survive in a thin envelope of nourishing gas, very thin. So thin that, with effort, it is possible to climb up to where the life-giving components of this atmosphere simply vanish and death shows its face with eyes pecked out. This atmosphere in which all of us live and love and fight and struggle and play and worry is less than five miles thick, at the extreme. Measured where it provides comfortable living, this wind-blown, gaseous, and delicate blanket is no thicker than Manhattan is wide. On that alone, our survival will be told.

"Life always waits for some crisis to occur before revealing itself at its most brilliant," said the writer Paulo Coelho.

God, I hope so.

Coelho had been my frequent companion on this climb. I read and reread his fantastic book *The Alchemist* during the ups and downs of acclimatization. For the adventurer, he is a charming, sly motivator. I stumbled onward, looking for the guy with the tea.

"If you think adventure is dangerous," he wrote, "try routine. It's lethal."

Amen. That will put a kick into your tired step.

I kept his book on my all-purpose, always ready iPhone along with my music, videos, other books, and my journal—so many pages I tapped out on that dinky keyboard during the expedition. See how much easier I had it than Mallory?

I was about halfway down the last scree slope leading into Base Camp when I saw him. Ahead. The man with the tea. That's him!

But it wasn't. It was Chombe, our Tibetan "kitchen boy." He was coming to meet me with a Coke. My delirium became reality. I gave him a huge hug. My climb was complete.

Interlude

Letters

I am not entirely myself in the high mountains. In some ways a little more, and others, a little less. Up here, in a tent, in the sparse air, wired on exhilaration and battling exhaustion—well, my thoughts usually wander even further than my body. Inevitably, I miss people back home. People I love. I feel the urge tell them so.

As I left Kathmandu for Everest, I wrote my son, Nathaniel, who lives in Kansas City with his mother, Sara. In hindsight, it seems maudlin and ridiculously dry fare to send to a boy of six. But I was thinking that if I didn't come back, this letter would be his last touch with me. I wanted it to be something that he could read again when he was older. I wanted him to know about my days as a Himalayan mountaineer.

Nathaniel, I have left Kathmandu and am in Tibet after driving up a horrible road for six teeth-rattling days to the Rongbuk Glacier and I am going to spend the next two months living here in a tent. Why am I going through so much trouble? I am going to climb Mt. Everest, the highest mountain in the world, via the North Col/North Ridge route. It is not the easiest route up the mountain and there is no guarantee of success. Ever since I was a little boy like you, I had three dreams in my life—to compete in the Iditarod Sled Dog race (but I discovered I didn't like dogs well enough to do it), to compete in the Ironman Triathlon (which I still would like to do), and climb Mt. Everest. All of my life I thought they were just silly dreams and I would never have the money or time or expertise or fitness to do them. Dreams are a wonderful way to occupy your imagination, but life requires that we work and so dreams can slip away from us if we are not careful. But life is also a crooked road and it leads us on paths we don't often expect. Even when I came to Nepal (which was a minor dream in itself), I never thought I would be able to climb Everest. But somehow circumstances came together to give me a chance. I am going to climb as a partial Sherpa—what does this mean? Because I am a good climber and have worked with a group of Sherpas doing my research here, I will help lead the climb and work with the foreign guests and I do not have to pay anywhere near a full price. This means I get to climb Mt. Everest as a climber and not a tourist. Also, I will be collecting data for my research while climbing.

This trip to Nepal has been the watershed moment in my career; I finally have the experience and a massive set of data that will allow me to conduct excellent research for years to come. When I applied to the Fulbright Fellowship program, it seemed like trying to win the lottery and that I had no chance of success. But I made it. If I had given up or not even tried, I would never have succeeded. Even if odds seem overwhelming, you only really fail if you give up and don't even try to compete.

Dreams have a funny way of working themselves into reality if you never forget them and keep striving forward. Even little things can help you achieve your dream if you keep working towards it and never forget. It is so easy to get seduced by a comfy bed or TV or drinking a beer, and your life spirals away into a blur of comfort until you turn around and you are fifty with nothing to show for your years.

I am writing this letter because not everyone survives Everest. As you grow up, I don't ever want you to think I didn't love you. I always wish we could have lived as a family. But your mother and I each followed our own directions in life—our dreams were different so we chose paths that diverged. You will make your own decisions as you grow and will find your own dreams. I love you forever and I dream of the dreams you will pursue. Life is meant to be lived and lived well. Don't ever let money interfere with pursuing your dreams.

With luck, I will see you again when I return to the States late this summer.

I love you, Daddy.

My mom was often on my mind. I worried because she worried so about me. I wanted her to understand what I did. In this e-mail, the long weeks of acclimatizing and setting up camps on Everest were over:

> Well, our climb has started! Yesterday we did the section from Base Camp, walked past Intermediate Base Camp (IBC), and came all the way to Advanced Base Camp (ABC) in one day. The whole climb from Base Camp to Summit is about 14 miles horizontally and 12,000 feet vertically. Of that, we did 12 miles and 4000 feet yesterday. A 12/4000 day in the US would be a good one, but nothing too incredible. But when you finish at 21,000 feet and carry a 45 lb. pack, it is a MONSTER day. We did the first half, up to IBC, pretty quickly—3 hours—and ate lunch there. I still felt really strong and was moving pretty fast considering the "trail" is just a faint path in the middle of loose softball-sized and bigger rocks. You constantly slip and trip and they roll around under your feet. But once we left IBC and started hitting 6,000 meters

in elevation, the pack grew heavier and heavier and my legs grew leaden. I was moving faster than anyone else I saw, but I FELT slow as heck and my steps became more and more drunken and I struggled to move forward. The pack was this monster that cut off my circulation and breathing and I grew to hate it. I was carrying the satellite receiver, which is over 15 lbs, and I just wanted to dump the whole thing into the glacier melt river that flowed below our scree ridge.

I had forgotten how cold it is up at these elevations. Soon I was freezing in my synthetic t-shirt and Gore-Tex shell. Of course it had to start snowing with a very strong wind as I got close to ABC—too close to stop for more clothes, but not close enough to get there without freezing. I was so tired and spent that it took me 15 minutes once I reached ABC to finally make it to the tent. I stumbled over to it and plunged in—searching for warm clothes. After I had something warm on and my sleeping bag on top of me, I feel asleep! I took a nice little nap and didn't hear as the others slowly trickled in. When it got dark and the temperature dropped down to WAY below freezing, I had to force myself up for some dinner. But it was worth it as my aching muscles screamed for food.

Today has been a lazy day of laying in the tent and eating. We will rest two more days while the weather stabilizes and then head out on the 20th probably and will take four straight climbing days to reach the summit.

Fortunately the lousy cook who accidentally poisoned us with undone chicken is staying in Base Camp. I think this is the best news we had in a while! I had to take two poos on the hike up from his last bit of poison and two more this morning in the frosty air, but I think it is out of my system now! Hopefully for good . . .

Now the computer and satellite set-up is working well, so for the next couple of days we may be able to send and receive emails with no problems at all—what a luxury.

Johnny

My "forever" partnership with Narcisa was no more. She remained in
my thoughts, however, and we were still in touch. I sent her this e-mail
via satellite phone, describing the ups and downs of life on the great
mountain:

> We have been here at ABC [Advanced Base Camp] for several
> days and 6400 meters is pretty harsh at first. You just feel so
> lazy and lie around in the tent all day. Thankfully I have my
> good sleeping bag or I would be frozen. Ed is using two sleep-
> ing bags inside each other and is even more toasty than me!
> Both Ed and Kenny got sponsorships for the climb (Ed from
> Mountain Hardwear and Vango, Kenny from OR) and so they
> have lots of gear to play around with—which we need be-
> cause it is so damn cold. We are sleeping on about an inch of
> small sharp rocks on top of solid ice and are on the edge of a
> sort of a forest of ten-foot-tall ice pinnacles. Ed was laughing
> about what would happen if one of them fell on our tents!
>
> It has snowed every day since we have been here and the
> weather is very regular. The sun comes up in the morning and
> is super hot—probably 40 degrees—and so we wear just a
> pair of pants and shirt. We eat and work on digging platforms
> in the ice for tents or to drain the melt water (even at this
> altitude the glaciers are melting like hell) until we eat lunch.
> Then, around two o'clock, then sun disappears, it drops WAY
> below freezing, the wind picks up and it snows. Sometimes
> it snows only for a few hours, sometimes all night. But be-
> tween the super dry air and monstrous winds, it is gone from
> the ground by the next morning almost entirely—like it was
> never there! For drinking water, they just use an ice-ax and
> cut out chunks of the glacier next to the tent and melt it or
> gather a pile of the snow.
>
> Life here is pretty incredible—we have a dining tent
> with a table filled with teas, coffee, juices, drinking choco-
> late, etc. and two things of freshly boiled water at all times.
> You know I hardly ever drink anything normally but here I
> drink ten or more cups of stuff a day because it is so dry! We
> also get huge amounts of food because most people lose their
> appetites. Not a problem for Ed or me though! We eat fried

chicken and french fries and ham and vegetables and anything you can think of for all three meals. I may be getting fatter, not skinnier! Of course it is so damn cold that it burns quickly. I am sitting here at 3 pm writing and can see my breath. Last night at dinner it was below freezing even in the dining tent so you have to eat fast because the food gets cold.

Ed and I are going to start our high climbs tomorrow and will climb up and then come back down and then higher and back to here for the next week or ten days. Then we will go back to basecamp to recover and can use the sat phone there again. Otherwise there will be no email for a while and I am sorry, but it is a super long climb to get there!!

The cold is draining the laptop battery at an incredible rate so I have to go. I will try to write later if we can keep everything working under these conditions.

I love you and miss you so much *iubi* [Romanian for "my love"]. I have been reading The Alchemist by Paolo Coelho, and had forgotten what a stunningly great book it is—I recommend getting it if you can and reading it. It seems very pertinent to me as I am climbing and freezing.

I wish I was more coherent—the stunning cold has reduced life and my mind to the basics. I think a lot about what you are doing and hopefully the fun you are having.

Chapter Nine

The Unknown

In the collection of the New York Public Library, a five-inch copper sphere provides a glimpse of our world as Westerners understood it five hundred years ago. This famous Hunt-Lennox globe contains a notation describing the equatorial region of East Asia this way: "*Hc Svnt Dracones.*" Over the years, this became a popular notation for cartographers to signify mysterious, unexplored places on a map: "Here be dragons."

It was a powerful idea. The sheer wonder inspired by terra incognita fueled an entire human epoch, the so-called Age of Discovery, and captivated people, at least in the New World, into the nineteenth century. Today, although many scientific mysteries remain for us, the physical geography of our Earth is thoroughly mapped and exhaustively traveled. In comfortable coffee shops in New York, in the pubs of London, on Caribbean cruise ships, T-shirts shout out their owners' journeys to once-exotic lands: Annapurna Base Camp, Blue Corner Palau, Lamu Island, Saint Pierre and Miquelon.

But some mysteries remain even now. In 2013, the door to one of these forbidden and little-known places swung open. I had traveled widely in Central and South America. But this opportunity was different. Not only was the destination of our expedition difficult to reach, legitimate travel there had been off-limits for most everyone for decades. Our team of scientists was one of the first in the modern era allowed to enter—heading deep to the jungle mountains of Costa Rica and traversing the country from Pacific to Atlantic through the heart of this mountain rain forest. This was probably as close as I would get to the lair of mythical dragons. No T-shirt mementos from this place.

Our route would take us over the Cordillera de Talamanca, a mountain range that reached 3,800 meters (12,500 feet), impressive for Central America but not really an imposing altitude for mountaineers. The jungle terrain down low, however . . . oh, that jungle. It was almost the end of us.

From my journal:

> It never seems to end.
>
> No big snakes bit me last night and it was very refreshing to sleep next to the river. Rebecca really loves wielding the machete and cleared the site super well after the fer-de-lance incident. Everyone was moving slowly—Rebecca's arm is swollen and infected looking, Alistair said he has a swollen spot on his leg that is puffy and yellow and oozing pus. In his soft-spoken way, he said that if he collapsed or didn't wake up, that was the problem. Will's infected hands are better after he put the kerosene on them but are still twice normal size . . .

Rewind the story. One lazy day on an earlier trip to Peru, my colleague Rebecca Cole began talking about her dream project. Rebecca was a superbly credentialed ecologist and the research director of the American Climber Science Program. She was also a native of Costa Rica and had been immersed in trying to understand tropical flora and fauna since childhood, really. For her PhD, she studied forest restoration in her native country and came to know most of Costa Rica's ecosystems. Everywhere, that is, except for the Cordillera de Talamanca in the southern reach of the country adjoining Panama. As it happened, she spent her childhood within sight of these mountains—but never set foot in them. A joint Costa Rica–Panama national park, called La Amistad, or Friendship Park, had been established there to protect the resources of the range. But it was not the kind of place one normally associated with the word "park." Violent drug traffickers had stalked the mountain trails since the days of Manuel Noriega and posed such a threat that scientific and other lawful travel had been

off-limits in the Talamancas for all of Rebecca's life. As a girl growing
up, she could only stare into the mountains and wonder. Now, as an
adult and an accomplished scientist, her wonder only intensified.

In scientific terms, there be dragons.

More compelling still was the realization that during these decades when most legitimate travel into the Talamanca region was restricted, Earth had sustained extreme El Niños, widespread drought,
mighty hurricanes, rising temperatures and a 40 percent increase in
human population, with the attendant increase in energy and resource
consumption. What had been the consequences in the Talamancas?

"Let's go," I said. "Our next expedition."

I don't believe in savoring ideas, allowing them to stew and ripen.
Things get lost, forgotten, they fall by the wayside. When I see an
important opportunity, I don't hesitate. Then and there, we started
roughing out a plan.

Our expedition would come under the auspices of the American
Climber Science Program and we would begin in just a few months—
during the winter of 2013–2014. Rebecca would be the organizer, co-
ordinating with officials at La Amistad International Park and other
Costa Rican scientists. Years ago, she had moved away from home to
work at the University of Colorado and then the University of Hawaii,
but her connections to her homeland remained deep. Her father was
an American who had moved to Costa Rica years earlier to live near
his wife's family. He purchased a mountain farm between the Panama
border and the forested highlands. In time, he converted it to a research station devoted to sustainable agriculture and the study of forest restoration. As in much of the tropics, large areas throughout the
region had been cleared and eventually degraded through poor farming practices. "Loma Linda," as he called it, thus became a long-term
ecological laboratory for environmental recovery and served as the
inspiration for Rebecca's career as a scientist. With this expedition,
she would be going home.

There were more than mountains to see and analyze in this region. I proposed an ambitious undertaking—a full coast-to-coast
transect of the country, an environmental-data-collection expedition
from the Pacific to the Atlantic. We'd call it the C2C. In sea kayaks,
on mountain bikes, and on foot up grueling jungle climbs, we would
explore the southern wonders of this country that had become so

popular with eco-tourists. We would measure and record a variety of environmental parameters and see what we might learn from indigenous peoples about ecological adaptation.

This would be a far deeper look than anything I'd undertaken in previous Latin American trips. Those were mere glimpses by comparison. Now, we would put the place under a scientific microscope—truly explore this landscape, mile by mile, from one horizon to the other. And guess what? No frostbite—oxygen as plentiful and rich as anywhere—no having to melt snow for water!

Hey, I thought to myself, *I've been focusing my expeditions on the high mountains for years now. A winter in the tropics, with oceans and jungles—what could be a more welcome respite?* All expeditions are a mix of the 4Ds—danger, delight, drudgery, and discovery—and I figured this one would have the proportions just about right. This was a trip where I would get stronger instead of wearing down. Or so I blithely assumed.

Before long, I'd have reason to recalibrate my thinking on this, a lot. But for the moment, the tropics made the case for themselves. I had begun my studies of climate-change adaptation in warm ecosystems, and this expedition would take me back to my intellectual start. There was serious reason for our work here. Climate change is often calibrated by measuring the melting of glaciers and icefields, or by charting creeping desertification in Africa. But by disrupting precipitation regimes, climate change should have an equally powerful effect in the world's tropical rain forests. These areas are home to some of the richest biomass on Earth. These biomes, in turn, are critically dependent on abundant rains falling in historical patterns. Droughts here are not always immediately visible to the eye, but they are devastating to flora and fauna. At first, the ecosystem suffers in subtle ways. Soils dry. Trees are weakened and become vulnerable to insects and disease. Animals are displaced. The altered environmental conditions do not so much kill organisms directly as leave them debilitated or forced into unfamiliar behaviors, so they wither and perish just the same.

I don't recommend it as a strategy, but I always wind up starting expeditions dead tired. Occupational hazard, I guess. Grading the last of the semester's exams would keep me on a schedule of all-nighters, on top of getting the house ready to shutter for months. Or maybe it was just habit. Anyway, I inevitably wound up deferring that first sweet rush of excitement to the imperatives of old-fashioned exhaustion. So it was when I arrived in Costa Rica's capital city of San Jose. By the time my late flight from the States landed at Juan Santamaria International Airport and I staggered into my hotel, it was a bleary 2:00 a.m. I had just four hours until my bus was to leave for the southern city of San Vito, 175 miles away through the interior of the country. I don't remember my head hitting the pillow.

Groggy and only partly replenished by rest, I met up with two members of our team in the lobby as we gathered our bags and headed to the bus station. Will Leith was a young engineering and physics student and an up-and-coming hardcore ice climber. He would be undertaking a rather unique study of animal diversity on this expedition and was also assisting Rebecca's husband, Carl, an atmospheric physicist, in his study of black carbon, this time in runoff rather than ice. Canadian Alistair Chan, who aspired to be a doctor *and* a Navy SEAL, would serve as the expedition's medic and was excited to work with our audio recording equipment and see what we could learn about species habitat and distributions from listening to the forest. Both young men were at watershed points in their lives and answered the call of purposeful adventure—primarily to understand what a major twenty-first-century wilderness expedition entailed. The American Climber Science Program attracted any number of such highly motivated young people, and when they were as strong and determined as Alistair and Will, we were delighted to have them along.

Costa Rica was changing. From my view out the bus window, I could see the lowlands were becoming heavily developed and more "modern," that is, more universally nondescript, than when I had been here a decade earlier. Industrial-scale factory farming had become a larger presence. Contemporary architecture created a bland "anywhere" kind of feel. Along the center of the country, the "quaintness" of the rural past had been swallowed up by economic bustle.

Even though I was far from caught up on my sleep, excitement pushed exhaustion aside as the three of us talked over the rumble of the diesel bus. Our preoccupations would be familiar to almost any international adventurers—the gear we brought, the gear we needed, the challenges awaiting, and what we hoped to accomplish. By such conversations, we followed in the footsteps of generations of explorers and adventurers and forged the bonds necessary to hold the group together later, when all we had was each other. I was particularly taken by Will's interest in the expedition's equipment. He was practically as obsessed as I was, which I considered a good sign. I should have guessed that he would go on to make a career in the outdoor gear business.

From San Vito, we made our way to Rebecca's home, the Loma Linda research station not far from the Cordillera de Talamanca rain forest, that misty green land of the jaguar, the poison frog, the bullet ant (so named because the bite felt like getting shot), and the pit viper *Bothrops asper*, also known as fer-de-lance—and, in our minds anyway, the mythic dragons of unknown places. Green exists in many environments, but here it all but screams out, Green! Lush and dense, shiny or dull, canopies over canopies of flora pumping oxygen into the moist air to mix with the inescapable rich odors of jungle compost.

Two objectives awaited us. We had to fine-tune our small group of individuals into a functioning team. And we needed to finish outfitting ourselves for the long transect of the nation. Both were straightforward undertakings; the everyday stuff of wilderness expeditions, a joyful time of tingling anticipation. We had little idea of how much the jungle would demand of us.

Rebecca's qualifications to lead the scientific inquiry were unique, in the true sense of the word. She had the academic chops, the deep sense of place that only locals can accumulate, plus the strength and the drive. She also had connections, so we were joined by her longtime Costa Rica research associate, Marvin Morales, a field technician who amazed us with his knowledge of the flora and fauna of the country, both the friendly kind and the not-so-friendly. He kept us from some very bad potential encounters with the latter. Our final team member was Rebecca's husband, Carl, who was attending a conference in Europe and would be joining us in a few days.

Even though our team could claim substantial local experience and plenty of muscle, success would still lean on the knowing shoulders of a guide. That was the way of the world, and particularly important in this mapless terrain. Ours was Zenon, of the indigenous Bribri people of Costa Rica. He lived in a village on the edge of La

Amistad International Park and was virtually the only person to have firsthand knowledge of our proposed route. Zenon, who went by one name, as was common among Bribri, was old now but had first-hand knowledge of the routes through the mountains since boyhood, having accompanied his father into the Talamanca years earlier and then leading trips himself before the area became restricted. He was excited to be a part of our expedition and welcomed the opportunity to contribute to science—having seen how the rainfall patterns had changed here over the years. The Bribri understood climate-change nuance in the tangible, dinner-table way that agrarian peoples do. And it worried them.

Because Zenon's long experience of Talamanca trips with his father had instilled such powerful memories, he tried to pass along the same sense to his stepson, Yordi, by enlisting him to join us on this expedition and get his first taste of the mysterious mountains.

From my journal at Loma Linda:

> Finally I slept. Last night was so good and profound a sleep, my entire body eased. There was a slight rain falling gently on the steel roof that blended with the crickets and frogs into a soft Costa Rican lullaby. When I finally woke this morning I had coffee, mango, papaya, and a warm fresh raisin bread for breakfast. Everyone was milling around the house dealing with gear and I joined the disorder . . .

Assembling the supplies and equipment to sustain ourselves turned out to be a bigger challenge than I'd expected. Rebecca arranged roadside support to haul our gear and food for the approach to the Talamanca Range. This part of our route covered 250 miles, and we would travel it on mountain bikes. We guessed that would take us five days. After that, though, we would be on foot and entirely on our own. Because our planned route over the Talamanca mountains had been so little explored or traveled, we didn't know how much time it would take us to cross—what obstacles we'd face, how many miles we could travel in a day, how much water we would have to lug. That left plenty of guesswork, a circumstance that expedition planners like me find exasperating. We took a stab at it, figuring about 150 to 200 wandering miles, maximum fourteen or fifteen days, without any support whatsoever. All we really knew was that everything had to be carried on our backs. More, this mountain portion of the traverse would take us from hot, muggy conditions at sea level to over 2,700 meters (9,000 feet), where temperatures would be cool, if not actually cold.

We drove into town to buy food to supplement freeze-dried provisions that we had brought to Costa Rica with us in our swollen luggage. Mostly, we settled for old-fashioned staples: rice, peanut butter, pasta, cookies, and crackers. Not the lightest to pack, but cheap, available, and nourishing. To that, we added quinoa—a protein-rich grain from the Andes—and large vacuum packs of tuna. The weight of food added to our trove of essential scientific equipment and didn't leave much capacity for personal gear. Almost none at all, in fact. We made radical cuts in our gear lists. We allotted one set of clothes for each of us to wear sleeping and another for hiking, and that was it. Nothing warm aside from the meager warmth from rain gear. No tents—I brought jungle hammocks for us, which we would rig with mosquito netting and rain flies as our airborne tents free from the dangers of nocturnal visits from snakes or other unpleasant visitors. A sheet of plastic with hanks of rope would serve as a cooking and eating shelter. We brought ultralight water filters and stoves.

I carried a solar panel from Voltaic Systems, which has been our oldest and best sponsor. I hoped for occasional chances to deploy it in the dark forest understory. Otherwise, batteries would have to keep our GPS and satellite communication gear operating.

Then came the sorting. Upstairs at the research station, we opened the windows to the tropical breezes, and the smell of banana trees and tropical gardens filled the room. We weren't in Kansas anymore, for sure. Excitement flashed through us all, and I savored it. For these sweet moments, everything was ahead, anything was possible, life was good in our world. Anticipation. There was nothing like it. And just think, Christmas was only days away, and this trip was our present to ourselves, lucky us.

We spread everything out and made six piles—large ones. Each was a mix of shared science equipment, food, and community camping gear, such as stoves and water filters. They were divided by weight and size. Then people chose which one they would carry along with their personal gear. That was how my parents divided things between my brother and me: One of us made the split and the other chose. Hard to complain that way. As was only fair, Carl, when he arrived from Europe, and I, as the biggest guys, ended up with the heaviest loads—just over eighty pounds each. It would be a brutish burden. But facing a long interval of unsupported travel and research through steep, largely unknown jungle left us wondering if even this much would be enough.

I have been debating a question. Why are high-altitude mountain expeditions so sharply etched in my memory, when jungle travel quickly descends into the phantasmagoric?

The great German filmmaker Werner Herzog made the movie *Fitzcarraldo* about a man who wanted to bring an opera house to the South American jungle. While filming, Herzog gave an interview that itself demonstrated the power of the jungle to squeeze down on one's thoughts. He described the jungle as *pain, misery, violent, base, unfinished country, a curse.* Then he cheerfully added, "I say this full of admiration for the jungle. It is not that I hate it. I love the jungle. I love it very much. But I love it against my better judgment."

I understood what Herzog was driving at.

We were ready.

We loaded our bikes and gear into Rebecca's four-wheel-drive and headed west to the Pacific coast. I had hoped we would begin our scientific sampling on the Osa Peninsula while kayaking across the Golfo Dulce, or Sweet Gulf, of the Pacific, a sheltered bent-finger bay just north of the border with Panama. But that proved too difficult to organize, so we used our day of sea kayaking as a conditioning test—acclimatizing, if you will, testing ourselves in the heat and humidity of the tropics.

> We had a 45 minute walk through the jungle this morning to reach the beach. Rebecca had to hire a local to "show us the way"—mainly so we wouldn't get shot by a gringo who doesn't like people legally accessing the beach across this property. Unfortunately when we got there, the boats were tiny—with every stroke my boat sank beneath the waves. Most of the others were OK, Alistair and I are the heaviest and we suffered quite a lot. It was like riding a child's tricycle while everyone else was on adult bicycles. The air

was still and calm with high cirrus clouds—pretty much the worst possible conditions because with the humidity and lack of breeze it was like a sauna where you are exercising super hard to get your tricycle moving.

We kayaked for seven hours past pods of dolphins and a silly romp of otters before reaching a mangrove thicket that led inland to our hotel. Afterward, Alastair and Will squeezed in time to surf, and we all gathered to enjoy the sundown sea breeze and a dinner of fresh fish. Our C2C expedition had started off on a high note. Here's to us, team!

We spent the second leg of the expedition likewise sitting down. This time on the stiff seats of mountain bicycles. We would be traveling roughly 250 miles on small, mostly unpaved roads crossing through the agricultural lowlands and would be collecting data about these heavily impacted ecosystems.

It wasn't long ago, I remembered, when I was expressing delight that Costa Rica would erase the worry of frostbite. I could now add an important postscript. Memo to self: Don't forget about the opposite. Heat. Heatstroke. Feverish. Torrid. Swelter.

Leaving the coast, we rode into ridiculous heat and stifling humidity. I could feel my brain sweating inside my skull. Icefields didn't sound all that bad after all. A mountain of them. I couldn't drink water fast enough. And it was usually tepid. Good gear could protect one from the cold. Good gear did diddly against the heat. Oh, and one more thing. High in the Andes or the Himalaya, there are no snakes. But here? This was snake nirvana. Snakes! Snakes gathered in Costa Rica the way New Yorkers gathered for a free concert in Central Park. Long, slithery snakes.

I want to make it clear that I am not a herpetophobic. Phobias are irrational. A wariness of snakes was entirely rational. I know. I know what it feels like to step on a big meaty writhing snake. This was not a phobia.

We began to encounter snakes soon in our journey. One of our scientific projects for this portion of the C2C transect was to carefully collect data about roadkill in Costa Rica. Will was our lead for this and he was working in cooperation with Clark University in Massachusetts. We logged the precise geographic location of all roadkill, comparing small gravel roads to large paved ones, roads through jungles to roads through plantations, dead snakes to dead mammals. Mostly snakes. The goal was to help science get a better sense of how roads fragment a landscape. Roads break habitat into smaller pieces and disrupt movement of fauna across a region. They make inbreeding more common and make species more vulnerable to other environmental disturbances. Roads are one of the factors that make a landscape less resilient to climate change. Our work would add to the base of knowledge, as we would be traveling many different types of roads slowly, taking their measure intimately. Of course, we left out the part about human sweating, gasping lungs, aching legs—or that common torment of hot climes, having to drink more than was comfortable, and all the time.

I couldn't get snakes out of my mind. Brilliant green snakes, mottled camouflage snakes, slender and fat snakes, long and short snakes—Dr. Seuss, where are you now? We identified many of them as venomous and recorded everything we could about them while still keeping our distance, fearing they might have one last desperate strike left in them. We identified one heavy, seven-foot brute with a flat spear-shaped head as a lancehead, or to use the French term, a fer-de-lance.

Crap, we hadn't even set foot in the real jungle yet. And already we're dealing with snakes. I began to dread the moment I would step on one. I knew it would happen when I was exhausted. Careless for just an instant. The sudden alive slithering under my boot. Then the scalding burn of its bite. My skin tightened, and I rubbed the snake tattoo on my calf, calling up what karma it might hold. I finished the last of a bottle of hot, stale-tasting water.

Several days before Christmas we were on the move at 5:00 a.m. to finish the biking section. No bread pudding, no pear trees, and no chestnuts roasting on fires (thank heaven). But food was very much on my mind. In my journal I noted that we came upon a fruit stand, where I shoveled Cheetos into my mouth and gulped Gatorade and cola, and savored a pineapple. Any calories are good ones when you are exhausted. For dinner, we shared a pizza. In between, I snacked on beef jerky and a bag of M&Ms. We set our alarms for 3:00 a.m.

With the bicycles now packed up and returned to Loma Linda, the easy part of the expedition was behind us. Ahead, the

Talamanca Mountains. The unknown. Dragons. Before sunup, we set out walking among farm hedgerows along broken ground that might have been a road some years before. Then, in the middle of this nowhere, a single random electric streetlight illuminated sugarcane fields and the loose rocks of this broken old road. Some things were not easily explained, and often humans had a hand in it. We walked.

The sky lightened. And warmed. It was going to be steamy, I could tell. We came to a corner and passed through a gate. Just like that, the cultivated farmlands ended. We set a course for the mountains. As if to emphasize the nature of what lay ahead, we came to a bridge, which a movie-set designer might have dreamed up if the script called for a primitive river crossing—two cables to hold onto, then hand-hewn planks wired together underfoot. It was perfect—everything but a weatherbeaten sign, saying: Dragons ahead. I wobbled across, while others watched and wondered if it would hold. Together on the far side, we started up a formidable, unending hill through spectacular natural savannahs on trails of eroded red clay. I began to lag in the heat and humidity but tried to stay attentive in case of snakes. My pack was gigantic and I felt like a beetle with a massive carapace. Each step all but staggered me.

The hill turned into a ridge that took us skyward. Hour after hour we slowly paced upward. Our vantage on the landscape broadened, but thankfully wisps of clouds blew in and shielded us from direct sun. As we gained still more elevation, we could feel the air cool even as the day warmed. Then a breeze sprang up to keep us even cooler. Despite these ideal conditions, I was not getting stronger. I couldn't keep up. I felt like Sisyphus under the weight of my pack. Marvin, too, was struggling. Together, we brought up the rear of our expeditionary band. A sad sight, I'm sure. Rebecca and Carl appeared and spoke encouragingly. But I was losing my focus, turning inward where I could dwell on my miseries. I had no food or electrolytes in my system. No energy. Depleted.

In getting this far, others had adopted a more relaxed approach and had taken a day or two or more off along the way. Not me. I was being obstinate in trying to fulfill the goal of C2C and had spent far more time biking than anyone else. Only I had come from the Pacific under my own power. Now I was paying for it. We climbed. Nothing ahead but the ridge aiming skyward. Minutes. Hours.

Finally, after maybe seven hours, we reached the rain forest, the real wild of the Talamanca. We had thought to set up camp near this point. But our guide, Zenon, showed himself to be a poor communicator and finally gave us the bad news that we were only halfway. I wanted to stop. Hell, I needed to stop. But Zenon explained that there was no water for perhaps another six hours. We had no choice but to move ahead. Rebecca relieved Marvin of some of his load, and we soldiered on, and up and up.

Lots of fires had burned through this area in the past, leaving thick, difficult underbrush. The going seemed to get harder and harder. I stopped worrying about the spectacle of the executive director of the American Climber Science Program, the man who had been atop Everest, tottering along like a rest-home resident. I almost stopped worrying about snakes, which itself was worrisome. If I worried about anything, I worried about slipping on the increasingly wet ground and never getting up, rolling over like a turtle with my pack beneath me and my limbs aimed heavenward. Finished. Downed trees added to my misery, forcing us onto our hands and knees to crawl underneath. The footing became more perilous even as my ability to concentrate evaporated. I reached that point of physical stress where I knew that if I stopped to rest, I wouldn't be able to move again. So when we finally reached the Continental Divide and others took their breaks, I just marked a GPS reference point, collected my suite of environmental observations, and kept going, this time downhill. They would catch up with me soon enough. I wondered if I'd still be standing.

Later, I asked Rebecca what she thought about the crossing— finally seeing the Continental Divide in person:

> One of the things that was so amazing about that point was the change in the forest! Going up the Pacific side, we were in sunlit beautiful, dry oak forest. Then we stepped across the continental divide and plunged into a forest turned suddenly dark and muddy, with new species of trees with sprawling trunks and branches that we had to crawl over and under, down the steeply descending muddy slope. The frustrating thing was that we could hear the creek that we knew we needed to reach but it was down deep in a ravine. To make things worse, it was rapidly getting dark and

finding a place flat enough to safely set up hammocks on the steep mountainside was becoming difficult.

The water we were looking for, the water that would allow us to stop and camp, was supposed to be "right there," but it never was. We kept plunging downward and found nothing. It was steep—and then steeper still. In the mud, we slipped with every step. No wonder drug runners could take refuge here. Who in their right mind would give chase? I fell. Others fell. We all fell. Step over a downfall log, fall. Slip. Dig your hands into the mud and try to regain your footing. I approached the wall in my head that signaled the limit of my endurance. I was thinking of how to say, I can't go on. Not how to say it to my colleagues, they were ahead, but to myself.

Then Will materialized. He took my pack and led me down to a creek. We had been moving for nearly fourteen hours. Zenon reported that we were still a long way from our intended camp. Was he out of his mind? It was nearing sundown, and in the tropical latitudes, darkness comes on quickly. We went back up the hill about twenty minutes to a spot where we found trees stout enough to hold our hammocks. Sort of. I set up the stove. Others strung hammocks. We ate and I crawled into my hammock. It was comfortable in that Ace-bandage kind of way that pressed in and made movement difficult. I started to shiver. We had climbed only one day, but the conditions had changed. There was a chill in the air. Without ground as insulation below, even the tropical rain forest seemed frigid. I lay and shivered for a while, then I had to get up. I put on my second set of clothes, everything I had, all of it packed when the heat was unbearable. Back in the hammock, I continued to shiver. But I was also exhausted. Day One. In the land of dragons, alone with my friends, my work, a thousand miles from anywhere . . .

I thought about the air I was breathing. Thick. Saturated with moisture, rich with oxygen, ripe with vegetation. No need to gasp for breath here. It smelled of decay, and vaguely of danger. The firmament of the rain forest.

But where was the rain?

We had planned for the possibility of nonstop rain. In Central America, the winter months are dry on the Pacific side but wet on the Caribbean side. Having crossed the divide, it was more than likely that we would be subjected to long hours of chilly drizzle, if not massive downpours of rain and flooded rivers. In these mountains, it could always rain. Some months it was the rainy season on the Atlantic side of the mountains and other times it was on the Pacific side. Often it rained on both sides. But we'd felt just a spritz of rain here and there when the air got too heavy and moisture leaked out. It seemed the endless rainy season had chosen this December to end. Rainy season or not, we thought that drinking water would be abundant. Not so, however. Right away, we discovered that the Talamancas harbored fewer streams than we had imagined. Plants could hydrate themselves from fog and clouds, but we could not. We resolved to carry at least a gallon of water when we could find it—and hope that would be enough.

Rain-forest dreams of aching thirst followed me into sleep.

Science was a collective effort for the most part. But each of us had lead responsibilities. Alistair was in charge of our sound-recording equipment. In addition to recording birdcalls for researchers at the University of Hawaii to identify, perhaps to find some new species across this remote region, we intended to produce a recording of local birdcalls and forest sounds for local schools and conservation organizations. Will had finished his Pacific side of the roadkill inventory and was working with Carl in sampling black carbon in stream runoff. This light-absorbing carbon-residue material not only hastens the melting of snowfields and glaciers but is also the signature of historic fires. Carbon in waterways would be a sign of human activity in this region over the past several centuries and would give clues to the human history here. Rebecca, Marvin, and I were documenting the vegetation and collecting corresponding ground-reference data for later satellite analysis. Rebecca was also collecting soil samples.

From the first miles of Day One, we understood just how much work we'd bitten off. By Day Two, we were all but overwhelmed—at least I was. My clothes were clammy, the ground squishy, and my thoughts a little ropy, too. We slogged onward—and upward. In *Heart of Darkness*, the writer Joseph Conrad described the ethereal sensation of moving through jungle: "Nowhere did we stop long enough to get a particularised impression, but the general sense of vague and oppressive wonder grew upon me. It was like a weary pilgrimage amongst hints for nightmares."

Yes. But I think the nightmares belong to strangers, outsiders who dare venture into such places. Outsiders like me. The jungle spoke a different language to those who called it home. I remembered a girl I met years before on an earlier trip in the jungle of Ecuador, an adolescent girl. I had just ascended a pair of volcanoes in Colombia and crossed the western border into Ecuador, where I met up with a friend who was traveling to rid himself of terrible nightmares from service in Israeli Army Intelligence. He had silently resolved to seek his physical and mental limits as a way of overcoming his past. I was doing something of the same, so we teamed up. Studying the map of Ecuador, we found a likely river to explore—running through a deep valley far from roads. Cross-country hiking through the jungle in unknown territory seemed to be what we needed.

We took a bus and sat next to this gregarious girl who jabbered at us until the road ended. She got off and so did we. She flashed a good-bye smile and darted off. We shouldered our oversize packs and strode into the forest. Rains opened up. Hour after hour we plunged through the gloom and wet and mud. Once in a while we came upon a man or two on horseback. We asked how to find the river. Each time they seemed puzzled by our presence in this remote part of the jungle. "CIA?" they asked my blond friend and me in return.

After many long, confused hours, we plunged down the soggy, overgrown trail and reached the river. Tired, we plodded through the motions of pitching a tent and eating. The next day brought more of the same—rain, mud, and hard miles. We detoured around sheer slopes and crossed thundering tributaries as we followed the twisty canyon course of the river downstream. The challenge was physically and mentally absorbing, just what we wanted. On the third day, the clouds vanished and our spirits rose. We slogged on.

I saw a movement ahead. A deer? Another flash. A girl. When she heard our heavy steps, she stopped to wait. We stared at her in disbelief—it was the same talkative adolescent girl who had shared our bus three days before. How had she gotten here?

"I walked," she replied, matter of fact.

We started downstream again and she joined us. We saw that she didn't mean "walking" like we did, but rather skipping and loping through the jungle as her fancy directed. We asked, Where is your pack, your tent, your stuff?

"I have nothing," she replied, still smiling. We were thunderstruck. How? Why?

"My mother gave me money for the bus and said to go visit my grandparents."

We listened more. By our reckoning, her grandparents' village was still hours downriver. But for her, survival in the jungle was no more complicated than for a farmer to find his way to a coffee shop in Nebraska.

"I stopped to ask people for food or a place to sleep when I needed it and then walked some more," she said.

Not once did she mention the incessant rain—although she wore no more protection than a T-shirt. Soon after our young friend adopted us, her frail, dime-store shoes disintegrated. She kicked them aside and proceeded barefoot through the mud and tangles. It was not a big deal.

When we finally reached her grandmother's, we were in for another shock.

"Take her," said grandma, speaking to my friend.

What?

"Yes, you can marry her and take her back to your country, she will be happy with you."

We were speechless in witnessing this glimpse of jungle culture. A girl would be left free to travel alone in a landscape we felt was dangerous. When she became hungry, she stopped and ate with someone. When her old shoes fell apart, she went barefoot. If a strange man offered to take her to Israel, she would go. Life on the margin was one of adaptability. In this case, adapting to poverty. The more I thought about it, though, the more I doubted whether *poverty* was the right word.

My friend declined to offer marriage, and we left the girl behind. That didn't seem a big deal to her, either. The sparkle did not leave her eyes. It was simply another turn in life.

Christmas Eve in Costa Rica. I staggered into camp. Like most local people I have worked with around the world, Zenon did not seem to grasp the time it would take us to get from one place to another, and he never erred on the side of stopping early. I was whipped. Beat. Without paying attention, I stumbled around and lashed my hammock to a pair of trees. One turned out to be too small. I should have paid attention. It began to pull out when I put my weight on the hammock. I had to start over. Under ordinary circumstances, this would have been hardly more challenging than tying my boots. But I was weary to the bone. I got it done only because Rebecca and Carl came to my rescue. I didn't remember dinner even as I ate it. Then I was in my sleeping bag, sore, dopey tired, and melancholy. I shivered myself to sleep.

Morning. Merry Christmas.

Sure. Ho ho ho.

Maybe the Sahara Desert on December 25 has less of a Christmas feel than the Costa Rican rain forest. But not by much, I'll wager. We had been spared the anticipated rain for another day, which had buoyed my spirits. But, again, not by much. Only because Rebecca gushed that it "was the very best Christmas ever" did I feel my own mood lighten upward. She was such a good friend, and this trip meant the world to her. She didn't deserve a grumpy campmate. So, okay, Merry Christmas!

When I told Rebecca later that I felt so grumpy, she said:

> But, but, there were hundreds of fireflies all night that mixed with the stars and looked like Christmas lights. And, we were in a primeval, palm-covered valley that looked like a place lost in time next to a spectacular waterfall plunging down a vertical, fern-and-orchid covered cliff!

I had to admire her viewpoint.

My primary mealtime responsibility was to wrestle our old stove to life. We had been unable to find fuel for newer stoves, wouldn't you know. That was a common problem in the developing world, matching old and new technologies. So I began boiling water. We always made sure that we had enough clean water left from dinner for morning coffee. Without caffeine, even Rebecca couldn't have cheered us up. Others broke down camp and began packing. People traded turns at the dreary chore of pumping water through our ceramic filter. Streams here contained more sediment than we expected, so the small-capacity filter needed to be disassembled and cleaned frequently. Christmas offered no break from camp rituals.

As we had planned, each of us packed our own food for breakfast and lunch. Today with my coffee, I had a measure of dry cereal and a stale bagel.

We continued filtering water until we had enough to sustain us during the day—plus a second day's water in case we had to dry camp. Hammocks came down, Alistair retrieved the sound-recording equipment, we sorted and packed everything away. After gulping down the final swallows of coffee, we shouldered packs—now ever-so-slightly lighter on account of the food and fuel we'd consumed. Much of that, however, was offset by the growing quantity of Rebecca's soil samples. Time to go.

The disadvantage of camping near streams meant starting the day on low ground and having to climb steeply uphill. The topography of these mountains was canyon up, canyon down, 3,000 feet up, 3,000 down. Mountain ridges, which would have been much more pleasant to follow while traveling, wandered this way and that in too large a scale. We didn't have time for such a route—so we traveled more or less in a straight line, up to the top of a jagged canyon and then down to the tangled bottom of the next. It was a clearheaded idea, on a map. Doing it through the trail-less jungle, mile after phantasmal mile, was a hazier proposition.

Zenon led the way with his son right behind him. The man did not share our sense of time and schedule, but he was an artist with a machete, relentless, tireless, completely efficient. He took down each vine and seedling and succulent with exactly the force needed, never more, always conserving energy. For that uncommon skill, he stood tall in my admiring mind.

The flora was becoming thicker, more storied and more story-book jungle-like. Even without rain, the vegetation preserved moisture in the soil, so we struggled in ankle-deep, sloppy mud. My knees screamed. I fell. I fell again and again. I was too heavy, too tall, too weary for efficient jungle travel. On the steepest pitches, I pawed and pulled my way up.

As my spirits sagged, my mind wandered. When we reached a ridge, I ate the peanut-butter sandwich that I'd set aside for lunch.

Then I found myself wondering if that had actually just happened, or was I remembering from yesterday? We passed a second creek. It was 11:00 a.m. Or was it 3:00 p.m.? I forgot even as it was happening.

A story? Or a dream? That was Conrad's question.

Frequent recording of our position by GPS would provide a record of where we had been, but nothing of what it was like.

Why does the jungle work this way on the mind? Because we cannot see into it. Distance is feet and hours, no other visual cues. We struggled and moved, but we had little satisfaction of progress. The green gloom and shadows weighed down on us. Whack! Whack! The beat of the machete became as sharp as the pounding of a jackhammer. Traveling down was as miserable as going up. And going up was plenty miserable. You know that if you lose your concentration, you could reach for a tree root and find a coiled fer-de-lance. But wait. Then you realize that you have been daydreaming, not concentrating at all as you reached for one root and then another for . . . well, for a while.

We came upon the tracks of a jaguar. Will paid a steep price for standing too long in one place without thinking, without looking. A column of army ants swarmed up his leg and bit him ruthlessly. We watched a band of monkeys moving ahead of us as if they were leading the parade. We heard a waterfall. Everywhere trees were down. In the accelerated biosphere of the tropical rain forest, the process of life and death was accentuated and fallen trees crisscrossed the forest floor. Coming on such obstacles, Zenon took a respite from swinging his machete. No rest for the remainder of us, however. If the dead log was lying on the ground, we had to climb up, clear the ground on the other side, checking for snakes, then clamber down. Most downed trees were not on the ground. They were hung up on other trees or brush, and so they would rest at varying distances off the ground. The smaller members of our team could often duck underneath. But Carl is six foot three and I am six foot five, and we often ended up on our hands and knees in the mud, shoving our packs ahead of us to someone waiting on the other side.

Then we followed a ridge downhill. Then the ridge disappeared. The vertical drop ahead was about twenty to twenty-five feet. If we were in the Himalayas and facing such a cliff, we'd be roped together and anchored to ice or rock. Vague, wispy thoughts came in and out of focus—danger, exhaustion, ache. Then danger again . . . I noticed a jagged spear of a broken sapling below me. That was definitely danger. You do not want to be on unsure ground overlooking a spear point. However, I held a tree and my foot seemed solid on a root, so I crouched to take the next step down. And then I was falling. In a nanosecond of sick realization, I pictured the sapling driving into the brachial artery of my bicep. Instantly, I twisted so the spear point would not plunge straight into my arm but might graze along the skin. By some miracle, the gymnastics worked.

Instead of piercing my arm, ripping through muscle and a spurting artery, the branch gouged out an eight-inch ravine of flesh along the inside of my arm. It was a nasty wound, but not life threatening. I trembled. Carl and Rebecca hung close to me. I think they were worried about my strength. I was.

We bandaged up my arm and continued the descent.

At the bottom of the canyon, we found a roomy campsite. I rested my throbbing arm in my hammock and ate the last of my Cheetos and then passed around a secret stash of M&Ms and beef jerky I'd saved just for today. Hardly any Christmas present could have meant more at the moment; you would have thought I was Saint Nick himself from the delighted grins. We talked about our science work and wondered about the continuing lack of rain. Zenon had never experienced so long an interval without rain. Here and there as we climbed, he had hacked into a clearing and marveled at the vistas opened up by receding undergrowth.

"I've never seen it like this," he said, in wonder.

He also described it as "alien" to come across just one band of monkeys and no other mammals in such a wild place. The drought had driven them to lower elevations in search of more abundant water.

For dinner, Rebecca suggested we feast on one of our freeze-dried meals. Carl said he had a holiday treat for us. He produced the electronic tablet on which he was recording his black-carbon data. We gathered close together and, incongruously in this strange, mysterious jungle, watched Carl's favorite Christmas movie, *Trading Places*, on the tiny screen until we couldn't hold our eyes open. We collapsed into our hammocks. It was 6:30 p.m.

Yes, Merry Christmas.

uccessful adaptation to climate change will test humans in several ways: technological, political, social. But there's something more. It will test our humility. Can we reconcile ourselves to the power of nature and cope that way? I learned this lesson during an earlier Central America trip along the Caribbean Sea. I was in the so-called Mosquito Coast region of Honduras and Nicaragua, the swampy area that was the setting of the movie *Mosquito Coast* with Harrison Ford. The lesson was clear, and it stayed with me—the critical virtue is resiliency.

Simply, I saw that societies could make themselves strong by coping instead of resisting. The La Mosquitia area of the coast has been slammed again and again by hurricanes. When such storms reached the United States or almost any modern population area, lives were imperiled, property destroyed, if not devastated, and economic well-being disrupted. In fact, when Hurricane Mitch swept over Central America and Florida, 15,000 people were killed and damage exceeded $6 billion. Yet, the mighty storm had only minor impact when it landed at full strength at La Mosquitia. Why? Because people had adapted their lives in a way that made them resilient to the impact of hurricanes. They accepted the power of nature and did not fight, they adapted.

The main coping mechanism was in the native design of homes. Rather than trying to build hurricane-proof housing like we did in most developed countries, they constructed simple huts with strong poles in the corners and in the middle of the walls. The remaining walls were constructed of light wood that blew away during a hurricane. Possessions were cached in protective storage both inside and outside the house. When a hurricane swept over them, the structural skeleton of the house was left standing. The wind blew through. Afterward, it was a straightforward matter to replace the lighter components of the dwelling that had been carried off.

The specific design was not as important in my mind as the philosophy. In La Mosquitia, people had learned to bend before the wind, and thus did not break.

nward. My arm throbbed. My precious boots, sturdy on so many rocky mountain terrains, were disintegrating in the tropical

humidity. I wasn't sure how much longer they had left. But the Talamanca routine was unvarying. Make coffee. Filter water. Pack up.
Zenon still out front. Whack! Whack! Halt. Take samples. Measure
our location by GPS. If there were monkeys in the forest canopy
above, we might have appeared like zombies pursuing some mysterious, plodding rituals.

Onward. Physically we were a mess. My arm was wrapped in
a dirty bandage. My knee was sprained. Rebecca's arm was swollen
and unhealthy looking, bandaged in several spots after various nasty
scrapes and bites. And she had dislocated her thumb. Carl's toe was
broken, a consequence of slipping in the mud and smashing into a
root. Alistair's leg was still oozing pus from his insect bite that become
infected.

Onward.

From my journal:

New Year's Eve. We got down to the river and started moving
slowly: no breakfast food left other than some instant coffee and so
I have no energy to move faster. I tied my broken boot to my feet
with string and Alistair's crazy glue and athletic and duck tape. I
hopped and did everything possible to keep the broken sole out of
the water. It made movement slow but I kept moving. We hacked
our way along the river and after an hour or so, we saw some
men on the opposite side of the river staring sullenly at us—min-
ers or fishermen probably. We were looking at them and cutting
through the jungle and then suddenly we were in a banana farm.
We thought we were done because there was the barest trail—
which, after the past two weeks seemed like a highway. It was interesting walking—occasional stilt houses with scattered clothes,
hammocks, and not much else inside them. Pigs and sometimes
puppies were occasionally running around, but they didn't bark at
us at all. I saw three snakes today, but they all slid away. The first
one was tiny, the second was very long and skinny, the third was
fatter; but I had no fear at all of any of them. Perhaps I am too tired.
We also saw a poison dart frog—bright red and tiny. Rebecca was
careful not to touch it and caught it in a bag and then put it on a
rock face and I watched him climb. A pretty awesome sight that I
had been hoping for throughout the expedition and a fitting end to

the Talamanca section of the expedition. The last bit I walked with Alistair and we finally reached a one-room school and tiny store and bought Cokes and chips and juice. We also got 16 eggs and so I cooked up fried eggs with our last supplies of ramen and quinoa. It was a much welcomed protein blast. I could only cook enough for two people at a time because it was so much food, but no one turned any of it away. I thought it was pretty damn tasty. Finally I could cut the tape away and could take off my wet boots. We hung our hammocks on the first floor of the schoolhouse and slept next to the river again. It was actually a pretty good last day for sort of a bad year. My sprained knee ached sharply and I was super hot and tired, but I think next year will be a lot better . . .

This year's resolution?—"Succeed." I need to push and go that extra bit beyond just being Audacious (last year's resolution). Audacious was a step only, time to begin finding Success.

We woke at 4:30 a.m. Strange sounds. Not wild birds, but people. It was curious how rapidly the "middle of nowhere" had become somewhere—only a few more hours of walking to find electricity and gravel roads and wood buildings and the noise of people. How lovely. We had accomplished plenty, but we were beat up and ready for restaurant food and real mattresses. Someday I would miss the jungle, probably. But not now.

I was not anticipating a short or an easy final day to reach the Atlantic, even though we were back on more or less level ground. I ached all over. My clunky boots were wet and clammy as I pulled them on, and I tried to lash down the detached sole as best I could. Not very well, as was soon apparent. We followed a path that villagers said would lead to a bus stop. I could feel hot spots on my feet already, and I knew they would soon be full-fledged blisters.

The C2C team split up. The others waited for the bus. I walked on. I calculated it was twenty-six miles to the ocean. I aimed to be the only one to finish the full C2C on my own power.

I walked. Onward. I thought it important that one of us make complete the C2C under his own power. Call it dogged. A light rain began—the first rain of the trip. What a funny time to start.

After a while I started thinking about my teammates. They were at some village restaurant by now, drinking a beer and chuckling about what a stubborn fellow I was. That would be the word. Not dogged. Stubborn. Ha, but at least I had them carry my pack on the bus.

My feet were on fire. I am a steady, confident, and easy walker. Except when my feet are dying. I stopped at a roadside shack for chips and a Coke. But I didn't dare dawdle, or I'd never get going again. Onward. The rain intensified. Hours seemed to pass more quickly than the miles. I tried to calibrate my progress with the GPS. I was getting slower and slower. To my right I could see Rio Sixaola, the river that marked the border with Panama. I was sure my feet were bleeding now. The police passed me on the road several times but did not stop.

Finally, the gravel road turned into concrete and I found myself in the village of Bribri, named after the local indigenous people and the provincial capital, nine miles from the ocean. I was conscious of stumbling now. I was thinking I'd better get a bus, or I'd collapse. Maybe I'd be arrested as a suspicious character staggering in the street. Or they would find me face down in a gutter like a vagrant. I admitted defeat. So close. It wasn't even New Year's Day and I'd already failed at my resolution to "Succeed."

I glanced to my right. Like a miracle, there was a shoe store. The only building around. And it was open. The luck to find what you need just when you need it can make the difference between success and failure. This was a stroke of good fortune. I went in and, using gestures and my pitiful Spanish, explained my need. The proprietor brought out a tiny pair of shoes. I shook my head and he brought out another, just as small. I was too tired to be infuriated, but I was close. He kept it up. Finally, high up in the wall and covered with dust, I saw a huge pair of flip-flops. I pointed and he retrieved them. Painfully, I peeled off my boots. My feet were two raw stubs of suppurating meat. But damned if the flip-flops didn't fit.

My spirits rose. I could walk nine miles in these babies. I put my soaking wet boots on the store scale just to see. Nine kilos, or just shy of twenty pounds. I took time to bury them along a creek outside of Bribri. A good place. I always try to find a nice spot to bury footwear that has served me well. The afterlife and karma and God are all difficult things to know, but I believe if you treat people and things well, then you will be treated well in your turn. Good-bye boots and thank you.

It rained heavier and grew dark. I lapsed into a semiconscious trance. Onward. Then I heard it off in the growing darkness. Surf. I pulled myself into the present and waded into the Atlantic. Rebecca and Carl somehow materialized and we walked toward some lights down the beach to our hostel.

Costa Rica and the Cordillera de Talamanca proved more challenging than I'd expected, physically and mentally. A respite from frostbite, yes. But otherwise the jungle mountains tested us to our limits—more suffering per day than any expedition I'd been on to that point. But the rewards were significant, too. In a way that I never even considered beforehand: by penetrating these trail-less canyons, we caught a faint scent of ancient exploration—maybe the rarest experience of any I've ever had, and one I'm unlikely to duplicate. Slip-sliding, whack-whacking, huff-huffing through the mud, feeling half claustrophobic and half agoraphobic, relying on a native guide and without a map, we came close to honestly touching life in the Age of Discovery. As it happened, the spot where we met the Atlantic was just to the south of the bay where Columbus first anchored in 1502. On the West Coast, where we started C2C, we were not all that far north of where Balboa became the first European to see America's shore of the Pacific, back in 1513.

The scientific rewards pleased us, too. I've traveled in lowland tropical forests across the world and have seen that they have a lot of similarities—conditions are so rich for life that even large changes can get lost in the homogenous struggle for survival. But mountains always tell their own story, and the empty rain-forest canopies of the Talamanca told a striking one. When you take the "rain" out of the rain forest, environmental stress occurs quickly and dramatically. The historic precipitation gradient from the Pacific to Atlantic, lowland to highland, disappeared for the time we were there. A land lush with vegetation and teeming with wildlife grew silent. Plants wilted and suffered. It is water that nourishes the forest. Without it, we observed withdrawal symptoms appearing fast. None of us wanted to witness the first stage of a drought, but as scientists, we were fortunate to be on hand to record this swift descent into rain-forest distress. To the extent that climate change results in more and more frequent such episodes, we could confidently deduce that the rain forest would cope poorly.

We measured nitrogen and carbon in the soils throughout our trip, revealing that what appeared to be unbounded fertility of the region was much an illusion—the result of constant nourishing by rain, which obscured the essentially barren nutrient loads of the soils. Every time we tied a hammock to a large tree and unexpectedly pulled it over with merely the weight of a human body, we witnessed the essential fragility of this landscape.

The rain forest is the most diverse biome on planet Earth, but it would be a mistake to think that it is also the most resilient. Just the opposite is closer to the truth. Extreme competition for resources has driven each organism to evolve with greater and greater specialized capacity to carve out a niche for survival. Any significant change would put all of them at risk. Although the drought we witnessed only lasted two weeks, it had led to rapid, large-scale responses from the flora and fauna. What would a year-long or decade-long drought bring?

Much of our work was not necessarily meant to assess current conditions, but rather to build a serious baseline of data so that scientists will be better able to calibrate future changes with precision. That approach was a cornerstone of my scientific interest, and it's why the Costa Rican Park Service was an enthusiastic partner in our work, as were private rain-forest protection groups. One of our baseline, look-to-the-future projects was the making of acoustic recordings of jungle sounds—so that laboratory ornithologists could map species of birds that were present at different locations in and around the rain forest. Rebecca made double use of these recordings by producing a Rain Forest Sounds CD that we gave to park officials to use in schools.

I asked Rebecca Cole for her reflections on the expedition:

"Was it worth it?" Yes. In fact it might be one of the best things I have ever done. I grew up hearing stories about the Talamanca and it always represented something unreachable and mysterious. From legends of bloody battles between invading Spaniards and indigenous people to lost gold mines to terrified explorers emerging half crazed from the jungle, it was something the older folk in my village talked about with awe. As a biologist, it was one of the places that the more adventurous types liked to think about studying but almost never had the funding—or ability and commitment—to reach . . . [Now] we have one of the first publishable soil data sets from such a remote rain-forest region. We have the first-ever set of recordings of bird and frog calls. Given that this is one of the most biologically diverse mountain areas on the planet, that is barely scratching the surface! In addition to all the basic research that could be done to simply characterize the plants and animals and ecological communities, there is a whole world of exploration to be done there. I am particularly concerned about the impacts of climate change in mountainous areas with high numbers of organisms found nowhere else on Earth. And, of course, there are lots of possibilities for archeological research . . . and a lost gold mine to search for!

PART IV

SURVIVAL

Chapter Ten

Alive

The goal of physical training for alpine climbing can be summed up in one phrase: to make yourself as indestructible as possible. The harder you are to kill, the longer you will last in the mountains.

—Climber and author Mark Twight

men.

I looked heavenward from deep in Himlung's glacier and saw light shining. Snow overhead twinkled. A sunbeam shot down through the opening where I'd broken through, and I could see a distant splinter of sky. Around me, the ice glowed, glassy blue-white. This was fortunate. Without sun or a headlamp, I don't imagine I would have stood a chance.

My thoughts began to clear. In the aching stillness, my senses came into focus on the situation. My brain seemed to be undamaged, I guessed. I struggled upright, which hurt more than I thought I could bear.

The sentiment of a long-ago mountaineer seemed fitting: *Will I live or will I die?* Well, I won't know that until the end, will I? No, actually I knew. That this fellow climber of long-ago ended up putting that thought into writing, and the act of doing so answered the question, didn't it? Well, by heavens, I was going to write something about my experience down here—which meant naturally enough surviving it. This crevasse wasn't going to kill me, no way. Live or die? I'd live.

That left only the matter of how. How would I get myself up and out, exactly?

I took stock of my situation. I saw that I still held my ice tool in my left hand. The odds were getting better already. An ice tool was a refined, toothy version of the old climber's ice ax. I bought mine in Kathmandu before heading out to Himlung. It was the "LuCKy" brand. I couldn't pass on karma like that. Let's see what kind of luck you bring, Mr. LuCKy.

And damned if my second Black Diamond Venom tool wasn't here on the ledge, too, and my sunglasses as well. I did not have two functioning arms. But with two ice tools and a working left arm I might be able to sink one tool into the ice, inch up, set the other, shift my weight, and inch up again. It wasn't much of a plan, but it was something to work with. And I didn't have time to waste hoping to find a better one.

Seventy feet is not all that far, about as tall as a white oak in the suburbs. Not quite as far as the tallest ladder on a firetruck. Not all that far except when it's forever. I'd resolved to gain those feet, so that was settled. I could never have guessed, however, that later someone could search Google Images for "70 feet" and find selfie-photos of my bloody face.

For the moment, though, I was pondering what to do about a problem that was much more immediate: any movement, even just a twitch, sent electric bolts of pain through my body. My upper right side screamed nonstop. Broken ribs on both my left and right sides compounded the misery of something as simple, and essential, as trying to draw a breath. Fifteen broken bones, as it would turn out. All demanding relief.

I did the only thing I could bear to do. I rested.

At 6,000 meters (19,685 feet), the physical effort of just rising up required me to stop and recover, and that's without broken bones. And I was going to have to do a lot more than stand up. But your body's limits are flexible—and more so if you've prepared yourself physically and psychologically. Then, when put in a bad situation, you can draw on resources that you never knew were there. Meanwhile, however, hypothermia was only a short while away, then frostbite, and I would be a frozen slab before long if I didn't get moving.

For the moment, the frigid temperatures in the crevasse worked for me as much as against me. I felt around my face and found that my bleeding eye socket and the gash on my forehead had congealed, along with a glaze of snot that shot out of my congested sinuses into frozen lumps. The cold had improvised a temporary bandage of my injuries.

That wouldn't help my one working hand, however. I wore a lightweight pair of fleece gloves, and nothing more. These were basically glove liners—only good for the mountain sunshine. And they had become wet already in the first minutes and were beginning to freeze. All but useless. My precious hand was growing numb.

Icy air swirled up from the void below and set fire to my lungs. No more resting. I had to get moving, and keep moving, no matter how severe the pain.

I stared up at the hole I had left in the crust of the snow blanket above, and a second small opening I must have loosened. I recorded myself talking over my predicament on my Sony HX7 camera. Given the conditions and the numbness in my hand, it was a wonder anything turned out.

As I talked to the camera and took a 360° view of above, I concluded that my only option was to move to my right. I'd need to traverse hundreds of feet in that direction to gain the seventy vertical feet to the surface. Above and to the left, the crevasse was too wide for me to scale, considering my condition and my lack of equipment. To the right, the crevasse narrowed so that I could chimney up using both sides of the ice for leverage. Or so I hoped.

I tried to calculate how long it might take to be rescued from above. My teammates Jake and ailing Ulyana would not be coming back up until tomorrow afternoon at the earliest. Possibly the next day. They wouldn't be able to rescue me themselves, and probably—wisely—wouldn't venture far looking for me. They might not even realize there was a problem until dark, when I didn't show up for dinner.

No good at all. I was shivering. I wouldn't live through a single night down here.

My thoughts returned to my elemental choice. Climb out. Or die. And that was really no choice at all. I figured it would keep getting warmer on the surface until about 4:00 p.m. That allowed roughly six hours until conditions turned against me. Six hours to climb seven stories up.

No time to waste. I needed to get going.

Because my right side was useless and yowling with pain, I was going to have to reach across with my left arm for every inch as I moved right. And that would constantly push me off balance. My conversation with myself was not so much self-pitying as coldly calculating.

My abdomen began to feel stiff and swollen—a symptom of internal bleeding.

I moved.

I kicked the front points of my crampons into the ice in front of me. I sunk one ice tool about face height and the other as far above and to the right as I could reach.

I pulled myself off of my tiny perch. I gasped for oxygen in this thin air. Not much of it to be had. Pilots turn on supplemental oxygen at 3,000 meters (10,000 feet). I was twice that high—which meant proportionately a lot less oxygen here. Hardly had I begun than the rhythm felt unending. Move. Stop. Pant like a drowning man. Fight off the nauseating waves of pain. Move . . .

As I moved, I aimed toward another block of ice that had fallen and become wedged to the right where the crevasse narrowed. The alternative was a seemingly bottomless void, unquestionably fatal. Where I began, the width of the crevasse was seven or eight feet. In the other direction, a school bus could have dropped through.

I gave only passing thought to the eerie reality that I was climbing inside a moving object. Glaciers are never still. They advance. They recede. Crevasses open. And slam tight.

I concentrated on what I hoped would be a route out. I would climb from the ledge that broke my fall to the wedged block of ice ahead, then keep pushing toward the right flank until the crevasse narrowed enough so that I could pin my back against one wall and my legs against the other and chimney my way up. At least that was my plan.

I concentrated on each stab of the ice tools, each kick of a crampon. Unfortunately, you cannot "work through" broken bones the way you might for tight muscles or a sprain. I wasn't getting looser and stronger, but tighter and weaker. The pain wasn't going to ease. Sometimes, it came in jolts so excruciating that I closed my eyes and held my breath and wondered if I could endure it.

It took around thirty-five minutes to reach the block of ice. I was encouraged. I had definitely gained some height—maybe ten feet.

Ahead, though, blue ice gave way to wispy snow smeared over the walls. It had the texture of whipped cream—the result of condensation as moisture descended from the surface. I could not climb up it at all. It wouldn't hold. I had to keep moving right along the lower edge of this whipped-cream wall until the crevasse narrowed farther.

I looked. My left knee dragged a trail of blood across the wall of the crevasse with every move. Damn it. If I could keep from smashing it further, the blood would freeze into its own bandage. If.

I made a second short video, pocketed the camera, and moved. One foot. Two. Was this what it feels like to be hit by a truck? Ahead, I faced a fifty-foot span to another ice block that had fallen and wedged itself in the crevasse. Halfway along, panting for breath, I looked down between my legs. The glistening white walls grew shadowy as they disappeared into black. Suddenly I had a sickening vision of myself sliding down, unable to stop. Forever.

I heard what I think was death whispering in my ear. The pain was becoming unbearable. Surely I had run out of energy. In a fleeting instant, I saw my mom. Her sadness.

There was something left. I twisted my body. My left hand arced overhead and the ice tool glanced off the hard surface. I shifted my weight and swung again. It bit.

Right foot—kick in the points of my crampons. Ice crumbles and gives way. Kick again slightly higher. The points hold. Body screams.

Pulling with my arm, standing on my foot, I move. Shock of pain.

Left foot kicks . . .

Left arm swings . . .

Another.

Another.

Another.

Finally, my right foot steps onto a bulging outcrop on the side of the wall. Then my left. I can rest. Lungs like a bellows.

Ahead, the surface of the crevasse changed again. Textures emerged in the whipped-cream snow, bumps and ledges. Here the walls had not just cracked open, they had also smashed together as the glacier moved, leaving handholds and footholds that made it easier to balance. But the broken surface was not trustworthy. Each movement had to be tested and cleaned of broken ice. Each step had to be backed up in case the ice gave way. I reached and constantly pulled chunks of ice down onto my battered face and body. I was the bull in nature's china shop. Another video.

At least I was moving upward now. One foot vertical for every three or four to the right.

My body entered the final throes of survival mode. It could spare no energy for rumination. Time passed in a fog. Minutes turned into hours. Each step, each swing, each kick came slower. All I ever knew or remembered was pain and cold and this damn ice. The pressure of internal bleeding made me feel wide and heavy.

Then the walls narrowed. I could put my back on one side of the crevasse, lean into it, and chimney up. Although, in fact, my movements were more of a slow-motion wheezing crawl.

The glow of sunlight was thirty feet away. The walls of the crevasse seemed to get firmer. Or was my mind playing tricks?

My watch said it was after 3:00 p.m. I had to keep moving. I had advanced so far to the right that I'd lost sight of the large twin holes I made in the snow crust when I fell in. Solid snow overhead. No opening anywhere. But the surface radiated light above me. One last video and onward.

I was teetering now. Exhaustion was winning the fight with what remained of my will. I kept searching myself for more fight. Another push to survive.

Left foot. Kick into the wall. Ugh.

Set the right ice tool higher. Yeow.

Up.

Right foot, higher. Oh God.

Wiggle my back slowly up the ice as I pull with my left arm. Arggh.

Rest.

Left kick . . .

Each step higher required minutes, and the pain always got worse. But the glow of sunlight was coming closer, too. I reminded myself. Pain does not kill you. Pain is the affirmation of life.

I mistakenly loosened a chunk of ice—bigger than my body. I staggered as it bounced against me. I was on the very knife-edge of falling with it. But with a burst of adrenaline, I held on. The adrenaline ran out in only seconds, but that was all I needed. I was at my limit. I didn't think there was anything left.

Fifteen feet. Twelve. Ten. Eight.

My ice tool brushed the bottom of the snow crust. Panting for breath. Whatever was left, I called on it. I dug into the snow crust above as I climbed.

I punched through to the surface.

A tiny hole grew larger. Swing. Swing again.

There was no elation. No energy for that. I felt only agony, sharp unbearable broken-body misery for the last twenty minutes until my torso wriggled free.

I had dug myself out of my own grave.

Fresh air. Sunshine.

Then I was stuck. Exhausted. I tried to pull up and bring my legs to the surface. Impossible. Minutes passed. Half-in, half-out, I was all but paralyzed and began to fear that I would collapse and fall back down into the crevasse for good.

What a different perspective this was. Just forty-eight hours earlier, Jake and I had walked this area, scouting for crevasses and finding none. Now, he was down lower on Himlung, and I was wondering if the mountain wouldn't win this battle with me after all.

I gave myself a mental slap in the face. I said to myself, *You climbed up that damn crevasse and you aren't going to die here.* I pushed with all my might. There wasn't much might. But I flopped onto the snow.

Safe.

I got to my knees and lurched upright, and I fell face first into the snow. It felt like I broke whatever parts of me were still intact.

I was shocked. I'd spent most of my life walking. Walking was my natural position. Now I was so physically mangled that I couldn't stand and just walk the short distance that would get me down the glacier and back to the tent. I had used up my life force, burned every calorie stored in my fat, muscle, sinew. I was an empty husk.

I was a long way from being safe.

I tried crawling on hands and knees, falling forward and sliding through the snow when I could. I gasped for breath and looked around. I had gone maybe twenty feet in fifteen minutes.

But the downhill slope grew more pronounced. I could slide farther and easier. I realized that my panting wasn't just on account of altitude. My throat was nearly swollen shut from thirst.

Minutes again seemed to pass into hours. The tent came closer until I reached the flat ledge where we were camped. Crawling was becoming too painful on my broken ribs, so I would lurch again to my feet, and try to stumble three or four steps before collapsing, coughing and gasping for breath.

At the tent. At last.

I wonder.

Do I curse my bad luck for falling deep into a glacial crevasse and shattering my body?

Or, do I give thanks for my good luck in beating the odds and struggling back out alive?

I barely managed to crawl into the tent. My food bag was heaped down at the bottom end. Impossible to reach. No strength for that. No will power. I was empty. But alive.

I panted for breath—each one sending a jolt of pain through my chest. I became aware of something lumpy. I was resting against Ulyana's sack of possessions. I thought about that for a while. Then clenched my jaw, tightened, and reached. Her food was on top. In a wandering fog of thoughts I dwelled on the absurd realization that it requires two hands to accomplish almost anything. And I had only one. I could nudge my water bottle and feel that it was full. The contents sloshed. Unfrozen. Oh God, yes. But even using my teeth I couldn't twist the cap loose. Finally I managed to tear open three of Ulyana's GU Energy Gel packets—and the ice-cold gelatin burned my throat all the way down, but it provided a jolt of calories. I located a bottle of low-strength hydrocodone tablets and took two against the pain. Swallowing them dry was its own agony. These opioids were hard on my stomach and, for a time, made me forget my thirst and hunger.

Not knowing when Ulyana and Jake might return, I focused everything I had on sending word for help. On account of our bare-bones budget, we were not equipped with a full-on satellite voice-phone setup. Instead we relied on DeLorme inReach devices, which allowed us to send text messages via satellite. We used the system chiefly to post updates to Facebook. Thankfully, every outbound message carried a map and GPS coordinates. Even more fortunately, the inReach was within real reach. The time here in Nepal was afternoon, and people in the United States half a world away who might be following the expedition were probably still asleep. I could only hope someone was up, so I posted:

"Please call Global Rescue. John broken arm, ribs, internal bleeding. Fell 70 ft crevasse. Climbed out. Himlung Camp 2. Please hurry."

A few minutes later, I realized that people would need more information, so I sent out a second post:

"Global rescue phone number 6174594200. John All AAC member number 9890. Bad shape. Need help. Everyone else is safe below at Camp 1."

I had no way of immediately knowing the uproar I created. But I felt confident that I wasn't completely alone in the struggle anymore. Because I could operate the inReach with just one hand, I sent messages to my mom and my son. I told them how much they meant to me. I promised that I'd survive. I messaged a woman whom I had fallen for before leaving the states. My newfound affection for her, and my hope that we could transform our relationship into something more lasting, was one of the things that had spurred me on when I neared the end of my endurance climbing out of the crevasse. They messaged back with love and support. Yes, others were mobilizing.

Here, on the far side of the world—the far side of my world, anyway—I drew closer to this new woman in my life. I guess you can never feel so bad that love doesn't matter.

She messaged:

"We've got a lot of love and happiness to make."

I texted my dear friends Rebecca and Carl, and others who were important to me from the founding days of the American Climber Science Program, such as James Holmes and Carey Roberts, people I'd met through the American Alpine Club and whose support had blossomed into dear and lasting friendships. They, too, replied. Late-day shadows began to creep up the mountain. I could feel the deep Himalayan cold beginning to settle in. But this outpouring of affection and support warmed me for a time. Yes, damn it, I would survive. And live to tell them, each of them, that words never meant so much as theirs did now.

Global Rescue was not equipped to respond with the swiftness of a military medevac, no matter how desperate my circumstances. The Kathmandu lifesaving team was unable to mobilize before dark, so I would have to endure the night on the mountain—a long one.

I sent a text to Facebook, which I meant to be reassuring:

"Unless the bleeding inside gets me, I should live."

My challenge now was simple, and nearly impossible. I had to get the tent zipped closed properly, take my boots off, and climb into my sleeping bag before the cold became too severe. I could not survive a night this high in the Himalaya dressed as I was.

Dad to the rescue. My father and I went shopping before I left, and we bought a large, heavy-duty Gerber knife. Dad was a gadget and knife kind of guy. Now, I grabbed for it and put it to use. I couldn't get my boots or crampons off one-handed, so I began the agonizing process of trying to cut them off. Left-handed, I began sawing away. I was either going to be carried off the mountain in a helicopter or die. I wouldn't be needing them. And even though they had served me well, I was in no condition to give them a proper burial.

Every move was misery. And this process took me a half hour, grunting, wincing, and trying to stay focused with that razor-sharp blade in my hand. Finally, they were cut away. I gagged down another hydrocodone tablet and began to try to close up the tent. I shut the fly and got the zipper door partially closed. But that was all, and that would have to do.

Finally, I had to try to move onto my side and get covered up. I rolled left and my ribs exploded. The pain was blinding. But without the warmth of the sun, I would freeze without insulation. I needed to get onto my sleeping pad. In this thin air, my breath came in ragged gasps— each a reminder that my abdominal and chest muscles had been torn and bruised. I tried to balance my dislocated and broken right arm on my right side, but it meant fighting back paroxysms of pain. Whatever relief the hydrocodone provided, it was not enough. Not nearly enough. I dragged myself to the left and got my chest slowly onto the pad, then my left leg, and finally my entire body. I dragged my pack forward to keep my body at about at a 45° angle, which provided some measure of relief.

A text. My mom was busy on the other side of the world. She passed along someone's advice to raise my legs because of internal bleeding. So I used my toes to drag a bundle of something over and propped my feet onto it. Several times I accidentally bumped my water bottle and heard the contents sloshing around inside, maddeningly unreachable. Finally, I draped my sleeping bag on top of myself as well as I could. Another hydrocodone and I settled in for a long wait. Oh for morning. Oh for the whack-whack of a helicopter. Oh hell.

Another text from Mom. And Carey. Same message: Don't fall asleep, they said, because of internal bleeding. For the first time, I wanted to laugh out loud. Fall asleep? Maybe I could lapse into a delirious trance, but sleep in this agony was the least of my worries. Never fear, Mom: I'm in far too much pain to drift off.

Hour after hour. I could focus my thoughts on little beyond the pain. It hurt to hold still. It hurt to try and move, even a little. But I had to shift. Which was worse? I argued the dead-end question with myself. It hurt, period.

Silence was occasionally interrupted by the rustle of wind. Then it was still again. And cold. I could smell the cold, even over my own stench. If I had the strength, I'd probably be shivering. But I didn't. I began to worry about the battery, so I shut down my inReach. I'd need it tomorrow. Now I was alone again. Hour after hour.

I could stand it no longer. At around 3:00 in the morning, I switched on the inReach and sent another general-circulation Facebook post.

"Bleeding inside feels better but so cold. Pain meds running low. Longest night ever."

Separately, I sent three other texts—to my son, to my parents, and to this new woman in my life whom I couldn't get out of my thoughts.

They responded with encouragement. But it rang rather formal to me, only deepening my despair. I know they were trying not to convey panic, but I was hoping for more . . . for more hot-blooded emotion. I needed someone who could hear my silent screams.

On and on. This longest night would just not end. I'd never endured anything like it, or even imagined anything like it. Finally I realized that things were changing. The walls of the tent took on a glow, faint but enough to signal the coming of dawn. Maybe 5:00 a.m.

I knew the helicopter was still hours away, but I had to check. I needed them to understand that I was no longer able to move. They were going to have to get me from inside the tent. I sent two texts to make certain they got the word to the pilot. They acknowledged. But they also reported a delay in the rescue flight. Uh-oh.

The rescue folks were negotiating prices for the helicopter, and it was cloudy in Kathmandu. I was told to expect liftoff at 6:30 a.m.

Then 8:30. I think my eyes watered for a moment. I had been so close to the end for so long. I was dying. I needed help.

From a daytime high near 30°F, the temperature had fallen to −20°F during the night. Now it was rising. But −10°F was not really that much to cheer about. Muscle cramps had gripped me during the night but had then just faded into the general miasma of agony. I was slipping into paralysis. I texted every hour, asking when the helicopter would arrive.

"Soon."

"We are working on it."

Nine o'clock became ten o'clock. Finally—the text from Global Rescue:

"Mission launch, helicopter is on its way!"

The flight would take two hours, unless there was a problem en route. The tent walls glowed brighter. Finally, I could feel the warmth of the sun. It was the first good thing I'd felt in nearly twenty-four hours. And it provided a boost. I begin sorting some gear with just my left hand, trying to move nothing else on my body. I would need my passport and wallet. I wanted to bring my camera to see if the movies from inside the crevasse had turned out. My iPhone never left me, and I knew I would need to write about my experiences. And of course the inReach. With my left hand, I scratched a nearly illegible note for Jake and Ulyana telling them that I had fallen into a crevasse and was on my way to Kathmandu. I asked them to take my gear down if they could and wished them luck on their summit bid. At that point, I assumed they would carry on the quest and gather the data that we'd worked so very hard for.

Then the far-off sound of the helicopter. It was down low in the valley but slowly grew louder. I smiled. Good to my word, I would survive. I began to say thanks to all the people who had assisted. Some of the tension began to drain away. Nineteen hours had passed since I slip-crawled into the tent.

The sound disappeared. The pilot probably stopped at Base Camp. Then I heard the blades again fighting for purchase in the thin air. The sound grew louder, and louder still. They had to see the tent. But the crew seemed to be searching elsewhere, first one side of the ridge, then the other. What the hell? Now the helicopter sounded like it was right on top of me. But still it did not stop. The pilot circled and then moved higher up the mountain. I wanted to scream, "I'm here in the tent, god damn it!" Wasn't the pilot thinking? He'd been told I was in the tent and couldn't move.

Fifteen minutes. The once happy sound was growing fainter. Panic gripped me. Twenty minutes. Now it grew louder again. Once more it circled. I begged it to land. And it did.

I was nearly overwhelmed with relief when I heard the tent door unzip and the face of a Nepali man appeared. I tried to tell him I couldn't move. But my voice sounded like a croak. He grabbed the bottom edge of my sleeping pad and pulled. I just about passed out—it was a new level of pain. He dragged me at a fast walk directly to the helicopter. I couldn't bear the stabs of pain with each bump. This was the worst yet. And I couldn't make myself heard to slow him down. Finally, we reached the helicopter.

The pilot jumped out and they levered me to my feet. The helicopter had no doors, just openings. There was a seat for the pilot and then just floor space. Everything that could be left behind had been removed to lighten the craft. We were at the very edge of its capability. I fell forward onto the floor, and the two of them hoisted my legs in after me. I either passed out or was close. The pilot got back into his seat and the single crewman strapped me down. I croaked again, begging for water. The pilot gave me his half-full water bottle and it was the most wonderful liquid I ever tasted. My voice seemed to be returning. Still raspy but perhaps intelligible. Why, I asked, did they not land the first time? Were they worried about being too close to the tent?

"No," he told me. They were searching for a sign of where I'd fallen into the crevasse. The pilot, a European who spoke with a strong Germanic accent, said he understood I was in a crevasse. Besides, he figured if I had been in the tent, I would have come out. Yes? He said he stopped on his return down the mountain purely on impulse. The flight had been long and he hated returning empty-handed.

My stomach tied itself in a knot. I'd had about enough of these razor-close calls.

He powered up the engine and it was a short hop down to Base Camp. My Sherpa friends looked grim and near tears. They brought me water.

The pilot and his crewman refueled with five-gallon jerry cans they had cached. They reattached the doors they had left down here.

And we departed on one of the most satisfying and beautiful flights of my life, zigzagging past the towering peaks of the Annapurna massif and down peaceful-looking Himalayan valleys. We skimmed low over a ridge, and three mountain sheep bolted at the sound. The pilot knew this terrain and wasted no time getting me to help.

The crewman talked cheerfully during our journey, but I found it difficult to listen through noise and the waves of pain that came with the jostling of the helicopter. He was not a medic but had been prepared to descend on a line into the crevasse searching for me, or my body. He had quite a mountain résumé, having summited Everest five times. I think he said five. Under better circumstances, it would have been a delight to hear his stories and maybe share some Nepalese moonshine.

We whirled out of the mountains and descended quickly. The temperature seemed to soar unbearably. After weeks in the dry cold above 5,000 meters (16,404 feet), Kathmandu at 1,400 meters (4,600 feet) was steaming. I sweated nonstop, and I gave off a smell that was enough to make me gag. I could only imagine the effect on others.

We landed. My thoughts began to shift from events past to questions about the struggles ahead. This wasn't going to be easy. Four hospital orderlies approached. The pilot and the crewman joined them in flinging me onto the stretcher—at least that's what it felt like. I almost lost consciousness as the rough handling awoke every damaged tendon, bone, muscle, and organ of my body. They squeezed me into an ambulance and had to lift my legs in the air and bend them so that they could close the rear door. The ambulance had not been made for someone six foot five. I begged the attending doctor to stabilize my arm and shoulder as we bounced down the city's potholed roads. There seemed no escape from the sharp bolts of agony.

At the hospital, my dear friend Sujan waited. I was given more painkillers, rushed through an ancient-looking X-ray room, and placed on my back. A mob of people surrounded me, half of them holding me down and the other half trying to wrestle my dislocated shoulder back into place. I screamed, and the doctor called for an injection of something stronger.

Mercifully, I vanished into unconsciousness.

I awoke and the bustling attention continued. Sujan was at my side, room after room. He sent updates to Facebook, telling my family and others that I had been helicoptered to Kathmandu. I needed food desperately. The medical staff wanted to administer more oxygen.

Neither one of us got our way. The oxygen was plenty heavy down here; I couldn't bear more. I shook off the oxygen mask every time a nurse tried to affix it to my face. My begging for food was denied again and again, presumably in case I might need immediate surgery. But I hadn't eaten in fifty hours and was getting frantic.

I wanted out. I wanted to get home. I wanted to be in the arms of this new woman in my life. Because of the way things turned out, I've left her name out of this book, but she was the one who occupied my thoughts during my delirium.

Sujan, no longer just a friend but also now a brother, became my guide and all-around fixer. My internal bleeding seemed to have stopped, and I had been pumped full of antibiotics. The doctor assigned to my case advised me to have emergency surgery on my arm and shoulder, but when I declined firmly and repeatedly, he agreed to release me after only one endless night in the hospital.

I paid a steep price for insisting on leaving, however: the doctor, in what I thought was an unfair disregard, provided me with only ibuprofen and Tylenol for pain, neither of which was up to the task, not by a mile. Sujan wheeled me out of the hospital and arranged a room at a hotel.

My videos had turned out pretty well. I posted one to Facebook, and the reaction was immediate. My friends shared the grisly story and video, and by word-of-mouth I was swamped with new friend requests. So the whole family could see, Mom asked me to post all four videos on YouTube. That brought on a siege of news reporters. Within twenty-four hours, I'd spoken to journalists all over the world.

In the curious way of things, I'd earned a moment of fame and a global audience, not for the good things I'd done, or the things I'd done well, but for an inexcusable blunder and bad luck. But I had lived, and I trusted that curious people would move past the single event on Himlung to the larger issues that absorbed my life. My struggle, I told myself, would underscore how important it was to understand and deal with climate change.

The trip home to Kentucky took forty hours. Krishna Shrestha, a Nepali professor and friend, found a sling for my arm. Sujan and my parents made flight arrangements.

Two opposite things absorbed me—the sharp pain of a mangled body and the uplifting gush of love and support from family and
friends. I hoped to recover quickly from the former and never, ever,
forget the latter. The new woman in my life met me at the airport. I
couldn't have been more optimistic. I had pursued worthwhile goals,
and I'd lived to tell about it. This was my reward.

But recovery did not come easily. Or fast. I existed on a diet of
painkillers—six large Percocet capsules a day, plus Valium, then Am-
bien. It was a combination that left me a shambling, often confused
zombie. People close to me said they could not recognize my broken,
wandering thoughts and deadened emotions. It was a terrible time
of fear and rejection for them. I underwent surgery for my arm and
shoulder, and wound up in a high-riding, winged shoulder brace. No
one had ever thought of me as fragile. Now even my mom did. The
drugs may have helped the mending, but they left me blurred and
often empty. And still in pain. I lost nearly six months of memories.

The young woman who was so important to me up there on the
mountain took this especially hard. She had given me everything.
I had nothing to give back. She had been my vital ally in the battle
between life and death. An angel of hope at my darkest moments. I
couldn't repay her feelings because I felt so dead inside. Trying to regain my life was more difficult that I realized. Without ever reaching its potential, our love foundered. I knew even then that I'd spend
many months wondering what I could have done better.

A couple of months passed—spent lying on the couch in a daze as
my body knit itself back together. Then the pain began to relent. With
it, the need for painkillers tapered off. I began to hear, over and over
again, the comment, "You are starting to sound like yourself again."

But I wasn't myself. My relationships with my fellow teammates
in Nepal was wrecked and beyond repair. My absence left a mess in
South America with the American Climber Science Program, and only
the devotion of my fellow leaders—Rebecca, Carl, and Ellen—held it
together. On the Internet, critics faulted me for being alone in such a
place as high Himlung without asking about the circumstances that
had led me there.

My body strengthened, my mind cleared, but the ensuing months
continued to be the worst of my life. Gaps opened up in the basic who,
what, why, when, and where of my life. I looked back with regret and

ahead with uncertainty. Before, I'd never had enough time. Now it seemed I had too much.

I wrote poetry and felt sorry for myself. Then, after nearly a year, I found myself arguing that poetry was fine, but self-pity wasn't. I had set upon a life's work to contribute to our collective understanding of our planet. And there was life left in me.

Physical therapy was painful. Then it was cathartic.

Slowly, very slowly, the future began to make sense. When someone congratulates me on my survival, I smile and nod. I don't bother explaining my discovery: life and death aren't entirely either-or matters. Some of my old self had indeed perished up there high in the Himalaya that spring. For a long while, I only spoke of events on Himlung from the third-person viewpoint to keep my heart rate under control. But I was liking the part that survived. I owed apologies and I carried regrets, yes. Still, I had reason to be proud of what I'd accomplished. All in all, what remained of me seemed a pretty good foundation on which to build. Maybe a little less invincible, maybe a little wiser.

Interlude

Harry Potter

Knowledge carries an obligation. If you're fortunate enough to learn something worthwhile, I believe you're obliged to share it—to be an advocate for learning, to encourage excitement about the quest for understanding, and to set an example by putting what you know to good use. That's why, when I'm not off somewhere in the wild, you'll find me in the classroom. Two sides of the same valuable coin. Hey, it worked for Indiana Jones, didn't it? I'm no Harrison Ford, but I am the itchy-footed son of a professor and I'm a lifelong student myself. The campus is my habitat and teaching feels as natural as breathing.

Environmental science is what I teach. But I believe a good professor must be a master of both esoteric and applied knowledge—the "how" and the "why" as well as the "what" of things. The battle for grades ends long before life does. I know, that sentiment is a real cliché. But take my word for it, please. It's no less true for being repeated a million times. And I had that fact knocked into my head at the bottom of a Himalayan crevasse.

I want young people to treat their education as a great gift and to seize the opportunities that arise out of it.

Live with passion. Pay heed to duty.

Sometimes I talk to students about the book *Tom Sawyer* and the passage when Tom walks in on his own funeral. Just as I crawled out of my own grave on Himlung, I urge them to imagine something similar happening to them. What if they unexpectedly died, today? What would sadden them most about life cut short? What dreams and loves and friendships deserved more from them? What regrets would fill their eternity? Then, at that moment when they found they hadn't died, that they were not done with life, that they had another chance, what would matter most to them? How would they reset their expectations for themselves each day?

My own answer has been to take on the challenges of life as a Berserker—an unreasoning, fearless Norse warrior who cannot quit until the fight is done. This made it possible for me to do what I could not do when I needed to do it. Wind me up and I've been known to go until I get to the summit and back to Base Camp, and then pass out. I teach my students that, yes, evolution rewards those who do not exhaust themselves. But evolution also gave us the sloth and the earthworm. Sometimes, you need to aim a little higher.

I always smile when I realize it was a baseball player and coach—Tommy Lasorda—who observed: "The difference between the impossible and the possible lies in a person's determination."

I'm alive today because of this approach. But I'm not speaking of merely breathing alive, eating-your-peas and taking-up-space alive. But tingly alive; kick up your heels alive. If *it's worth doing* . . . that old thing.

Many people praise the *Harry Potter* books because they engage young readers so fully. But contrarian that I am, I challenge that easy assumption.

I figured I would ruffle a few feathers with a convocation speech I delivered at Western Kentucky a while ago, expressing impatience with young Potter's apathy.

What a lousy role model. He KNEW Voldemort wanted to kill him. He KNEW Voldemort killed his parents. But the first few years he was at Hogwarts, he just screwed around playing quidditch and eating magic jellybeans. I would have been learning every defensive and offensive spell possible. He only survived through incredible dumb luck. In real life, preparation is how you succeed . . .

To my surprise, nearly 6,500 freshmen gave me a standing ovation for those comments. The university president told me it was the first time had ever witnessed such a response for a convocation speaker. And during the next semester, random students would say hi to me on the quad or greet me in the gym.

Grab on to life. Bite down on it. Suck the marrow from the bone. The campus may be a safe place to begin adulthood—but let's remember, risk awaits us all. Meet it, head on. As our world becomes more technological and the pace of change increases, our need to respond wisely rises with it.

Once you have prepared fully and conditions are right, you still need commitment to succeed. Like paddling a surfboard into the surge of a wave, or stepping off a cliff with a paraglider on your back, or saying "I love you" to someone for the first time, sometimes in life there is a second of irreversible commitment. Seize and embrace that moment.

So forget the wizards and wands. Get yourself a fedora, an old leather jacket, a bullwhip if you need one, and head out into the world.

Chapter Eleven

Findings

Once we look around and accept that Earth isn't what it used to be, and indeed seems to be less so all the time, we need to stand back and explore two questions. Together, in broad terms, they are the foundation of my work, the focus of what I teach, and the motive for my fieldwork. They are the "So what" questions. First: "So what" if the climate is changing? It has before, and may again. Already, a good many consequences of these changes are apparent, and more are sure to come. So, "So what?" Secondly: "So what" are we going to do about it?

Let me begin with the first.

The surface of planet Venus is hot enough to melt lead, to boil away oceans, to set afire everything we would call life.

Okay, but compared to Earth, Venus is closer to the sun, so of course it's hotter. End of story.

Well, no, it isn't.

Venus is also hotter on average than the planet Mercury, which is nearer still to the sun.

Some background: Venus and Earth are roughly the same size. Planetary scientists believe both were created in the same fashion from solar dust. Compared to Earth, Venus is about 28 percent closer to the sun.

It's important to note that carbon dioxide, CO_2, is plentiful on both planets. The big difference: much of Earth's CO_2 is locked away in rocks that make up the planet's crust or in the fossil fuels that now power our societies, in sediments on the ocean floor, in permafrost, and in the very soils that provide our food. Venus, by contrast, suffers from a "runaway greenhouse effect."

To take a quick step back, the "greenhouse" phenomenon begins when sunlight reaches Earth. A portion of this energy is absorbed on the surface or in the atmosphere. The remainder is reflected back skyward. Some bounces out into space, and some is trapped in the atmosphere, where this captive energy serves to cloak the planet in a blanket of warmth like glass over a greenhouse. It is a decidedly delicate balance of sunlight absorption and reflection that maintains Earth's livability.

Add more CO_2 into the atmosphere, and the balance is thrown off. More solar energy is trapped by this gas, and temperatures rise. The process is called radiative forcing. In general, warmer temperatures liberate pools of carbon stored in the soil and geology of a planet. As things get hotter, more carbon gas is released into the atmosphere to trap a greater share of the sun's radiative energy. The "greenhouse" warms, which releases still more CO_2. The temperature continues to rise. At some point this cycle "runs away" out of control and becomes an unstoppable and catastrophic process of physics.

That, in short, is one of the great fears for planet Earth.

Both planets have the same amount of carbon and oxygen present, but the atmosphere on Venus is nearly 97 percent CO_2. The energy of the sun becomes trapped in this dense gas, and surface temperatures soar to more than 850°F. Water has cooked off the planet's surface, so mists of sulfuric acid comprise the only rain on Venus. On Earth, by contrast, atmospheric CO_2 is about one-half of 1 percent. But—and this is a really big "but"—Earth's atmospheric CO_2 has increased 24 percent since the middle of the twentieth century, and that rate has been accelerating, according to the National Oceanic and Atmospheric Administration and every scientific instrument on our planet. Scientists estimate that if all Earth's stored carbon were released into the atmosphere, our air would be much like that on Venus.

In any system as big and complex as our atmosphere, there are variables galore. But let me emphasize that greenhouse gases and their effects on temperatures are not theory. This is not something to be countered by religious belief, economic ideology, or the rap of a committee chairman's gavel. This is hard fact. It is chemistry, physics, geoscience.

That some gases absorb energy is as well established and immutable as, say, gravity. Indeed, if they did not, life would be impossible on Earth just as surely as if there were no gravity. If some share of the sun's radiation was not captured, the Earth would be frozen solid and virtually lifeless. So we owe our existence and the wonders of life around us, like farms and forests and rivers and oceans, to the fact that the greenhouse of atmospheric gases holds on to a portion of the solar energy beamed our way and keeps Earth at a livable average temp of 59°F.

This trapped solar radiation does far more than just blanket our planet in warmth. It provides the energy that drives winds, fuels evaporation, and churns up weather. Because this is the world we know and in which we have prospered for millennia, we can say a word of thanks for the greenhouse gases that are our savior and friend.

But more is not, in this case, better. You may have a vague memory of the *I Love Lucy* episode on TV where Lucy learns that adding more yeast to the dough does not create better bread. Instead, it makes a helluva mess. The same with greenhouse gases. If you want to know how climate change will affect Earth, just imagine adding more energy to our atmosphere, more yeast in the dough. More power in the hurricane, more heat in the drought, more favorable conditions for disease-carrying insects, bigger wildfires, stronger blizzards, super-tornados and their eerie offspring "firenados." An increasingly hyperactive atmosphere. A helluva mess.

Human enterprise has made itself felt by altering the fragile climate balance of Earth for centuries. We humans use, and therefore alter, the land underfoot according to our needs, our cultures, and population densities. The most widespread of human land-use changes has been the conversion of natural landscapes—many types of them—into agricultural production. Today, more than half of Earth's potential agricultural land is in use. These transformations, say, from forest to farm, carry important consequences for our climate. To take just one that has been under way for centuries: cutting down forests to open the soil to sunlight for cultivation. This means the dark-green forest canopy is replaced with lighter and more reflective shades of soil. This alters the albedo of the Earth's surface. *Albedo*— isn't that a great word? It's the measure of the reflectivity of the Earth's surface—how much solar energy is reflected, and consequently how much is absorbed. A white T-shirt has greater albedo than a black one in the hot summer sun. And thanks to albedo, no one walks barefoot on black asphalt in Tucson in July.

Some scientists—including the noted Carl Sagan, whose *Cosmos* television series impelled me toward science as a child—have theorized that the Little Ice Age in Europe, from about 1300 to 1870, was partially caused by the regional clearing of European forests for agriculture and the resultant albedo effect—less dark forest canopy to absorb solar energy and more cultivated fields to reflect it back outward and thus cool the landscape.

Today, because of the increased concentration of greenhouse gases, more of this reflected energy does not escape the atmosphere but is trapped, and the result is just the opposite—global warming.

With that, the global water cycle is being altered. This is the timeless process in which water vapor precipitates out of the atmosphere onto, and into, the Earth and then drains away to return via evaporation and transpiration. Science reminds us that as the air warms, a corresponding increase in evaporation occurs. Thanks to global warming, we will see drier soils and heavier loads of H_2O in the atmosphere to precipitate out as rainfall. The consequence? Some areas of the planet grow drier and others wetter. Ironically, greater floods *and* droughts await us in the future.

An even more dramatic kind of accelerated feedback loop can be measured in the Arctic Ocean. Not so long ago, this ocean was capped in ice that sent much of the sun's energy back into space. Skiers and mountaineers know the power of albedo—they see it in severe sunburns after hours on a blinding mountain. The ice and snow covering, meanwhile, stays comparatively cool. But warming atmospheric temperatures have upset the balance. The reflective ice melts and is replaced by water. Like a dark-colored car on a hot day, this ocean water absorbs more of the sun's energy in the form of heat. The warming seawater melts more ice, and the loop continues, accelerating and gaining power until the ice and snow vanish. Eventually, the oceans grow hot, and . . .

Bad ending.

And that accounts for the mounting urgency in our civic and political conversations. If we merely stumble onward, quarreling and stalling and pushing the problem into the future, conditions will get worse, people will get more desperate, and we will reach a tipping point where the process cannot be stopped or undone: the runaway greenhouse effect. Technology may be our friend, but once the greenhouse effect becomes a runaway cycle, technology cannot fix things any more than technology can repair a bridge after it starts to fall into the river.

For more than a century, the word *survival* has carried dual meanings. The British Society for Psychical Research uses "survival" as the term to describe life after death and has done so since about 1900. Today, the society maintains a Survival Research Fund with the purpose of supporting scientific inquiry "into the fundamental question of whether some aspect of consciousness or personality survives the death of the body."

As an adventurer and a former search and rescue team member, I'm very interested in the other kind of survival—in which we overcome ordeals and crises to maintain a mortal presence a while longer. It's obviously personal, as you've seen from my adventures, but it's also the rationale for my work. It's the kind of survival we consider in the context of climate change. This is the second part of the "So what" question. So what are we going to do? Will we survive? Will our way of life, our cultures and values, prove wise, lucky, and adaptable enough to survive? Will joy and opportunity survive? Will our coastal communities survive? Our farms on marginal lands? Those suburbs and retirement communities tucked into forest canopies?

Some days, the headlines seem to lengthen the odds. Both in what they say about Earth's climate, and what they tell us about ourselves. About Earth: 2015 was the hottest year ever measured; and fifteen of the sixteen hottest years ever measured have occurred since 2001. About us: in 2016 the Supreme Court, at least temporarily, blocked regulations to control CO_2 emissions from coal-fired power plants because of industry objections.

Meanwhile, for those who pay attention, "climate change" is becoming "climactic change" for our planet.

So, are there solid, rational reasons to be hopeful about the future?

Yes.

Survival is a pretty good human motivator. Fewer and fewer residents of our world are untouched by climate changes. More and more of us are feeling these changes in tangible, even emphatic ways. And only the foolhardy think they've seen the end of it.

The world's credible leaders, speaking with increasing vigor and conviction, are drowning out the banalities of those who defend the status quo. Just as significantly, when we behold the great entrepreneurial power so characteristic of human progress, we see ever-more-energetic shifts in the direction of climate solutions and away from climate problems.

The UN Intergovernmental Panel on Climate Change shared the 2007 Nobel Peace Prize for "efforts to build up and disseminate greater knowledge about man-made climate change, and to lay the foundations for the measures that are needed to counteract such change." The Peace Prize, yes. Because environmental dislocations, water distribution, and economic upheavals are gigantic potential flash points for conflict.

The Nobel Prize citation warned:

> Indications of changes in the earth's future climate must be treated with the utmost seriousness, and with the precautionary principle uppermost in our minds. Extensive climate changes may alter and threaten the living conditions of much of mankind. They may induce large-scale migration and lead to greater competition for the earth's resources. Such changes will place particularly heavy burdens on the world's most vulnerable countries. There may be increased danger of violent conflicts and wars, within and between states.

The first, and easiest, steps in building the "foundations" for surviving climate change rest on the perfectly sensible, indeed unassailable, idea of "no-regrets policies"—actions that reduce greenhouse gases while also generating other important benefits. Or, if you prefer, actions that produce profit, jobs, and social gain while mitigating activity that contributes, or could contribute, to climate change and bring the world closer to the runaway greenhouse effect. In common vernacular, win-win. No better call to action.

In the United States, leaders of both political parties have embraced "no-regrets policies" in one way or another. And little wonder. The strategy is the very essence of sober-sided, opportunity-minded conservatism. How can you argue, really, with policies that promise to pay dividends while strengthening society and securing future prosperity? Just the same, no-risk policies virtually define the kind of payoffs promised by progressive action—that is, "progress" toward common and worthy social goals. Traditional liberal ideals of social justice are similarly advanced with actions that safeguard the most vulnerable among us.

Alternative energy, such as solar, illustrates both the promise and the contemporary challenge of "no-regrets policies."

By moving away from fossil fuels, we reduce the emission of greenhouse gases and help stabilize our atmosphere. We also take a bite out of acid rain, rein in smog, lower lung cancer and asthma rates, lessen environmental and human-health consequences of coal mining, and so on. Bushel baskets of positive benefits are there for the taking. And many people are reaching for them.

In the meanwhile, it's personal to me. I emerged from Himlung's crevasse with renewed determination to do whatever I can to hasten the inexorable movement toward humanity's inevitable adaptation to these changes.

When my recovery allowed, I loaded up my possessions and moved across the country to Western Washington University to expand the work I had begun with the American Climber Science Program. I set out to found a new and bigger academic organization dedicated to helping us understand and adapt to the here-and-now of our rapidly changing planet. Consistent with my long-standing goals, an important ambition of this new Mountain Environments Research Institute created toward the end of 2016 is to expand the ranks of climate scientists who are willing and able to penetrate, and study, the world's most difficult terrain.

I think this Institute came into sharp focus down there in the blue-white icelight of that ancient Himalayan glacier. That's when you indulge those fatalistic foxhole promises: *If I live through this . . .* if, if, if.

But the basic idea of such an organization had been marinating in my thoughts far longer. I can trace it clear back to my youthful days when my father took me west from Georgia to lonely, lovely Wheeler Peak in Nevada's Great Basin National Park. The power of that 3,982-meter (13,065-foot) desert mountain spoke to me, and so did my father. With his words and by his example, he passed on to me the very

strong belief that whatever I wound up doing, it should be for a mean-
ingful cause.

When I went into the wild, it would be not to conquer but to
understand.

S een from our contemporary vantage point, geology seems to be an
easily defined branch of science. To wit: the study of Earth's physical characteristics and the processes that affect the planet. Add to the
list matters such as climate, resources, stewardship, and the like, and
we call it "geoscience."

But geology didn't always answer to a consensus definition. Indeed, the discipline has a stormy history, which is worth a moment's
reflection. Just a couple of centuries ago, two rival approaches were
advanced on how the study of Earth should be framed. On the one
hand, the "catastrophists" were absorbed with studying how Earth
was shaped primarily by, what else, catastrophes—volcanoes, earth-
quakes, the rise of mountain ranges, and so forth. Religious views
sometimes figured strongly in this line of thinking. To wit, the great
biblical flood of Noah's day. On the other hand, "uniformitarians,"
or "gradualists," preferred to study the small, timeless processes—
such as erosion and sedimentation—that create much of what we see
around us. You can put Charles Darwin in this camp.

Today, almost everyone of thoughtful bent accepts that both ideas
have things going for them—that Mother Earth is a slow-moving, drip-
drip kind of planet, punctuated by occasional explosive catastrophes.

If two lines of thinking converged to give us the science of geology, climate change is also the sum of two similar categories of
impacts. The first involves alterations to norms. Example: an overall rise in temperatures, degree by degree, from "norms" measured
over decades. Second are changes to patterns of disturbances—
stronger hurricanes, more violent terrestrial storms, fiercer wildfires,
and more-widespread plagues. Changes in the norms are generally a
slower "gradualist" process. Earth spins toward uninhabitability over
a span of time. By contrast, disruptions in the patterns and intensities
of disturbances can occur much more rapidly—catastrophes that hit
with a massive boom.

Imagine, for instance, a 10 percent annual reduction in food. Starvation comes slowly. But deprived of water, we perish in a week. Eliminate oxygen, and humans survive less than fifteen minutes.

In my research expeditions, I've investigated both kinds of impacts. In the Himalaya, rising temperatures are bringing about the retreat of glaciers and extending alpine growing seasons. These are changes to norms. And while consequences downstream will be significant, and eventually huge, they can be measured in intervals of years, interspersed by localized calamities, like Everest's 2014 killer icefall. By contrast, our expedition into the rain forest of Costa Rica's Talamanca brought us face-to-face with the rapid, two-week onset of widespread drought. In most of the world, such an event would barely be noticed. But in the rain forest, wildlife fled the hills almost immediately to search for water and water-dependent food. Plant cover showed signs of deep stress. In the tropics, the complexity of biotic specialization and interactions left the environment vulnerable to catastrophic collapse in short order. I witnessed an even more dramatic example of the phenomenon a decade ago on a trip to hike to the top of Cerro Chirripó, the tallest peak in Central America at 3,820 meters (12,533 feet). Drought had weakened trees, which invited an invasion of insects that promptly killed them off. Then a quick-moving fire had burned through and many of the dead trees fell. This array of downed wood became efficient fuel for the next fire. In only a few years, the forest vanished—nature's version of a clear-cut, thanks to changing patterns of rainfall, and the response of insects and fire.

As I see it, knowledge drives policy. Or at least, solid data help farsighted leaders sell wise policy. That's why gathering baseline information from these hard-to-reach environments is so important. Without data, environmental changes are matters of anecdote and, sometimes, of argument. With firsthand data in a field book, changes become fact.

Another fact: although the dogmas of catastrophism and gradualism are each partly correct, the opposite is also true. Both are partly wrong, and this cannot be overlooked in our policy discussions about climate change. Catastrophists are dangerously off base to frame climate change as a pop-up or cyclical natural process against which we can do nothing, or need not bother. Gradualists are equally reckless to think of such changes as occurring over spans of time that stretch to the horizon rather than mere geologic eyeblinks. Doing so mistakenly suggests that we enjoy breathing room to evolve our way beyond fossil fuels at a relaxed pace.

I climb mountains, cross jungle mountains, crisscross savannahs, and wear out my boots not just to chart what is changing and why, but to try and calibrate how rapidly it is happening. Black carbon illustrates matters, although there are other ways. Our expeditions measure the distribution and concentrations of these energy-absorbing carbon particles because they are trail markers of industrial growth. Natural wildfires give us a historical baseline for black-carbon deposits. Beyond that baseline, any increases reflect the quantities of fossil fuels we use and fields we burn. The balance—there's that word again—is upset by this additional black carbon spewed into the air to be spread across the planet by winds. The effect is particularly noticeable on ice and snow, where black carbon changes the albedo and draws ever more solar heat to these surfaces and accelerates melting. You don't need a fancy calculator to see how quickly gradualism becomes catastrophic—particularly if you live in places like Miami or New York City, where your expensive house may be destined to become part of tomorrow's oceanic continental shelf rather than your family's inheritance.

Velocity is one consideration. Time the other. The burn of the fuse. The ticking of the clock.

Mountaineers enjoy, and suffer, intervals of down time. It's part of the undertaking. Waiting out a storm in a tent high on the flank of a peak, say. Or slowly reducing snow to water on a dinky one-burner stove. Or merely acclimatizing.

We fritter away some of this surplus time, pining for lost loves, gazing at sunsets, that kind of thing. But there are stimulating intervals, too. Free time allows us to ponder the matters pinging around deep in our minds. Being a climate scientist, when I curl up in a puffy sleeping bag, I'm apt to brood about human adaptations to change.

I was resting at a camp during a climb of North America's highest peak, Denali, in Central Alaska, when I began to dwell on the idea that most of our lives are engineered to allow no time to ponder much of anything. In particular, our high-speed culture just doesn't provide the intervals during which we can adequately acclimatize our minds to the changes under way in our environment. How many times have you heard, "I don't have time to worry about it"?

We should allocate some. Popular meditation strategies ask us to find time to clear our minds of thoughts. I prefer the Denali strategy. Let's find time to acclimatize our thinking to the changes under way and those to come. After that, our actions will follow, I'm sure of it. Otherwise, we take our chances.

With time to ponder, both individually and as societies, we'll recognize that old climate patterns are fading into memory. We will abandon the idea that next year and the years after will be much like recent years past. Instead, we'll prepare by building social and eco-logical resilience to perturbations. In practical terms, such strategies will include improved efficiency for agricultural irrigation, infrastruc-ture reinforcement to protect us from severe storms, cost-benefit anal-ysis that may lead to planned retreats from hurricane-prone coastal areas, revised zoning to lead people out of harm's way as the oceans rise, investments in civil-defense and public-health capacity for ex-treme events, and stepped-up efforts to preserve biodiversity. That's for starters.

Something else we'll recognize: none of these ideas is likely to turn out to be wasteful, no matter the ultimate course and pace of en-vironmental changes. That's why they are known as "no-regrets poli-cies." They make sense for their own sake, regardless of the twists and turns of climate changes. Think Pascal's wager.

On every level—as individuals, communities, and societies—no-regrets opportunities abound. We can waste less food and produce food locally. That makes agriculture more efficient, saves money, and uses less water, chemicals, and energy for transportation, among other things. There are credible estimates that one pound of food out of every three becomes waste. Imagine reducing that. Energy-and water-use efficiencies at home, from new types of light bulbs on up, are good for our pocketbooks and for our society. As of 2015, at least one-third of the US population did not recycle—a regrettable outcome for one of the simplest no-regrets opportunities.

Some no-regrets actions involve investment. Some require public subsidy. Others ask little more than that we change our habits. How well society embraces these kinds of opportunities will create the outline of our tomorrows.

And something else. "No-regrets policies" prepare us for a future in which we will need to be fast on our feet. Simply stated, as we become accustomed to changing the way we go about our lives, we become more resilient to the phenomenon of change itself.

Increasingly, psychologists find resilience a juicy subject of study. Why do some people overcome adversity and others do not? What makes a person resilient? When "you're faced with obstacles, stress, and other environmental threats," as the writer Maria Konnikova framed the question, "[d]o you succumb or do you surmount?"

Trying to grasp the nature of resiliency is the flip side of the more traditional societal inquiry about adversity. Instead of asking about the nature of human vulnerabilities and how to assuage pain, psychologists search for characteristics that enable some people to succeed despite tribulation. Maybe those traits can be taught.

Broadening the questions of resiliency from individuals to societies goes to the heart of how we can hold ourselves together to meet climate change. How can we make our nations and cultures more resilient? How can we avoid the dead-end contagion of social helplessness and futility that sometimes arises in the face of the unknown? How can we reframe climate change to make sure that we don't overlook opportunities, too?

Resilience is gaining currency among climate scientists and political leaders alike: you'll find it in a growing array of scientific studies on climate change. Even the word itself, *resilience*, is being studied in the context of climate change—the question being, which word motivates people more effectively, *resilience* or *adaptation*? Personally, I use the two together. If you can adapt to changing circumstances, you're resilient. And vice versa. But I do not take lightly the formidable power of words, or ideas, to shape how we see the opportunities and dangers ahead. That is, whether we succumb to climate change or surmount it depends, at least in part, on how we come to regard it.

Again borrowing from the journalist Maria Konnikova:

Frame adversity as a challenge, and you become more flexible and able to deal with it, move on, learn from it, and grow. Focus on it, frame it as a threat, and a potentially traumatic event becomes an enduring problem; you become more inflexible, and more likely to be negatively affected.

So, in tangible terms, what is climate-change resilience? It's architecture. It's agriculture. It's transportation. It's public health. It's infrastructure. It's marketplace incentives and budgetary subsidies. It's optimism and resolve, and some daring, too. It's a refresh in the social contract so that climate change does not become another means for "winners" to subjugate "losers."

One gets deep very quickly in these discussions, and it becomes realistic to wonder if one of the biggest changes will be in the way we humans perceive and relate to our world. When we find ourselves, broken and in pain, deep in the bottom of a pit, will we find the resolve and strength to climb out? Or will we let the darkness overtake us?

Climate change is the ultimate parable for the age of environmental reckoning. We are now writing the opening chapter.

Acknowledgments

As we created this book, every step of the way someone helped move things forward and this book would not have been possible without so very many people. . . .

Aunt Cindy has been asking me to write a book about my travels for years—often enough that it moved from being a vague idea into something more pressing.

Steve Yool, my PhD advisor at the University of Arizona, taught me the fundamentals of compelling science writing.

After my accident, Carey Roberts was amazing and helped me conceive this work as a way of healing the physical and mental wounds.

Bonnie Nadel saw the potential and helped me navigate the murky waters of finding a publisher and selling the book.

John Balzar forced me to think beyond the events and visualize how the book and the ideas within could be structured—and then helped me do it.

Ben Adams and the amazing crew at PublicAffairs made it all happen and look fantastic.

My colleagues at Huxley College of the Environment were incredibly supportive while I was distracted with both healing and writing.

Finally, the CDC, NWS, USAID, NSF, WKU, and Fulbright Program have graciously funded my work over the years.

John All is a global explorer and PhD geoscientist, specializing in climate change research in remote locations. His work is broadly focused on fragile, indicator environments, in particular the world's highest mountains, where changing climate has profound consequences. He is an advocate for adaptive strategies to cope with changes now occurring.

A lifetime fellow of the Explorers Club in New York City and Fulbright Senior Scholar, All is also cofounder and executive director of the American Climber Science Program (www.climberscience.com), which brings together scientists from many disciplines, along with students and mountaineers, to expand global research at high altitudes. He is founder and director of the Mountain Environments Research Institute at Western Washington University.

All successfully summited Mt. Everest via the North Col/Northeast Ridge route without crampons. He has climbed Denali, Artesonraju, Mt. Blanc de Tacul, Alpamayo, El Capitan, and hundreds of other mountains around the world. He has led expeditions on five continents to extreme locations—from deep caves to tropical rain forests; remote deserts to the great mountain ranges of Asia and South America.

He holds a doctorate in Geography, Applied Anthropology, and Global Environmental Change, and also a JD in International Environmental Law and a Master's Certificate in Environmental Ethics. He served as a program officer for the Climate Change and Human Health Initiative of the United Nations and has taught at Tribhuvan University in Nepal, Rutgers University, the University of Arizona, and Western Kentucky University, as well as his current position on the Environmental Science faculty of Western Washington University. He is the author of more than forty published scientific works, and has received nearly $2,000,000 in research and exploration grants. He serves in on scientific and conservation committees for the American Alpine Club and the American Association for the Advancement of Science.

John Balzar is the author of *Yukon Alone: The World's Toughest Adventure Race*, named a *Los Angeles Times* Best Book of the Year. His magazine work has been collected in anthologies, including *Wild Stories: The Best of* Men's Journal. A veteran newspaper journalist, he was awarded the Scripps Howard Ernie Pyle Award for human-interest storytelling. He has sailed across the Pacific, has worked as a river boatman in the Arctic Wildlife Refuge, and holds Science Diver certification from the National Oceanic and Atmospheric Administration.